£ 3-0
GGN

03/20

The ILLUSTRATED ENCYCLOPEDIA of
GOLF

The ILLUSTRATED ENCYCLOPEDIA of GOLF

ROBERT GREEN

Foreword by

SEVERIANO BALLESTEROS

CollinsWillow
An Imprint of HarperCollinsPublishers

'For my sons Ben and Sam, with fondest love'

First published in 1987 as
Golf: An Illustrated History of the Game

This revised and updated edition published in 1994 by
CollinsWillow
an imprint of HarperCollins*Publishers,*
London

ISBN 0 00 218458 3

Designed and produced by
Cooling Brown, Hampton-upon-Thames, Middlesex

Printed and bound in Great Britain

CONTENTS

FOREWORD

by SEVERIANO BALLESTEROS

For those of us who play the game professionally, golf is the means by which we make our living. For most of you, golf is a game you play for fun, something that gets you away from your daily jobs. But because you play golf for fun does not mean you don't take it seriously. You want to perform at your best every time you play.

Similarly, because professional golfers play the game for a living does not

mean we are incapable of appreciating how lucky we are to have a life in golf. Like you, we enjoy the game – the thrill of hitting the perfect shot perhaps a little more often than you do – and the pleasure of having an environment as attractive as a golf course in which to conduct our business. The difference is that, in our case, a ball in the water or a three-putt green is more than an aggravation. It costs us money. More heartbreakingly, it can cost us victory.

In this book, Robert Green covers not only the champions and the championships of golf but also its

history and development. In paying tribute to some of the great courses around the world, he highlights the beauty of this wonderful game. Believe me, when he says that Augusta National, the home of the Masters, is not only a beauty but a beast as well, he's right. And I should know! I've experienced both sides of that course's character.

I have known Robert for a long time, both as a friend as well as a journalist. He has spent many years studying the game and is one of the experts we touring pros consult for facts and figures. Golf, with its traditions and integrity, is rich in sporting culture, and its best qualities are brought out in The Illustrated Encyclopedia of Golf. It is essential reading for any serious enthusiast of golfing history. I hope you enjoy it as much as I have.

Severiano Ballesteros

INTRODUCTION

Several years ago, in the book that in many respects was the precursor to this one, I compared Nick Faldo to Seve Ballesteros, Bernhard Langer, Sandy Lyle and Greg Norman with the words: "*Faldo has not, at the time of writing, attained the heady heights of the other four, but he may yet.*"

That was on June 1, 1987, a date by which Faldo, unlike those contemporaries, had not won a single major championship. By June 1, 1993, he had won five.

I have recounted this prediction not simply from a flagrantly immodest desire to see how impressive it looked in print but because it is indicative of how much the competitive golfing scene has changed in such a short period of time. For example, by the summer of 1987, no Britons had won the Masters. By the summer of 1991, the title had been swapped around between Lyle, Faldo and Ian Woosnam. Henry Cotton, who died in December 1987, would have revelled in that.

Between September 1987 and October 1992, Europe won the Ryder Cup in America and Great Britain & Ireland did likewise in the Walker Cup. Far from being outshone, the women amateur golfers of Great Britain & Ireland first retained and then regained the Curtis Cup, while in the Solheim Cup, which started in 1990, Europe's women professionals emphatically won the 1992 match after being embarrassed at the first attempt.

Elsewhere, golf threatened to make it into the Olympic Games of 1996, until controversy and politics scuppered that scheme; a Senior tour in Europe got off to an improbably propitious start; and whereas prior to 1993, on only four occasions had 70 been broken in all four rounds of a major championship, in 1993 alone it was done six times.

There have been amendments in the laws governing rules and

equipment in the intervening years, too, the most significant being dealt with in Chapter 2, although lately no one has emulated astronaut Alan Shepard (pictured left) by essaying a few shots on the moon or some other planet.

This book takes in all elements of golf, from its very beginnings somewhere deep in the mists of time – whether those mists be enveloping some court in ancient China, a frozen Dutch canal or a rudimentary Scottish links – to the flamboyant glories of Augusta National and the flamboyant performances of Greg Norman's golf swing.

As Norman and his rivals know, golf is essentially about the battle with oneself – and with that small white sphere. "*That little ball won't move until you hit it, and there's nothing you can do for it after it has gone.*" Thus spoke Zaharias, Babe Zaharias, one of the greatest women golfers in history, whom you will encounter in these pages. She had a good point, of course, although that doesn't stop us trying to defy common sense. As Horace Hutchinson, a 19th century golfing sage whose perceptive and humorous – and somewhat misogynistic – opinions you will also find inside, once pointed out: "*If profanity had an influence on the flight of the ball, the game would be played far better than it is.*"

A.A. Milne got it partly right when he observed that "*Golf is so popular simply because it is the best game in the world at which to be bad.*" But if only a little swearing was all it took to make us good …

Robert Green, London, May 1994

CHAPTER ONE

SEVEN CENTURIES OF GOLF

St Andrews has a world-wide reputation as 'the home of golf'. Nothing can alter that now because it is how the 'auld grey toun' is perceived by millions of golf's devotees all over the globe, even if they have never been there and are never likely to. But St Andrews has at best a tenuous claim to the accolade: it is not even the home of the first golf club in Scotland; it cannot be said with any certainty that it is the place where the game began in Scotland; and what's more it is a matter of doubt that golf is of Scottish origin at all.

So when and where did golf originate? In a sketch in a stained-glass window at Gloucester Cathedral, illustrating scenes from the Battle of Crécy in France, a man is apparently preparing to strike a ball in a golf-like manner. It dates from around 1350, and perhaps it shows not golf but the game of *cambuca*, a popular pastime of the day enjoyed by the English, and similar to the earlier Roman game of *paganica*. Both involved someone standing side-on to a ball, intent on striking it with the club in his hands. The ball in *paganica* consisted of leather and feathers, in *cambuca* it was of wood. In the ancient Flemish game of *chole*, the ball was made of beechwood and it was struck with clubs forged from rigid shafts and iron heads. Since the colourful windows in Gloucester Cathedral are concerned with battle campaigns in France, it may be instead that *chole* is the game depicted.

Chole could be a genuine forerunner of golf. Still played occasionally in southern Belgium, it is a field game in which the ball is hit by a team towards a distant target – sometimes very distant, literally miles away. The target can be anything from a door to a tree, a pole to a stone. The team has three strokes to make progress before standing aside while its opponents, known as *decholeurs*, have the next blow with which they attempt to dispatch the ball as far backwards as they can, or into a spot which will make matters as

awkward as possible for their rivals. And so it goes – three steps forward, one back.

This obviously sounds more like large-scale croquet rather than golf, and one of the great difficulties confronting anyone who delves into the earliest days of the sport lies in deciding how many, if any, of these potential candidates actually spawned the game of golf we now know. Even back in 1338, German shepherds were granted special dispensation to mark out their territories by striking a pebble with their crooks, the distance which the shot covered being the extent of their grazing rights. Could that be said to have anything to do with golf? Probably not. Quite simply, if a man has a club in his hands he will look for something to hit with it: hockey, shinty, polo and lacrosse are just some of the games which evolved from the same basic instinct.

The late Dutch golf historian Steven J. H. van Hengel, acknowledged as one of the foremost experts on the origins of golf, felt that it probably developed via an amalgam of the implements used in *chole* and the rules of *jeu de mail*. The technique of the latter was similar to golf and it was played on a court prepared specifically for the purpose. It started in Italy and was taken up by the French, becoming especially widespread in the early 17th century. It went out of fashion some 100 years later but until 50 years ago it

THE ROYAL AND ANCIENT GAME *Charles I (above) pauses from his game at Leith Links whilst receiving news of the Irish Rebellion in 1641.*

GETTING THE EARLY BIG PICTURE *The Flemish artist Paul Bril painted this scene of* chole *players (left) in 1624. The implements are similar to those of golf, although the clubs are on a rather larger scale.*

BUT IS IT GOLF? *This detail from the Great East Window of Gloucester Cathedral has led some people to declare that golf must have been known in England around 1350 – the time this stained-glass image was made. In fact, that is highly unlikely. It is probable that the medieval English pastime of* cambuca *or the Flemish game of* chole *are depicted in this intriguing roundel.*

A ROYAL DISTRACTION
Mary Queen of Scots was a keen player of both golf and jeu de mail *(an imported variation from Europe). This picture shows her at St Andrews in 1563. Four years later she was seen playing golf at Seton House shortly after her husband's death – a fact used at her trial as evidence of her complicity in his demise.*

remained a regular activity in southern France as *jeu de mail à la chicane*, a cross-country version of the same game.

Incidentally, *jeu de mail* arrived in England from France. Translated, it was known as 'pall mall', and the original course in London was laid out in what is now the busy one-way thoroughfare of that name. Charles I was a keen disciple of the game around the same time as it was celebrating its halcyon days in France.

Golf had already been played in Scotland for centuries by the time Charles I came to the throne. He followed the example of Mary Queen of Scots in enthusiastically enjoying golf and *jeu de mail*. Mary was vilified for playing both shortly after the suspicious death of her husband, Lord Darnley, in 1567, and this apparent lack of grief at his demise did her chances of avoiding an appointment on the executioner's block no good at all.

However, this is getting rather ahead of the story (pun intended). I have, to be honest, slightly misrepresented the researches of van Hengel in saying that in his opinion golf emerged from a combination of *chole* and *jeu de mail*, both of which date from the Middle Ages. He doesn't say golf but *colf*, also known by other medieval phrases such as *spel metten colve* (game with club), but essentially *colf*.

It doesn't require an international interpreter to make the connection between *colf* and golf, but van

Hengel had a fundamental advantage in tackling the wealth of information available to golf historians in the Low Countries. The fact that he was a Dutchman meant he was able to investigate the old archives of pictures, maps and other materials written in medieval language with an ease which can only come to one who has the current version as his mother tongue. The task for Britons is as forbidding as it would be for a Frenchman, however conversant with modern English, to understand Chaucer.

Van Hengel traced *colf* back to Boxing Day 1297, to Loenen aan de Vecht in northern Holland. Then the local townsfolk played four 'holes' measuring a total of 4,950 yards to commemorate the relieving of Kronenburg Castle exactly one year previously. The castle had been the besieged refuge of two noblemen wanted for murder; that they were eventually captured and summarily dealt with by the crowd was deemed cause for celebration. The fact that *colf* was chosen to mark the occasion is, suggested van Hengel, proof that it was already popular by 1297, though not even he could say for how long.

Holing out at what might today be known as the Kronenburg Country Club was not performed by putting into a hole of 4¼ inches diameter. The targets consisted instead of four doors – respectively in a kitchen, a windmill, a castle and a courthouse. This unique ritual continued until 1831, when the castle was pulled down, but golf has remained.

Landscape artists portraying life in contemporary Holland towards the end of the 16th century regularly included golfers, or *colfers*, in their works, unquestionably because they were a common sight. The game was played in both matchplay and strokeplay form, to use the modern terms, and contested by singles, foursomes, fourballs or even, in that pre-slow play era, eightsomes. It was predominantly practised in spring, autumn and winter (hence the apparently surprising number of paintings which depict the game on frozen canals and lakes) because in summer the grass was too long and in those days there were no prepared courses, except for one at Haarlem. Doorways were gradually substituted by a hole in the ground, often with a pole protruding from it, as the ultimate target.

SCOTCH ON ICE? *Adriaen van de Velde's oil painting of 1668 shows a frost scene at Haarlem but it has been suggested that the Scots, not the Dutch, invented golf. The man about to strike the ball is wearing a kilt, but it is very possible that he was supposed to be an itinerant trader or soldier. The date is not very helpful either, since it is certain that the Scots had been playing golf for at least two centuries by then.*

Colf continued until the early 18th century when it suddenly fell out of fashion. There are no satisfactory explanations for this, but it was quickly replaced by *kolf*, a considerably shorter game, played on a course of some 20 metres in length. *Kolf* was popular in the Netherlands until just before the turn of the last century when the Scottish version of golf was imported.

And so back to Scotland. To suggest to a Scotsman that the game was not the creation of his countrymen is as dangerous as saying to a gurkha that his ancestors were cowards. And maybe he would be right to take offence. Then again, it all depends on what one understands by 'golf'. Though the Dutch were familiar with golf as a game with a hole in it, it is probable that the Scots have never played it any other way. To that extent they could be said to have invented golf as we know it; and St Andrews, despite the optimistic claim to have fostered the game that is inherent in the label 'home of golf', was indubitably responsible for 18 holes becoming established as the norm for a full round, a step taken in 1764. But van Hengel's theory of *colf* begetting golf is supported by the frequent trading links between Holland and Scotland from medieval times. These presented an abundance of opportunities for the game to travel across the North Sea, and therefore it is perhaps no surprise that the strongest indications are

that the movement was from east to west.

Until well into the 19th century, golf in Scotland was almost confined to the east coast, where the sandy turf among the dunes along the shore made for ideal golfing ground. Had the game begun in Scotland it is likely that it would have enjoyed a greater geographical spread, such as was to be found in the Low Countries, though granted the North Sea coast was favoured there, too. Furthermore, it is reckoned that around 1650 golf was played in only about 12 locations in Scotland – at Dornoch, Banff and Aberdeen in the north; at Montrose,

ON A PLATE *Golf began to be portrayed on ceramics sometime from the 17th century onwards. This Dutch scene dates from that era and is taken from an encaustic dish.*

THE EARLIEST LINKS *One of the first paintings of golf in Scotland. This water-colour by Paul Sandby was completed in 1746 and is entitled 'View of Bruntsfield Links looking towards Edinburgh Castle'.*

THE OLDEST GOLF CLUB

The Honourable Company of Edinburgh Golfers is recognized as the oldest golf club in the world. Edinburgh Town Council marked its foundation in 1744 by presenting a Silver Club to be contested annually by the members. This engraving after a drawing by David Allan illustrates the Procession of the Silver Club in 1787.

THE PROCESSION OF THE SILVER CLUB

Carnoustie, Perth, St Andrews and Leven further down; and at a few spots around Edinburgh – whereas there were over 40 places in Holland where there is incontrovertible proof that *colf* was practised by then. The first documentary reference to golf in the Netherlands dates from 1360 (though that is not to deny the truth of the previously mentioned splendid saga at Loenen); and in Scotland from 1457. In short, the odds are that Dutch traders introduced *colf* to the Scots, who in turn refined it into golf and eventually spread the gospel to the world.

Before we settle for calling this dispute an honourable half, we ought at least to acknowledge the existence of the Chinese claim that golf originated in their country. Called *chuiwan*, which means 'hitting ball', the first reference to it can be traced back to 943. Allegedly, the game involved hitting a ball into a series of pits. One theory, albeit extremely tendentious, is that this game was imported into Europe by tradesmen who did business in the Orient. However, although *chuiwan* was apparently the favourite sport of the Emperor Huizong – making the Chinese pastime both royal and ancient – there is no reliable evidence that it made the journey to the west and later became *colf*, golf or anything else. The Scots regard the suggestion not so much inscrutable as insulting. As for recent

research indicating that the genuine grandaddy of all stick-and-ball games, one which bears some resemblance to golf, was initiated in the Egyptian court of Pharaoh Tuthmosis III in the 1400s B.C., we will leave that one for scholars of the arcane only.

That first Scottish reference to golf, in 1457, was contained in a parliamentary decree promulgated by King James II of Scotland, declaring 'that Fute-ball and Golfe be utterly cryit doune, and nocht usit'. His Majesty was worried that these two sports were keeping his subjects away from precious archery practice, which was needed to repel the frequent incursions of the English – hence the order.

The date is instructive for two reasons. First, no such law would have been necessary had the game been played by only a few. Second, a similar enactment of 1424 prohibited 'fute-ball' but not golf, thus indicating that the latter had enjoyed significantly increased popularity in the intervening years. Interestingly, Edward III of England had issued a similar Act in 1363 banning *cambuca*.

Post-1457, references to golf gradually become more common, even in England. Catherine of Aragon, the first of Henry VIII's six wives, wrote to Cardinal Wolsey in 1513 that "*all his [Henry's] subjects be very glad I thank God to be busy with the Golfe for they take it for a pastime*". In 1552, a local licence made it plain that the people of St Andrews had the right to play golf, among other things, over the now-hallowed ground; though even as late as 1593 a luckless couple called John Henrie and Pat Rogie were apparently jailed in Edinburgh for 'playing of the gowff on the links of Leith every Sabbath the time of the sermonses'. The spelling of 'golf' in those days was, as you can see, anything but uniform.

There is evidence that in 1608, five years after King James VI of Scotland had also become James I of England, a seven-hole course was laid out at Blackheath, London, by Scottish courtiers who were homesick for their beloved game. This gives rise to Royal Blackheath's claim to be nearly 400 years old, although in their comprehensive work, *Royal Blackheath*, Ian Henderson and David Stirk suggest that a club was not formed there until 1766. It is, nevertheless, the oldest golf club in England, notwithstanding that there are references to golf being played at Molesey Hurst near Hampton in 1758.

Dating golf clubs is a hazardous business, partly because of the identity of the founders in those bygone days. Most of the earliest societies were established by freemasons. The inherent secrecy of the masons meant that when the golf clubs were eventually opened to those outside the fraternity, many of the existing minutes of meetings and other documentary materials were destroyed. For example, the Royal Burgess Society of Edinburgh Golfers was apparently formed in 1735 but there are no minutes to support the claim. Similarly, no records can be traced to substantiate the belief that Musselburgh was instituted in 1774 rather than 1784, as is suggested by the minutes.

Accordingly, the distinction of being recognized as the oldest golf club in the world falls to the Honourable Company of Edinburgh Golfers, now based at Muirfield on the Firth of Forth to the east of Edinburgh but in 1744 located at Leith, just outside Scotland's capital city. The club has maintained continuous records since then, although the scene of its members' activities was moved from Leith in 1831, initially to Musselburgh in 1836 and eventually to Muirfield in 1891.

The Honourable Company also bequeathed to the game its first set of Rules: 13 articles of faith which have multiplied and been embellished in the ensuing years, ostensibly of necessity but, it must be said, to the dismay of many people – including the late Henry Longhurst, the eminent British journalist, who felt the basic principles of golf could comfortably be accommodated on the back of a matchbox. The original 13 Rules devised by John Rattray (the club's first captain) and his colleagues captured the spirit of the game, with its reliance on trust and on the honesty of its adherents, and that remains the underlying theme of the Rules today – albeit with suitably severe penalties to deter would-be transgressors.

In 1744, to mark the creation of the club, Edinburgh Town Council presented the Honourable Company with a Silver Club to be contested by the members. Thus was born the first club competition. Rattray was the winner and hence became captain. The

SETTING THE STANDARDS
This painting of by Sir George Chalmers depicts William St Clair – the man who reduced the length of a round. It was his scoring exploits in 1764 which caused the Old Course at St Andrews to become an 18-hole layout, thus setting a standard which endures today. Note his firm grip and exaggeratedly closed stance, the preferred method of striking the feathery ball.

GOLF ON THE OLD COURSE *Though times have changed, in many respects the scene has hardly changed at all. Anyone familiar with golf would immediately recognise St Andrews from this 1798 illustration of players on the first green.*

event (matchplay, of course, since strokeplay was in its infancy) was played over Leith's five-hole layout, a forbidding test with holes measuring 414, 461, 426, 495 and 435 yards, respectively. Given the nature of the equipment back in 1744, that represents an equivalent of around 600 yards per hole by modern standards.

It is immediately apparent that the long game was then the thing, putting playing nowhere near so dominant a role as it does now. The notion that these days too much emphasis is placed on putting will never wilt for want of advocates, but they have been fighting a losing battle since the invention of the mechanical mower in the first half of the last century. The scythe gradually became redundant as an instrument of greenkeeping and the quality of putting surfaces improved rapidly. Putting became an art, rather than a case of hit-and-hope, on these new manicured surfaces, and through the 19th century 4¼ inches became the accepted diameter for the hole size.

It is likely that this seemingly random size was just that: it happened to be the width of the implement used to cut the holes at Musselburgh. It was obviously considered of satisfactory dimensions for general application because in 1893 the Royal and Ancient Golf Club of St Andrews (the R & A, as the club is now universally referred to in shorthand) decreed that a 4¼ - inch hole was mandatory. Thus it has remained.

That we should find the R & A handing down judgements and delivering verdicts on what was acceptable may appear surprising. After all, the Honourable Company at Edinburgh was in existence beforehand, and its members set down the first Rules

of Golf, which were copied with only one minor amendment when 22 *"Noblemen and Gentlemen, being admirers of the ancient and healthful exercise of the Golf"*, banded together at St Andrews in 1754. The usurpers even nicked the Silver Club idea; the members of the new society each subscribing five shillings to purchase the prize, claimed in its inaugural year by one Bailie William Landale.

But it did not take long for St Andrews to display its influence. In 1764, William St Clair covered the 22 holes of the Old Course in 121 strokes. It was decided by the St Andrews Society of Golfers, in the face of this contemptuous treatment of the links, to amalgamate the first four holes into two. Since the shared fairways and double greens, which today distinguish St Andrews from any other course, were already an integral feature of the design, that involved reducing the round to 18 holes. From small acorns…

As I have already mentioned, Leith had only five holes at this time. For that matter, the North Inch course at Perth – which is considered by some experts to be the first golf course in Scotland which was recognizable as such – had just six; Montrose, on the east coast between Dundee and Aberdeen, had 25. It wasn't until 1858 that the R & A stipulated *"one round of the Links or 18 Holes is reckoned a match"*. There had previously been a distinct trend towards 18 holes being the norm, and the edict merely gave legal effect to popular practice. It meant that golfers confronted by a six-hole course played it three times while a nine-holer was toured twice.

By 1858, there had been other considerable changes in the upper schools of golf and in the overall development of the game. In the struggle for supremacy, St Andrews had dealt the Honourable Company a mortal bow. In 1834, Murray Belshes, soon to become Captain of the St Andrews Society of Golfers, had approached King William IV, asking him to agree to be their patron. The King not only acquiesced to that request but permitted the society to rename itself The Royal and Ancient Golf Club of St Andrews. Since the Honourable Company had left Leith, which was soon to deteriorate, and had not yet re-established itself at Musselburgh, its members were in no position to challenge the concurrent claim made on St Andrews' behalf by the R & A to the title 'home of golf'. From that moment, the authority and eminence of the R & A has been undisputed (except in the United States and Mexico, where the US Golf Association is the governing body). The R & A assumed responsibility for formulating the Rules of Golf in 1897. In 1919, at a meeting in Edinburgh, the most prominent British clubs appointed the R & A the *"supreme ruling authority for the management and control of the game"*. And St Andrews has become the most revered golf course in the world, the inspiration to countless others.

At a humbler level, too, things were stirring. More clubs and societies sprang up along Scotland's east coast: at Aberdeen, Crail, Bruntsfield, Burntisland, and into the 19th century at Perth, North Berwick and, in 1851, at Prestwick – home of the first dozen Open Championships. A certain William Mitchell formed the Old Manchester Club at Kersal Moor in 1818, making it the second oldest club outside Scotland after Royal Blackheath.

It wasn't long before the British Empire began to feel the impact. A club was founded at Calcutta, later to become Royal Calcutta, in 1829. This was the first golf

club outside the British Isles, and it was followed in 1842 by another course on the opposite side of India, at Bombay. Appropriately enough, the Indian Amateur Championship, which began in 1892, is also the world's oldest national tournament apart from the British Open (1860) and Amateur (1885), but before then golf had also taken root on the continent, at Pau in the French Pyrenees.

That occurred in 1856, eight years after the invention of the gutta percha ball (more commonly known as the 'gutty') had helped to revolutionize the game. It flew further than its predecessor, the 'feathery', rolled truer and was more durable. Its influence was vital. From this point on, golf became increasingly contagious.

Despite the events I have already mentioned, golf was not terribly popular until after 1850. Certainly, it had attracted a loyal band of devotees before then, but they were, in terms of the entire population, small in number and predominantly a wealthy minority – giving golf a reputation as a rich man's game which it still finds hard to shrug off in some quarters. Compared to the boom that golf was to enjoy in the second half of

THE FRENCH CONNECTION
The continental breakthrough proved to be something of a false dawn. Pau Golf Club in France was founded in 1856, the first course on mainland Europe, but it was over a century later before the French began to take to the game in earnest.

EARLY PROFESSIONALS

Some famous names at Leith in 1867. From left to right: Davie Park, Bob Kirk, Jamie Anderson, Jamie Dunn, Willie Dow, Willie Dunn, Alexander Greig, Old Tom Morris, Young Tom Morris and George Morris.

the 19th century, the growth of the game was almost stunted. Van Hengel went as far as to say: "*It is in fact a miracle that golf ... survived the 18th century at all.*"

Van Hengel congratulated the masonic societies for keeping the flame burning, though golf itself was often simply regarded as an excuse for gluttony: "*a good exercise before sitting down for their sumptuous meals*". But even the most eager Bordeaux buff might draw the line at following the example set by golfers of the 1770's, as described by Tobias Smollett: "*they never went to bed without having each the best part of a gallon of claret in his belly.*"

Some 120 years later, golf had become distinctly more than a gourmand's delight, and for rather more people. Figures indicate that in 1850, around the time of the birth of the gutty, there were 17 golf clubs and societies in the United Kingdom; by 1890 this had leapt to 387, playing over, approximately, 140 different courses. The inauguration of the Open Championship in 1860 helped to publicize the game and within the ensuing decade three major English clubs were founded: Westward Ho! (now called Royal North Devon) in the south-west, formed in 1864 and the oldest English club still using its original course; the London Scottish Club at Wimbledon, London (1865); and the Liverpool Golf Club (today also honoured with the Royal prefix) at Hoylake in 1869. The latter hosted the first Amateur Championship in 1885.

The first and third of these were, like the majority of early Scottish clubs, built on linksland; that is, the sandy strips of otherwise useless ground which were left along the coast when the seas withdrew after the last Ice Age. It was considered (indeed, still is by some purists) sacrilege to refer to any other type of course as a 'links', and eventually the term 'golf course' was coined to describe non-links golfing grounds. If St Andrews was now to be just as readily described a 'golf course' as a 'links', that terminology would be guaranteed to disturb a few graves; as would the tendency to describe any course with a view over salt water as a links.

But our forebears would doubtless be amazed rather than appalled at the way golf has developed in so many ways, and not just in the modern extent of its geographical base. For example, fewer than 20 golf books had been written 100 years ago but today golf has an enviable collection of literature devoted to it. In 1890, the world's oldest extant golf magazine, imaginatively named *Golf*, was published in London. It changed its name to *Golf Illustrated* in 1899, and to *Golf Weekly* in 1992.

It was also in 1890 that the first edition of *The Badminton Library – Golf* appeared, edited by Horace Hutchinson. This volume contains a great deal of fascinating material, such as Hutchinson's comments on the mores of the contemporary professional:

" *Especially to be reprobated is the practice at some clubs of offering a 'drink' to a professional at the close of a round. If you leave him to himself there is no danger of his damaging his health by drinking too little. No golf professional is recorded to have died of thirst. On the other hand, the lives of many have been shortened and degraded by thirst too often satiated... .*"

"*On the whole, the professional is not a bad fellow. He has little morality; but he has good, reckless spirits, a ready wit and humour ... He is apt to be insolent in order to show you that he imagines himself to have some self-respect which is a self-delusion – but if you can endure a certain measure of this, he is a good companion. Never, however, bet with him; for so will it be best for him and best for you, as he is unlikely to pay you if he loses. This he is apt to do, for he is a bad judge of the merits of a golf match, a point which requires a delicacy of estimate usually beyond his powers.*"

Hutchinson was a golfer of no mean ability: four times a finalist in the Amateur Championship and twice a winner but, as that brief pedigree demonstrates, he was an amateur, in cricketing parlance, a 'gentleman' as opposed to a 'player'.

If he believed the professional to be beneath him, the *Punch* cartoons of the era depicted the pro as a tyrant blessed with an acerbic wit, as exemplified by exchanges like:

Pupil: "What am I doing wrong now?"
Pro: "Standing too near the ball – after you've hit it."

And again by this one:

Pupil: "I say, d'you think I can go?"
Pro: "Go? Why not? There's no-one in the bunker."

Sometimes the instructor's advice was countered with a logical retort from his luckless charge:

Pro: "The secret of putting is never to lift your head until you hear the ball rattle in the tin."
Pupil: "That's silly. You can't keep gazing at the ground for the rest of your life."

But generally the last word was left to the crusty tutor, who emerged as a man with the compassion of Genghis Khan and the brain of George Bernard Shaw.

This was the age when professionals were not permitted to enter clubhouses. It was enough that they breathed. Privilege was a word outside their dictionary – Hutchinson would doubtless have said outside their vocabulary. It is only relatively recently that the club pro has been regarded as a human being, and indeed even the star pro's between the wars, such as Walter Hagen and Henry Cotton, caused numerous ructions with their demands to be treated civilly. Hagen declined to enter the clubhouse at Troon for the presentation ceremony after the 1923 Open, where he had finished runner-up to Arthur Havers, because he and his colleagues had been refused admission during the championship.

Attitudes at the turn of the century especially were a far cry from the way Messrs Palmer, Nicklaus, Ballesteros, Faldo & Co are feted and chased today. Then the pro

was good for a few lessons and maybe the odd round. He could win tournaments or perhaps design a new course, but think of him as an equal? Really!

And then there were the caddies. It is one of golf's most repeated truisms that many of its finest exponents have graduated through the caddie ranks. That is hardly surprising. When Hutchinson was writing, the caddies would often be professionals who did not have an 'engagement'.

The word 'caddie' is derived from the French cadet: the son of a gentleman. The Scots mischievously traduced its meaning by using it to refer to those who carried the bags of the gentlemen who played golf in the earliest days of the game's history. In the strict Scottish vernacular, 'caddie' meant 'scrounger', and that is hardly the severest criticism to which caddies have been subjected down the ages. Their popular image has been recently upgraded into a kind of pseudo-profession by their regular attachment to the leading tournament players, as seen on television, but previously tour caddies were commonly dismissed as dirty, drunk or – in circumstances of extreme politeness – eccentric.

So much for the elite. The caddie most of us get on a visit to a strange club may be a thoroughly pleasant young chap, a boy or youth in between school or university terms, but the quaint image is of the gnarled old figure who says of one's good shots *"we hit a beauty there"* and of the bad *"you made a right mess of that"*. This is another mode of behaviour suggested by

WESTWARD HO! *The 10th green of the Royal North Devon Golf Club at Westward Ho! The photograph was taken in 1905, 41 years after the course was opened. It was a pioneering club in the cause of women's golf and it boasts the oldest links in England. The course itself now looks much as it did then.*

PUNCH-EYED VIEW *Golf as seen by a Punch cartoonist at the beginning of this century. Such jokes as this reflect many non-golfers' perception of golf as a good walk spoiled (to quote Mark Twain). The British humour magazine published articles and cartoons about golf for over 120 years.*

Tennis Player (from London): *"Don't see the Fun o' this Game – knocking a Ball into a Bush, and then 'untin' about for it!"*

Punch and other periodicals and books of around 100 years ago. The impression handed down the generations is of a unique band of men with a religious respect for the game, as in:

Player (after bad shot): "Golf's a funny game, isn't it?" Caddie: "Aye, but it's no' meant to be";

and a severe lack of patience:

Lady golfer (who has missed the ball six times with various clubs): "And which am I to use now?" Caddie: "Gie it a knock wi' the bag!"

Whatever the caddie may have thought, golf is in fact a funny game. Go back a century and the pro and the caddie were frequently the same person, but if not, united anyway in being a target of disrespect for the well-to-do golfer; a necessary evil for playing the sport. They were also comrades in displaying derision at the efforts of those who were their social betters but golfing inferiors. *Punch* intimated, probably erroneously, that their minds shared a sublime sense of sarcasm and, more correctly, that their shoulders bore the burden of an intolerable weight of chips.

How times have changed. They have long since gone their separate ways. The top tour professionals are sporting heroes now. They can afford to buy clubhouses. The club pro, too, is welcome within and has become a respected member of golf club life: a skilled craftsman, club repairer, teacher, salesman, even a friend.

The caddie? Well, signs ordering caddies to stay out of the clubhouse are still to be seen all over Britain and elsewhere around the world.

One century back, while the professionals and caddies were struggling along, golf was flourishing. Many famous golf clubs which now bear the proud title 'Royal' were created in the last two decades of the 19th century: Lytham & St Annes (1886), St George's (1887),

Ashdown Forest and Birkdale (1889) in England; Belfast (1881), Dublin (1885), Portrush (1888) and County Down at Newcastle (1889) in Ireland; Porthcawl (1891) and St David's (1894) in Wales.

These are just the tip, albeit a distinguished one, of the iceberg. Scotland, of course, was already well endowed with important clubs and there was ample room and demand for more, such as Gullane (1882), Nairn (1887), Luffness New (1894) and Western Gailes (1897). Throughout this century golf has expanded to the point where there are over 2,000 clubs in the British Isles, while the latter part of the 1800s is particularly significant as the time the game departed for the rest of the world.

It was British expatriates who took the game to Asia, via India in 1829. From 1888 to 1890, courses were built at Taiping in Malaya, Bangkok in Thailand, and in Hong Kong. It was almost exclusively the expats' domain, though the Asian nation which today is most associated with golf – Japan – has no history of colonial rule. The first Japanese golf course was opened in 1901 on the slopes of Mount Rokko, near Kobe.

Golf got off to a stuttering start in Australia and New Zealand. Royal Melbourne, dating from 1891 and now the owner of what is universally recognized to be one of the world's truly great courses, can boast the longest continuous existence of an Australian club, though earlier attempts to import golf had met with limited success in Adelaide and Sydney, and in New Zealand at Dunedin and Christchurch. South Africa led the way on the Dark Continent; the Royal Cape Golf Club at Cape Town celebrated its centenary in 1985, and the country now has several outstanding layouts.

Other countries, dotted all over the vast land mass, have taken to the sport, often in a climate which taxes the ingenuity of the best greenkeepers. In South America, the game took off because of the railways; to be specific, because of the British golf enthusiasts who were employed to lay down the railway lines as part of a huge investment programme in Argentina. In their spare time they founded the Buenos Aires Golf Club in 1878. Trains were also the catalyst by which golf was introduced in similar circumstances to Brazil, at Sao Paulo in 1890. It was a fitting way of reaching the unconverted since in Britain the railways were partly responsible for encouraging the game to prosper away from the major cities and towns. They provided a speedy and convenient means of transport to the seaside and other holiday areas suitable for the building of golf courses.

It is evident that Britain spread the word either via the Commonwealth or through the independent activities of small groups of its nationals. The latter took golf to Pau in France in 1856, although it was largely in northern and central Europe – Germany, Sweden, Denmark, Czechoslovakia (well before the days of Stalin, Yalta and the Warsaw Pact, let alone before the country was split in two in 1993) and, inevitably, Holland – that it received the greatest nourishment on the continent. Its more recent development along the Mediterranean, notably in Spain, was a response to the wishes of sun-seeking northerners. Despite the tournament exploits of Severiano Ballesteros and others, and some gradual signs for optimism, the game in Spain is still mainly the preserve of the Spanish rich and foreigners, as is golf also in Portugal.

Finally, in the last century there was, literally, a new world to conquer. The British shipped golf to North America in 1873, when a club was established at Montreal, now Royal Montreal, in Canada. An emigrant Scotsman, Alexander Dennistoun, takes the credit, and

ANCIENT LINKS *This scene of Hoylake Links, painted in 1895, shows the view looking west towards Kirby.*

A FAIR GAME FOR THE FAIRER SEX *While women are by no means welcome at every golf club in Britain today, they did play the game with gusto even in the last century.*

THE FATHER OF AMERICAN GOLF? *John Reid posthumously – and by default – assumed this title after forming the first club in the United States.*

within ten years there were further courses at Quebec, Toronto, Ottawa and Niagara. Another Scotsman, John Reid, is lauded, though more controversially, as the man who instigated the biggest breakthrough of all – the taking of golf to the United States.

Intriguingly, though golf is generally acknowledged to have taken root in the United States only 100 years ago, one has to go all the way back to 1650 to discover the first mention of *colf* in the court records of the justices at Fort Orange in New York State. They dealt with perhaps the first documented instance of a brawl over who was to pay for the after-round drinks. One Jacob Stol was fined 20 guilders or 2½ beaver skins for his part in the fight: an unusual penalty, the currency being explained by Stol's nationality and the fact that the Dutch West India Company had based a settlement there, and the skins being appropriate since that was the prime commodity in which it did business. But the Dutch obviously took *colf* to America with them as well, and it was hardly their fault if the natives were reluctant to take it up in earnest, albeit as golf, for over another two centuries.

In between times, there were desultory indications of golf making gradual inroads into American society. Henderson and Stirk, in another remarkably researched

book, *Golf in the Making*, uncovered a reference in the Port of Leith records to a consignment of 96 clubs and 432 balls being sent to Charleston, South Carolina, in 1743. There are documents showing that a golf club was formed there later, in 1786, and around that time there was also a golf club at Savannah in the same state. The source of that evidence – an invitation to the club's members to attend a ball – is all the material that bears testimony to Savannah's existence and it may be that it was really a social club which just fancied the word 'golf' included in its name; a kind of legacy from the masons.

Whatever the substance of these stories, the early clubs of the south-east perished during the American Civil War. Several other courses claim to have had a life prior to 1888, including Douglas Field at Chicago (1875), Oakhurst Golf Links (*sic*) in the Allegheny Mountains of West Virginia (1882), the Dorset Field Club in Vermont (1886) and the Foxburg Country Club in Pennsylvania (1887). Their advocates may have a good case or not, but – as with St Andrews' somewhat dubious claim to be the home of golf – John Reid seems destined to be regarded as the man who introduced golf to the United States, thereby lighting a candle that has burned ever-stronger ever since.

Reid was born in Dunfermline in 1840 and had learned the game at Musselburgh. He was living in Yonkers, New York, when he requested a friend, Robert Lockhart, to purchase a few clubs and balls for him while on a visit to Scotland. This Lockhart duly did, from the shop of Old Tom Morris at St Andrews, and after Morris had shipped them across the Atlantic as ordered, Lockhart dispatched them on to Reid. On February 22, 1888, Reid and a few friends used the recently arrived equipment to negotiate a rudimentary three holes he had cut in a field close to his house. The date was the anniversary of Washington's birth. As the American writer, the late Charles Price, remarked in his book, *The World of Golf*:

"Thus, on the birthday of a man who is alleged never to have told a lie in his life, was played the round which presaged a pastime that has since created more lying Americans than any other save fishing."

The same is true the world over. On November 14, Reid and his cronies formally drew up a constitution for their golf club. They called it – surprise, surprise – St Andrew's, although at least they had the grace to insert the apostrophe.

Reid's reputation as the Father of American golf is frankly undeserved. He did nothing to foster the infant game. He resisted uprooting to a more suitable site until the local authorities of Yonkers drove a road through his course, forcing the club to shift to a 30-acre orchard (from which his group derived the sobriquet 'The Old Apple Tree Gang'), where they played over six holes. Eventually, and with some unwillingness on their founder's part, the club moved again to find room for a nine-hole course. Not until 1897 did they have a full 18, and that was only after further peregrinations.

By then, golf had progressed rapidly. By 1891, there were 12 holes at Shinnecock Hills on Long Island to the east of New York city. The course, built on genuinely links-type turf, was a masterpiece of design, particularly for its day. The identity of its creator is a matter of some dispute. It was either laid out by an Englishman, Willie Davis, or a Scotsman, Willie Dunn. Whatever the historical confusion, there is no doubt that Shinnecock hosted the second US Open Championship in 1896.

The attraction of Shinnecock was not confined to its course or its views over Peconic Bay. Atop the hill overlooking the holes was erected an elegant clubhouse designed by the famous American architect, Stanford White: a man of the style, time and place so compellingly evoked by F. Scott Fitzgerald in *The Great Gatsby*.

All these facets conspired to make Shinnecock the first American golf course that looked like one. Not that it was widely known. One marvellous cameo scene was enacted in 1892 when John C. Ten Eyck, a leading figure at Reid's St Andrew's club, met Samuel Parrish, a founder member of Shinnecock, at the latter's Broadway offices. Ten Eyck commented that he had heard people were playing golf on Long Island, a situation he presumably considered odd in view of Reid's stubborn stance of not having anything

to do with popularizing the sport. Parrish's innocent reply shows that both men were equally startled by the truth. "*Why, yes,*" he said. "*Does anyone else play golf in this country?*"

Hundreds of Scotsmen, and some Englishmen, now began to arrive in America, some as teaching professionals, others as greenkeepers, architects, ballmakers – anything. A Scottish accent in particular was a passport to a job. It was a great opportunity for the emigrants and it was the reason why the United States was so overwhelmed by golf in such a short space of time.

Golf course construction provided the best barometer. In 1890, Reid's cow pasture was the country's only golf course. By 1896, the figure had risen to over 80. Four years later, there were 982. This phenomenal explosion meant that by 1900 there were more American courses than British ones, though, with very few exceptions, none worthy of being mentioned in the same breath as the famous existing links of Britain or the magnificent inland courses among the pine trees and on the heaths which would soon be built in England. This was primarily due to the prevailing philosophy, 'quantity, not quality'. One Tom

FIRST IMPRESSION *John Reid's rudimentary course near his home in New York. Reid is on the extreme right in the photograph, which, taken in 1888, is the earliest known photograph of golf in the United States.*

INFLUENTIAL US PIONEER

One of the founders of the St Andrew's Club in the US, Henry Tallmadge was also the first secretary of the USGA.

FIRST US AMATEUR

Charles Blair Macdonald is in the centre of this photograph at what was supposed to be the first US Amateur Championship, in 1894. When Macdonald didn't win it, however, he had the result erased from the record books.

Bendelow in particular has been heavily castigated by many writers for the number of 'quickie' courses he laid out, apparently without care or scruple, but it is likely that he was merely fulfiling the wishes of his paymasters within the budgets he was allocated.

Golf was a perfect sport for America in the Gay Nineties. Its upper-class genteel image fitted perfectly the thriving economy and the rise of that most American of symbols, the motor car. The United States was ready for golf; whether golf was prepared for Charles Blair Macdonald is more questionable.

Macdonald was an American whose grandfather lived in St Andrews (Scottish version). Young Charlie went to St Andrews University, met the great men of the game and assiduously studied the great British golf courses. His labours in the latter respect bore fruit when in 1909 he unveiled his pride and joy, the National Golf Links, right next door to Shinnecock Hills. Every hole on it was directly inspired by those he had seen and most admired on his travels throughout England and Scotland. Earlier, in 1893, he had designed the Chicago Golf Club, the country's first purpose-built 18-hole course.

Macdonald was a tremendous traditionalist, adamant that American golf should maintain close links with the game's founders. He was also an over-

powering bull of a man. In 1894, the Newport Golf Club on Rhode Island, also on the eastern seaboard, staged what was intended to be America's first national amateur championship, over 36 holes of strokeplay. All was well until Macdonald collapsed in the second round with a score of 100 to lose by a stroke to a Mr Lawrence. He protested that he had been unjustly penalized by a controversial ruling, and that in any case no self-respecting national competition could be held at strokeplay, as manifested by the fact that he, the best golfer in the land, hadn't won it. Duly cowed, the members of St Andrew's agreed to hold a matchplay event a month later. This, too, was denied a place in the annals of the sport when Macdonald lost in the final to a Mr Stoddard after narrowly failing to overcome the combined effects of a late-night party thrown by Stanford White on the eve (and indeed the morn) of the last day, plus a bottle of champagne quaffed at lunchtime in a bid to drown his hangover.

Call it charisma, nerve, bombast or something ruder, but Macdonald's acerbic criticisms of the calibre of the victor were upheld again. The championship did not count. Mr Stoddard went the way of the hapless Mr Lawrence before him and out of the record books. Macdonald bequeathed many things to the generations that followed, but sportsmanship and good manners were not among them.

The 1895 US Amateur was more successful. It was the first run under the auspices of the United States Golf Association (USGA) and its first president, Theodore Havemeyer. To quote Charles Price again:

"It became clear to some of the level-headed players that American golf was fast on its way to becoming nothing more than an offshoot of Charlie Macdonald's mercurial personality."

Accordingly, Havemeyer and two colleagues invited representatives from the nation's five most prominent clubs – St Andrew's, Shinnecock Hills, Chicago, Newport and The Country Club at Brookline, Massachusetts – to join them. John Reid and Macdonald were among these men, and out of this organization has grown the USGA, the American equivalent of the R & A.

The first 'official' US Amateur at Newport was also a success because it was won by Macdonald, though

there were a few glum faces at the outcome. He pasted Charlie Sands, a Newport member, by 12 & 11 in the final, but Macdonald didn't suffer from an economy-sized ego and he wasn't satisfied at that. He was determined to set a new course record. He had the local pro hauled out to partner him for the remaining holes, apparently unaware that it wouldn't have counted anyway as the contest had been at matchplay and not everything had been holed out. Having said that, who's to say he wouldn't have bullied the newly-founded authority round to his opinion had he managed to set a new 'record'?

On the day after the Amateur, the first US Open was played on the same course and won by Horace Rawlins, an Englishman, by two strokes from Willie Dunn. There were no complaints as to the validity of this 36-hole event because Macdonald didn't bother to enter.

From 1895 onwards, golf caught hold in America. It blossomed in the Roaring Twenties as it had in the Gay Nineties and for similar reasons: an economic boom. It survived the Great Depression and the Second World War to be revitalized in the 1960s by Arnold Palmer, President Eisenhower and television, though not necessarily in that order.

The impact of these factors and others – Walter Travis being the first American-based player to win the British Amateur in 1904; Johnny McDermott being the first native-born American to win his national Open; Francis Ouimet's improbable and romantic triumph over the best of British, Harry Vardon and Ted Ray, at the 1913 US Open; Walter Hagen's domination of the British Open in the 1920s and then Bobby Jones's domination of the whole game – are best dealt with in more appropriate sections of this book. So, too, in the next chapter, is the way in which America quickly cornered the equipment market, perhaps notably with the arrival of the A. G. Spalding Company on the scene in 1894, and the subsequent invention of the rubber-cored ball by a Cleveland chemist, called Coburn Haskell, in 1901.

But it is apposite to note here how the east coast influence was gradually diluted in the face of a comprehensive conversion to the faith. If by 1900 there was at least one course in each of the then 45 states of the Union, the Golden Age between the wars saw a

"What's wrong here?"

CHICAGO   TWENTY CENTS A COPY   TWO DOLLARS PER YEAR

staggering increase along the Pacific shoreline and the creation of fabulous and luxurious resort courses on the mainland, especially in Florida, and on the glorious off-shore islands of the Caribbean. The boundaries of agronomy have been relentlessly pushed back. New strains of grass have been nurtured to cope with the enormous range of climatic conditions encountered across the United States. Even the inhospitable desert is today home to verdant golf courses which present an unbelievable contrast to their bleak, rugged surroundings.

Golf in the United States has never been a seaside game in the strict sense in which it began in Scotland, but the Americans have patented a new set of hallmarks typified by lavish clubhouses, country clubs where golf is but one of several amenities, and real-estate development funding the cost of building a neighbouring resort course. As Peter Dobereiner, the widely respected British golf writer, has said of its development in the early 1900s:

"The game which had started as an informal knock-about on the sandy turf of a Scottish fishing town 450 years previously was now full grown and under new management."

A POPULAR PASTIME

The popularity of golf in the States grew rapidly at the beginning of the century, as witnessed by these popular journals of the time.

CHAPTER TWO

EVOLUTION & INNOVATION

*Golf is intrinsically the same pastime it was centuries ago but there have been major changes to the way
we play it. Some of these developments may be regrettable – like the six-hour round and the proliferation of
golf carts – but most have added to our enjoyment of the game.*

First, consider the fundamental implements of golf – the ball and the club. It is axiomatic, given the facts outlined in the previous chapter, that there are earlier references to the clubs and balls of golf – or *colf* – in the Low Countries than in Scotland. There are several 15th-century references to both club- and ball-makers in Holland, and records show that the Scots imported balls from across the North Sea, literally by the barrel-load, as long ago as 1486.

The Dutch *colfers* originally played with wooden balls, generally of elm or beech, which had negligible aerodynamic properties. They gradually adopted a ball made of white leather and filled with cow's hair, which was used in the local game of *kaatsen* (hand tennis). It is possible that it was the *kaatsen* ball that inspired the Scots to invent the feathery sometime in the 17th or early 18th century as a substitute for the wooden ball which was probably the popular ball of the day.

The feathery consisted of a leather casing, usually bull's hide, soaked in alum and crammed with goose feathers which had been softened by boiling. This was then knocked into shape (round, of course!) and painted white to make it more visible and more resistant to the elements. On drying it became tighter and firmer. It weighed about the same as the modern ball (that is, 1.62 ounces) and was usually a similar size, though in those days there was no uniform diameter.

The feathery had two diverse effects. First the good news. Whereas the cumbersome wooden ball could seldom be propelled more than 100 yards, distances of twice that and more were regularly achieved with the feathery. Samuel Messieux, a Swiss schoolteacher based at St Andrews, boomed a measured drive of 361 yards over the Old Course in 1836. Conditions were slightly favourable

BALLS OF A FEATHER *Two early examples of the basic feathery ball: one by Allan Robertson (above, left) circa 1840; the other by D. Marshall, 1830.*

VANITY PAIR *Mirror, mirror on the wall, who has the fairest swing of all? Nick Faldo and David Leadbetter work on getting the right image (opposite).*

– a frosty ground and a helping breeze – but the prodigious blow emphasized the qualities of the feathery. In wet weather, when it became rather soggy, its advantage over the wooden ball was not so marked. It is worth noting that the very act of stitching up the finished product inadvertently assisted its flight because the seams fulfilled a similar, if cruder, role to that played by the dimples which help the modern ball get airborne.

But the feathery had a downside, too. It made golf far too expensive for the ordinary man. One feathery cost twelve times the price of the old boxwood ball and, astonishingly, about the same as a wooden club. Even the most skilled craftsman struggled to produce more than four a day, which accounted for its apparently exorbitant price, and the average player may have used that many balls a round due to the feathery's tendency to split or get too damp. It could also, of course, in the time-honoured manner, be lost.

The less wealthy no doubt had to make do with wooden balls for decades after the coming of the feathery, and it is from this era that golf's image as a rich man's preserve still lingers. In Scotland it has managed to retain a name as a game for the common man, even though that has not always been the case. But from the moment that the Stuart kings took the game south to England with them, golf has always been exported with a designer label. The introduction of the gutta percha ball in 1848 may not have eradicated golf's snobby reputation but it did an enormous amount to restore it as a genuinely popular game.

Gutta percha is like sap, a gum which can be tapped from trees indigenous to Malaya. The substance is malleable when boiled in water and becomes hard on cooling.

There are mixed accounts as to how gutta percha came to find its niche in golf,

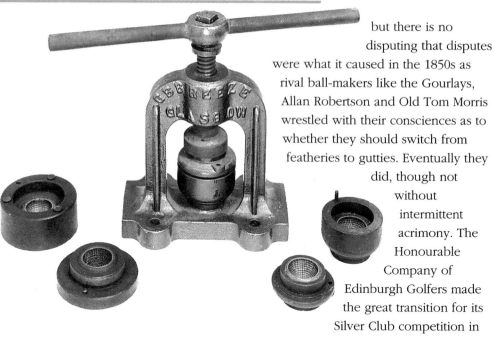

THE WAY THEY WERE
This rudimentary implement is a golf-ball mould from late in the last century.

WELL STUFFED *To make a feathery ball, manufacturers would fill a top hat with feathers, usually from a goose although chicken feathers were also suitable.*

but there is no disputing that disputes were what it caused in the 1850s as rival ball-makers like the Gourlays, Allan Robertson and Old Tom Morris wrestled with their consciences as to whether they should switch from featheries to gutties. Eventually they did, though not without intermittent acrimony. The Honourable Company of Edinburgh Golfers made the great transition for its Silver Club competition in 1865. With that, the last feathery had flown.

Its demise was not so much due to the greater distance that could be attained with the gutty as the difference in cost. Because the process involved in the manufacture of the latter was a great deal simpler, it was approximately a quarter of the price of a feathery. At a shilling a ball, with clubs at 3s 6d (17½p) each and the highest subscription in the land standing at three guineas (£3.15), this was the age when golf in Britain became more of a game for everyone. The increased leisure time created by the prosperity of the Industrial Revolution was another vital ingredient that enabled the sport to catch the imagination of the nation.

The gutty could be remoulded if badly damaged, which was just as well since in the early days it was prone to break up in mid-air, thus forcing the rules to accommodate this tendency by allowing the golfer to play a fresh ball from the point where the largest fragment had come to rest. This would be by no means the last occasion on which the Rules of Golf had to be amended to legislate for the properties of the golf ball. For the remainder of the 19th century, the new ball was repeatedly modified to make it more durable, and its outer shell was indented with a hammer after it was observed that the ball flew better when it had been cut or marked than when in its smooth, pristine state.

As quickly as the gutty came on to the scene, it was superseded. In 1901, the rubber-cored ball made its British debut. It was the invention of the fledgling American golf equipment industry. The idea belonged to Coburn Haskell, an employee of the Goodrich Tyre and Rubber Company in Ohio. Elastic thread was wound around a rubber core under extreme tension and then encased in a patterned outer cover of gutta percha. Although there were a few initial teething troubles not unlike those that beset the gutty, it had the inestimable advantage of covering a reasonable amount of ground when mishit, whereas the less lively gutty went nowhere and left a stinging sensation in the fingers if topped.

The Haskell ball was dubbed as being only fit for hackers by the great Harry Vardon – largely, one suspects, because he could see that it would scupper the prospects of the Vardon Flyer, a Spalding-made gutty ball he had launched in America on a mammoth promotional tour in 1900 – and derided by others as a 'Bounding Billy' that would ruin the finer arts of shot-making. If the ostriches could not see that a ball capable of compensating for a mishit was a gift from heaven to most golfers, in 1902 they were shown what a difference it made to the best players when Sandy Herd played four rounds at Royal Liverpool in 307 to beat Vardon and James Braid by a shot for the Open. Herd used the same ball for all 72 holes. It was a Haskell, and he was the only man in the field to play with one. Goodbye gutty.

From that moment, the Haskell ball has been improved to such effect that it has spawned a host of dicta from the R & A and USGA, the dual arbiters of the integrity of the sport. In 1920 they agreed the ball should weigh no more than 1.62 ounces and have a diameter of not less than 1.62 inches, a radical move since until then there had been no restrictions whatsoever, although the earlier enforcement of a 4 ¼-inch hole obviously ruled out ridiculously large spheres. Both bodies pledged to "*take whatever steps they think necessary to limit the powers of the ball with regard to distance should any ball of greater power be introduced*".

MOULDY OLDIES *The two boxes (left) contain a selection of gutty balls, while the four individual ones (featured far left) are two feathery (to the left) and two hand-hammered balls (to the right).*

But from January 1931, the USGA turned its back on collective responsibility and opted for independence. The 'big ball' was introduced, having a minimum size of 1.68 inches and a maximum weight of 1.55 ounces. A year later the weight stipulation was raised to 1.62 ounces and that remains the position.

The idea behind the big ball had been to provide "an easier and pleasanter ball for the average golfer" but, as with Haskell's invention, the big ball was soon perceived to be better for professionals as well. It sat up more invitingly on America's predominantly parkland courses (unlike the smaller ball, which had evolved in the windy conditions and tight lies prevalent in British links golf) and was easier to chip and putt well with – all benefits for the club player. However, it was also less forgiving of bad shots. American professionals therefore had to improve their striking technique in order to master the big ball.

In 1951, the USGA rejected a proposal, advanced by a special committee of its own and R & A members, that each ball should ordinarily be legal on both sides of the Atlantic, though they agreed to the suggestion for players in international team competitions. Subsequent attempts to settle for a uniform ball, perhaps of 1.66 inches, failed, but the American belief in the supremacy of their ball has since been justified. The Professional Golfers' Association (PGA) in Great Britain, swayed by the persuasive voices of those who attributed the American dominance of golf to their employment of the big ball, announced in 1968 that it was to experiment with the 1.68-inch version in its tournaments. Soon it was mandatory. In 1974, the R & A made the big ball compulsory for the Open Championship. Under the rules revisions that came into effect in 1988, the R & A outlawed the small ball altogether.

In still more recent times, the ball has - literally - gone from strength to strength. The original gutta percha shell of the Haskell has given way to new and refined compounds. Millions have been spent researching the properties of various formations of dimples. Winding has got tighter. Wound (three-piece) balls now compete with solid balls for their share of the market, though the solid ball of today is far removed from the solid wooden ball of the past. It is a two-piece composition which used to be considered particularly suitable for the average club golfer, but technology is rapidly breaking down such previously accepted barriers of expertise. The old distinctions, such as between balata and surlyn covers, are becoming ever-more blurred.

In the modern era, that R & A/USGA pledge of 1920 has become very meaningful. The young lions, or gorillas, of professional tournament golf hit the ball so far that many experts are worried that hundreds of the world's best courses are in danger of becoming obsolete. The imposition of velocity and distance standards have not stopped players like John Daly (OK, there's no one else quite like John Daly, but he is just the lord of a legion of long-hitters) reaching 500-yard-plus holes with a drive and a sand wedge.

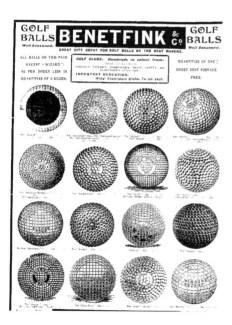

RANGE OF BALLS *Golf ball advertisements (right) were crammed affairs around the turn of the century. Notice that the Vardon Flyer is included in this one.*

This sort of hitting, though more powerful and prevalent among contemporary golfers, is not an entirely new phenomenon. Back in 1966, Henry Longhurst, the famous writer and broadcaster, recognizing that excessive distance is only undesirable when given to professionals and is actually the biggest boon of all for mere mortals, advocated *"a special and shorter 'tournament ball' for 'them' and another, the present one, for 'us'."*

That is a cry frequently echoed nowadays, but talk of a standard tournament ball is invariably resisted by the players and manufacturers. And distance isn't the only potential issue. A few years ago, the USGA banned the no-hook, no-slice Polara ball because it was considered to undermine the integrity of the game. The inventors engaged the USGA in bitter and expensive court proceedings which cost the governing body millions of dollars, but the prohibition was upheld. However, the marketing men and the scientists haven't given up. In 1993, Spalding announced the launch of its Magna ball. It has a diameter of 1.72 inches. Other companies have followed suit. (Remember, the current regulations only stipulate a *minimum* diameter of 1.68 inches.) In addition to the

THE PIONEER *Harry Vardon's action and grip (above) now look classical, but in his day they were unorthodox.*

THE PULVERIZER *John Daly is the biggest hitter in contemporary tournament golf, using modern equipment such as the driver shown here.*

manufacturers' claim that the ball supplies the average golfer with distance, accuracy and feel, its greater size also means less spin – which should mean that it slices and hooks less than a conventional ball!

Ball manufacturing today is big business indeed, far removed from the age when Allan Robertson was stitching up his featheries and muttering darkly about the gutty. What would he have made of today's day-glo pink, yellow and orange golf balls?

The mass production of the ball throughout this century has brought golf within the pocket and reach of millions of people all over the world, and the improvement in its playing characteristics has perhaps been the single largest factor in enhancing our enjoyment of the game. But a better ball would not be much use without better clubs with which to hit it.

It is man's primeval instinct to hit something with a stick. Clubs in all sports have been adapted for their specific purpose from this basic principle. Neither the Dutch nor the Scots can claim to have invented this innate desire, though the Scots can produce proof to show that they supplied wooden clubs to Holland around 1650.

Club-making came into its own with the advent of the feathery. Clubs no longer had to withstand the impact of striking a solid wooden ball, and artistry was given a free reign. Exquisite wooden clubs were fashioned from ash, thorn, apple and pearwood. The emphasis was on woods because irons would have inflicted untold damage on the delicate feathery. They

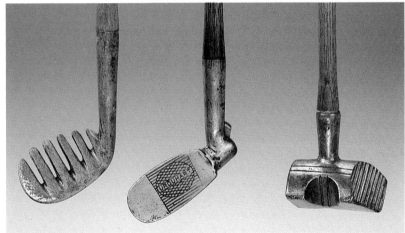

were generally used to extricate the errant golfer from the awkward lies to be found in cart tracks and on railway lines.

But irons were ideally suited to the less yielding gutty when it appeared in 1848, whereas the wood-makers had to run to harder materials for the clubhead, which became more rounded and less banana-shaped. The period up to the end of the 19th century is a marvellous tale of the skills of Scotland's master club-makers: the Dicksons, Henry Miln, Simon Cossar, Hugh Philp, Robert Forgan and others. It is a story admirably told by Henderson and Stirk in *Golf In The Making*, but sadly there is no room for detail here.

By the turn of the century, the Americans had not only produced the Haskell ball but also begun to dominate the club market. They had unlimited natural resources available and wooden clubs were their forte, though for a while they still looked to Britain for iron heads. Persimmon and dogwood were employed in the making of these new woods, and hickory replaced ash in the shaft. From that time until the present day, the United States has led the equipment field, though lately – as in so many fields of industrial endeavour – the Japanese have become increasingly influential.

These days, you can forget the simple distinction between woods and irons. Now both offer a wide range of shafts – for example, steel, graphite and aluminium – with different swingweights, flexpoints, kickpoints, etc. to suit. (This whole area is a delight to jargon fans, with phrases like 'frequency matching' and 'peripheral weight distribution' littering the manufacturers' advertisements.)

Woods don't necessarily have a wooden head. They could be made of metal, graphite, plastic or something more exotic, like the bullet-proof headed driver with a titanium shaft that John Daly wielded to bludgeon Crooked Stick in the 1991 US PGA Championship. The head might have a special section of yet another substance inserted into the clubface to fit the particular golfer's requirements, and the head itself may be out-size, mid-size or (rarely, these days, it seems) just plain normal.

Irons may be forged or cast. The former are blade irons, used by professionals and better players, while their cast cousins may be cavity-backed, peripherally-weighted irons that are generally classified as 'game-improvement clubs', ie. specifically geared for those players whose games need the most urgent surgery. From 1992, the Rules of Golf permitted the production of iron clubs with inserts of other materials in the face. Mostly, the manufacturers opted for graphite-based inserts. It was, of course, only a matter of time before someone came up with a graphite-faced iron that had a steel insert. By 1993, a Japanese company, Yonex, had done just that.

Some of these developments are doomed to be regarded by posterity as mere fads; others will change the game forever, as did the arrival of steel shafts. Steel didn't have the problems of high torque, or twisting, inherent in hickory, and it enabled accurately matched sets of clubs to be mass produced, an invaluable aid to the average player.

Steel shafts were not allowed until 1924, when the

THE SHAPES OF GOLF *Six clubs that were a familiar sight at the turn of the century. From left to right: Hammer Cross Head Driver; a hickory-shafted Hoe Putter; an Anderson Cross-Head crescent-shaped iron with the loft of a mashie; a Brown's Patent perforated iron; an Urquhart adjustable iron; and a hollow, brass-headed Nicola Putter.*

FIVE BEECH WOODS *These clubs (above) represent the craftsmanship of four men in the late 19th-century; from left to right: Thomas Dunn; Willie Park; Douglas McEwan; James Anderson and Dunn again.*

HARD SELL *Golf club adverts tended to be heavy-going text rather than picture heavy.*

USGA legalized them. At that time, the R & A ruled "*it is much to be deplored that players, instead of trying to master the use of clubs, should endeavour to overcome the difficulties of the game by using implements which have never been associated with it*". But by 1930 the R & A had acquiesced. Ironically, that was the year Bobby Jones won the Grand Slam playing with hickory-shafted clubs. It was effectively their last hurrah, but a defiant way to go out.

Club technology has repeatedly come under the microscope. In 1949, the Americans protested that the grooves on the British players' irons for the Ryder Cup match at Ganton were too deep. Ben Hogan, the US captain, requested that the clubfaces be filed down. His wish was granted. In 1977, Tom Watson was at the centre of a controversy when it was disclosed that the grooves on the clubs with which he had won so many championships were in contravention of the regulations. Should he retrospectively be disqualified for obtaining an unfair, if inadvertent, advantage, some purists asked? The answer, rightfully, was 'no'.

But that was by no means the end of the grooves disputes. Until April 1993, an American court had before it the case of the Karsten

Manufacturing Company against the US PGA Tour after the latter had attempted to ban all U-groove clubs, including Karsten's hugely successful Ping Eye2 irons, from its tournaments. But then sanity prevailed, and the two parties reached an out-of-court settlement that inevitably had both sides claiming victory, although allegedly the tour's insurers had to cough up close to $7 million. Either way, the ban against U-groove clubs was dropped.

Under the terms of an out-of-court settlement reached on January 27, 1990, after a similar lawsuit was brought by Karsten against the USGA, Eye2 irons purchased prior to that agreement remain legal in the United States and Mexico and will still be legal there after January 1, 1996, the date from which they will not be acceptable in R & A-approved competitions. Karsten had previously dropped its concurrent lawsuit against the R & A because of lack of jurisdiction.

It can be seen that schisms in the hierarchies of the game are a contemporary occurrence as well as being a thing of the past. It was back in the early years of the century that the R & A and the USGA went their separate ways over the notorious Schenectady (centre-shafted) putter with which Walter Travis broke the British stranglehold on the Amateur Championship in 1904.

There was a good deal of ill-feeling between Travis and the officials at Sandwich that week. When the R & A outlawed the instrument shortly thereafter, in what was widely seen as a fit of pique, they exported the unsavoury atmosphere across the Atlantic. Relations with the USGA were strained for a long time afterwards, perhaps accounting for the lack of agreement over the legalization of steel shafts and the breakaway over the ball specifications. It was to be nearly half a century before the centre-shafted putter was given the R & A's blessing, and when that happened it paved the way for Ben Hogan, who used one, to make his solitary but successful pilgrimage to the Open Championship, at Carnoustie in 1953.

Ever since there has been a hole to aim at, golfers have complained about their putters, often ignoring the obvious truth of the old proverb:"*It's a bad workman who blames his tools*". Putters used to be made of wood, but less so after the arrival of the gutty, when iron heads came into fashion. They have come in all sorts of weird and wonderful shapes; with mirrors attached, on wheels, on rollers – you name it, it's been tried. These crazy-looking contraptions aren't just footnotes in the history books either: the Basakwerd putter, with its blade fixed to the shaft in reverse, was in vogue for a while on the US Senior tour; two-time Masters champion Bernhard Langer has tried one with three plastic balls attached in line behind the head; Jack Nicklaus won the 1986 Masters with a weapon which resembled a vacuum cleaner; and since the early 1990s, the 'broom-handle' putter has been in vogue. Many eminent professionals abhor the fact that this club – with which the top of the grip nestles in the left hand under the player's neck, while the right hand makes the stroke – is even allowed by the rules. Until, or if, it is banned, the broom-handle seems well placed to maintain its popularity. At the 1993 Australian Masters, the top-three finishers all used one.

Clubs have had about as big an impact on the Rules of Golf as has the ball. In 1938, the USGA restricted a player to a maximum of 14 clubs in his bag, a decision ratified by the R & A in 1939. The situation was getting badly out of hand. Caddies were having to lug round 30 clubs or more.

The Rules of Golf have been amended considerably since the original 13 were enacted by the Honourable Company of Edinburgh Golfers in 1744.

The first rules were devised for matchplay and the one that was to cause the greatest argument was the original Rule 6, concerning touching balls. In 1775, 'touching' was redefined to mean within six inches of each other. The stymie had arrived.

The effect of the stymie rule was that the player furthest from the hole *had* to putt first. If his opponent's ball was dead on his line to the hole – assuming they were over six inches apart – it was too bad. He had to negotiate the obstacle as best he could. Some thought the stymie an abomination, an evil without merit since it could not be negated by the sporting gesture of putting out first. Others felt it was simply part of the strategy of golf, and this view was expressed with such ferocity that after the St Andrews' Society abolished the stymie in 1833 they felt compelled to restore it in 1834.

It was in 1834 that the Royal and Ancient Golf Club

UNLOVELY BUT LEGAL *Sam Torrance is one top pro who uses a broom-handle putter. In April 1993, he won a European tour event the same week that Rocco Mediate, also using a broom-handle putter, won in the United States.*

FIVE WAYS TO MAKE A PUTT *This handful of putters (below) all date from the early 19th century. They include a ladies' putter (second from right) and a Harry Vardon putter (far right).*

STYMIED! *This image of the dilemma posed by the stymie is after a painting by J.C. Dolman. As golf rules slowly evolved, one of the most controversial aspects that players had to contend with was the stymie, which grew out of the debate over the original Rule 6, on 'touching' balls.*

was created and soon its version of the rules was accepted throughout Britain and beyond in preference to those of the Honourable Company, the latter body gracefully acceding to the inevitable decline in its influence. The R & A presided over an increase to 22 rules in 1854, when St Andrews celebrated its centenary as a golf society.

In 1897 the R & A appointed its first Rules of Golf Committee but, as we have seen, its relationship with the USGA for over half a century was not entirely cordial – at best uncertain, at worst frosty. Differences in the formal decisions each body handed down meant that the understanding of the rules varied.

Accordingly, in 1951 a bid was made to heal the breach for the good of the game. A series of conferences was organized and the R & A and USGA arranged to meet regularly to review the rules in unison. They could not reach a compromise on the size of the ball but they did agree to jettison the stymie, thereby killing off a unique facet of matchplay. Subsequently, a Joint Decisions Committee was set up to ensure uniformity in interpretation of the rules and in the implementation of change.

Golf has changed in many other ways. For example, nearly 100 years ago Harry Vardon came to prominence, and he may be said to have revolutionized the golf swing. Vardon, who won the first of his record six Open Championships in 1896, not

only gave his name to the overlapping grip which he popularized – although at least one leading player, Johnny Laidlay, a Scot who won the Amateur in 1889 and 1891, had adopted it before Vardon – but also used a swing which was then decidedly unorthodox. He stood slightly open to the ball at address, whereas his rivals were closed, and he took the club away in an upright arc rather than with a long, low backswing. The consequences of these two moves enabled him to hit the ball from left to right. He could also hit the ball higher than most players if required.

Throughout this century, the best players have allied their individual actions to improvements in equipment and have worked on creating a swing that will stand up to the rigours of tournament golf. Nobody has ever done it with such flowing rhythm and style as Bobby Jones; no one has toiled so long on the range or hit so many perfect shots as Ben Hogan; no man has practised with such reward as Jack Nicklaus.

Those three golfers, together with Vardon, are surely the finest golfers in history, but the secret of golf does not lie in copying them since even they had, or have, idiosyncratic quirks which worked for them but wouldn't for others. As for Hogan's fabled 'secret of golf', it remains just that: a secret. Or maybe a fable.

It is a fact that fashions in golf swings will continue to come and go as the fortunes of the disciples of a particular method wax and wane. One year upright is in; the next might embrace the revival of the low, slinging action. Does the left or right hand dominate? Should one try to fade or draw the ball? Would the interlocking, overlapping or 10-finger grip be best? And what about unorthodox putting styles, as with the left hand below the right?

These and similar questions have been asked for the past 100 years and will be repeated for as long as golf is played. It is impossible to identify a certain style with a particular time, but we can sure than when Harry Vardon began seriously to tinker with the fundamentals of his golf swing, he was setting a precedent that has fascinated millions of less gifted practitioners ever since.

Through the ages, professional golfers who are tournament players have sought the advice and sagacity of professional golfers who are teachers.

Bobby Jones had Stewart Maiden; Jack Nicklaus had Jack Grout. Today, the most well-known and well-publicized association is that between Nick Faldo and David Leadbetter. In 1985, Faldo, who had been a consistent tournament winner from 1977 to 1984, decided he needed to alter his swing if he was to take the next step upwards. He turned to Leadbetter, an English-born, Zimbabwean-raised, American-resident pro. Between 1987 and 1992, Faldo won five major championships and established himself as comfortably the best golfer in the world. Who knows, maybe the fact that Britain's best golfer is happy to admit that even he requires lessons on a regular basis may drive more British club golfers to seek the assistance of their club pro, as happens more readily elsewhere around the globe. Hitherto, there has almost seemed to be a feeling in Britain that to take lessons is somehow unworthy. It was therefore perhaps no coincidence that in February 1993 the British PGA enlisted Faldo's support for a new campaign aimed at encouraging club golfers to consult their own pro more frequently.

If one was playing golf back in the hearty days of the masons, formal dress was as much a part of the ceremony as it is today at a grand dinner. A red or scarlet jacket was *de rigueur*, to be changed for a blue or grey one when it was time to get down to the serious business of eating and drinking.

This splendid idea of a uniform was enthusiastically taken up by golf's early exponents in the New World. Around that time, the likes of Vardon played championship-winning golf while sporting a buttoned, ventless jacket. Indeed, Vardon felt the constraints this imposed on the body were an asset in maintaining a sound, repetitive swing.

Climate was, inevitably, a major factor in the deregulation of clothing. Wearing a jacket to play golf in the August heat of the central United States made no sense at all, yet that is exactly what Vardon and Ted Ray elected to do during the 1920 US Open at Inverness in Ohio. What's more, Vardon should have won the tournament and Ray did. Even the American competitors that week, although dispensing with jackets, wore a shirt and tie, and plus-fours (with trousers tucked into knee-length socks or stockings) were heavily favoured. But soon ties were on the

decline, although the vivid colours that adorn the modern tour pro were not spotted on the golf course until Jimmy Demaret and Max Faulkner arrived.

Demaret won the Masters three times either side of the Second World War, but his clothes did not always meet with the same approval as his golf. Pink and violet, lemon and peach – he tried all sorts of combinations. At the 1949 Ryder Cup match he unsettled his opponent by stepping on to the first tee clad in a scarlet cap, salmon pink sweater and cherry red trousers. Faulkner, the 1951 Open champion, was similarly inclined to resemble a rainbow. Doug Sanders, who carried a vivid purple colour to disaster at the 1970 Open, continued the tradition and since then flamboyant dress has had to be pretty outrageous to be worthy of comment.

Today, the American Payne Stewart recalls the old days with his abbreviated plus-four socks (known as 'plus-twos' in Britain and 'knickers' in America, with sometimes embarrassing consequences in the UK). What was until recently conventional golf gear – brightly coloured or patterned V-neck sweaters, wide-collared shirts and polyester slacks – is now challenged by casual apparel, such as polo shirts and pleated trousers, straight out of the boutiques and fashion stores. Somewhere above, Vardon is probably looking down in disgust, Demaret with delight.

Finally, this chapter started with a reference to the golf cart, and it will end that way. The cart has, on the whole, been one of America's less glorious contributions to the game. It has simultaneously managed to reduce a healthy exercise to a motorized recipe for bad backs, weak hips and flabby bellies; slowed the game down when logic dictates it should have speeded matters up; and spoiled golf's visual appeal with ugly tarmac roads.

Golf carts are not all bad. They are marvellous for infirm or elderly golfers, they can be desirable in extreme heat, and they make a lot of money for the clubs that operate them, thus helping to keep other expenses down.

But generally speaking the golf cart is confirmation that change is not always for the better and proof that progress does not necessarily take us forward – especially if the damned thing is stuck in reverse.

SNAPPY SWINGERS *Payne Stewart (above) is a thoroughly modern golfer given to sartorial nostalgia. Jose Maria Olazabal (below) dresses in a smartly casual manner that would not look out of place in any non-golfing environment.*

CHAPTER THREE

HOUSEHOLD NAMES

The most widely accepted test of a golfer's greatness is his performance in the game's major championships. In the modern era, these comprise the Open Championship (or 'British Open' as it is sometimes referred to in this book in order to avoid confusion), the US Open, the Masters (held in the United States each April) and the US PGA Championship.

But there is more to being a 'household name' than simply the accumulation of titles, however prestigious those titles may be, and granted that winning them often involves skills that are far from simple. In short, a selection is inevitably subjective. Whatever principles one adopts in choosing who qualifies for inclusion in a category like this, the exercise is likely to prove invidious, even though it need not be specifically tendentious. And in this chapter, the featured players are not only the leading male professionals of this age or any other. It embraces both the amateur scene and women's golf, where the established criteria of excellence are less rigid, but no less present for that.

The 40 brief biographies that follow in this chapter will each, I trust, make the case for their subject's inclusion. All I can do now is apologize to, or for, those I have omitted. They have been left out due either to a) lack of space, or b) my poor judgement, depending on how you look at it.

Among the eminent players not included in this chapter but who have nevertheless made an impact on the glorious history of the game are Allan Robertson (the best golfer in the years before the Open Championship was inaugurated); Willie Park (winner of the first Open and three others); Willie Anderson (winner of four US Opens in five years just after the turn of the century); Jim Barnes (winner of two PGAs and an Open on either side of the Atlantic in 10 seasons from 1916); three-time major championship winners Jamie Anderson, Bob Ferguson, Tommy Armour, Denny Shute, Ralph Guldahl, Jimmy Demaret, Cary Middlecoff, Julius Boros, Billy Casper and Larry Nelson; plus a host of two-time major winners.

The aforementioned do not take account of outstanding amateur golfers like Walter Travis, Jerome Travers, Francis Ouimet, Lawson Little and Michael Bonallack; or prominent women players like Lady Margaret Scott, Glenna Collett Vare, Kathy Whitworth and Pat Bradley. And that's without mentioning more recent bright sparks like Fred Couples, Jose Maria Olazabal, Phil Mickelson, Paul Azinger, Betsy King and Laura Davies.

These golfers and more will be found elsewhere in this book. In the meantime, I hope you find this section, arranged alphabetically, to be interesting, informative and maybe thought-provoking. It has certainly not been devoid of thought.

THE GREATEST NAME OF ALL? *Jack Nicklaus, winner of 20 major championships (opposite and page 53), is the greatest player of all time if one is judging by the record books. His dogged determination and absolute concentration have played their part in making him a record-breaker. Moreover, he is also an accomplished golf course designer, and has been a fine ambassador for the sport and for sportsmanship generally.*

THE ROUGH AND THE SMOOTH
The crowds always flock to watch Seve Ballesteros (left and page 38) display his genius, often from the rough. His waywardness from the fairway may cause him to plough the odd rough track, but his astonishing powers of recovery and magical short game make him such an exciting spectacle for golf fans the world over.

PETER ALLISS

(Born February 28, 1931)

■ *The Voice of Golf*

The magazine *Sports Illustrated* in the United States once cruelly – but accurately – opined that a particular boxer wasn't even a household name in his own household. Alliss is a household name, in Britain and the United States especially, even among those who would not regard themselves as golfing *aficionados*.

In Britain, he is veritably 'the Voice of Golf', an undisputed position he holds by dint of his work as the BBC's chief television commentator. Across the Atlantic, his work for ABC has earned him international recognition. TV has been the medium through which Alliss's reputation has been forged since 1969, when he made the last of his eight appearances in the Ryder Cup.

These days, it is easy to forget, or even ignore, how good Alliss was as a golfer. His father, Percy, had been a formidable competitor, too, and in his prime Peter's long game was pretty well the equal of anyone in the world. For example, in 1958 he won the Italian, Portuguese and Spanish Opens in succession. But his short game was less reliable, and his putting was notoriously fallible, never more so than when, as a rookie, he missed two crucial short putts on the last three holes and thereby perhaps cost Britain the 1953 Ryder Cup. Despite that incident, Alliss deserves to be remembered as one of the best players to bridge the British generation gap between Henry Cotton and Tony Jacklin.

For Alliss, the swing – rather than putting – was always the thing.

ISAO AOKI

(Born August 31, 1942)

■ *Blazing a trail for Japanese golf*

Although Isao Aoki has been upstaged in Japan in recent years by his countrymen, Masashi (Jumbo) Ozaki and Tsuneyuki (Tommy) Nakajima, he was the first player from that golf-obsessed nation to make a significant impact outside the Far East. For that reason he has been chiefly responsible for proving that Japan is capable of being a serious force in golf. Although he went seven years between turning professional and winning his first tournament, his subsequent exploits have provided a stirring lesson to his compatriots. What they have to do is what Aoki, singularly, has achieved – win outside their lucrative domestic circuit, where Aoki himself has been triumphant on more than 40 occasions.

In addition to his victories at home, Aoki has won important titles like the World Matchplay Championship (in 1978) and European Open (1983) in Britain, and he provided a stunning climax to the 1983 Hawaiian Open on the US tour – he holed a full wedge shot for an eagle at the last to win by a stroke. His best effort in a major championship was in 1980 when, aged 37, he recorded the then second-lowest score in US Open history. Sadly for him, Jack Nicklaus returned the lowest.

At six feet, Aoki is tall by Japanese standards. By any standards he has been an outstanding putter, and while the magic may be fading from his stroke these days, even now he is a force on the US Senior tour. The example he continues to set should serve as an inspiration for generations of Japanese golfers to come.

More than any other Japanese golfer, Aoki set his sights on international titles.

JOHN BALL
(1862 – 1940)

First amateur to win the Open

In the 1970s and 1980s, Liverpool was the focal point for football in Britain. A century earlier, it was the English centre of golfing excellence – not least because of John Ball, who was born at Hoylake in Cheshire, home of the Royal Liverpool Golf Club. He shares with another son of Merseyside, Harold Hilton, and the greatest amateur golfer in history, the American Bobby Jones, the distinction of being one of only three amateurs to win the Open Championship.

Ball grew up on the Royal Liverpool links, and as a 14-year-old in 1878 he finished tied for fourth in the Open. He won the championship in 1890, thus becoming the first Englishman and the first amateur to capture the title. His breaking of the Scottish monopoly presaged a period of English domination. Ball also won the Amateur Championship that year, obviously making him the first golfer to win the Open and Amateur in the same season. Only Jones, in his Grand Slam year of 1930, has emulated that feat, and there is almost no chance of anyone else ever doing it.

Ball was a long-hitter at his peak, and also possessed a delicate touch with every club in the bag. Horace Hutchinson described him like this: "*In physique he is wiry and active, with sinews like whipcord, and is endowed with a heaven-sent wrist.*"

And Ball was clearly a fearsome competitor. His performances in the Amateur marked him as a golfer for the ages. From 1888 to 1912, he won it eight times, a tally which one can state categorically will never be equalled. These days, anyone who had the talent to get to four would have turned professional well before he reached that stage.

There is perhaps some irony in the fact that Ball was still considered an amateur during this period. He had collected a small sum of money for his high finish in that Open of 1878, but his subsequent application to enter the Amateur Championship was granted because 16 was declared to be the minimum age at which prize money could be received. Whatever one makes of all that, it is worth noting that Ball's record in the Amateur would probably have been even more formidable had he not spent three years away from the hurly-burly of the game, fighting in the Boer War.

In the 1880s and 1890s, all golf watchers had to keep their eye on the Ball.

SEVERIANO BALLESTEROS

(Born April 9, 1957)

◼ *Pure genius from a golfer born to the game*

If Arnold Palmer had not already made golf fans aware of the word 'charisma', Seve Ballesteros would have done it for them. He, together with Nick Faldo, is the best European golfer since Harry Vardon, and he makes golf as exciting to watch as did Palmer – with big hitting, a tendency to wildness, unbelievable powers of recovery and a nerveless putting touch.

Ballesteros is the successor to Gary Player's position as the game's foremost international competitor, having been victorious in a dozen different national Opens as well as winning nearly 70 times in 17 different countries. In 1979, he was the youngest winner of the Open this century, and in 1980 he became the youngest ever winner of the Masters. Through 1992, he had won at least one tournament every year for 17 seasons, a record only Player could better, but he did not win anywhere in 1993, his poorest season since he turned professional, which suggested he might not add to the five majors he had already collected. But then his win at the Benson & Hedges tournament in May 1994 indicated that he might.

Seve, the youngest of four golfing brothers raised by a farmer in Pedrena in northern Spain, has 'invented' more shots than any other contemporary golfer. His unique ability to imagine and execute improbable strokes is an invaluable legacy of learning to play the game with just one club. The chip shot he played to the final green of the 1976 Open indicated his genius; the 3-wood he played from a bunker to the final green of his singles match in the 1983 Ryder Cup confirmed it. However his career fares from hereon, the man is rightfully assured of being regarded by posterity as truly the Arnold Palmer of European golf.

Ballesteros was unquestionably Europe's leading golfer for 10 years or more, until Faldo assumed the mantle on the cusp of the 1980s and 1990s. It was Ballesteros who proved to other European golfers that the Americans are not invincible, even on their own soil and in their most cherished championships. He was the inspiration behind the European victories in the Ryder Cups of 1985 and 1987.

It has been said that Ballesteros was born to golf because his right arm is an inch longer than his left, making it easier for him to adopt the ideal stance. If so, it was a gift from God that he hasn't wasted.

Ballesteros's touch with the short game is legendary, as is the dramatic intensity he brings to the mundane act of lining up a putt.

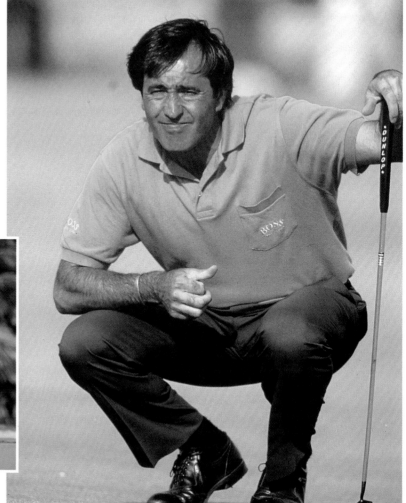

JAMES BRAID
(1870 – 1950)

Five-time Open winner

Scotsman Braid was capable of generating great length with apparently minimal effort.

James Braid, Harry Vardon, and J.H. Taylor were born within 14 months of each other and they remained such close contemporaries that, from 1894 until the outbreak of the First World War, they won 16 Open Championships between them. They dominated the Open so overwhelmingly that on the five occasions another man was able to win, one of the three – who have since been hailed as 'The Great Triumvirate' – was second.

Whereas Taylor was from Devon and Vardon a native of the Channel Islands, the traditionalists could rejoice that Braid at least was a Scotsman. While putting was never his strongest suit, he was not easily deterred by the caprices of fortune. In winning his second Open title, at St Andrews in 1905, he had to extricate himself from the railway line on both the 15th and 16th holes in the final round. These days, he would have been out-of-bounds; back then, those were just unfortunate breaks for Braid to overcome on his way to victory.

A powerful golfer blessed with a serene disposition, Braid won his first Open in 1901, when Taylor and Vardon already had three victories apiece in the championship. But by 1910, Braid had beaten both of them to five. He won all of them in Scotland, where his achievements as a course architect later included Gleneagles and Dalmahoy. But he ended his career in England, as the first professional at Walton Heath in Surrey.

JOANNE CARNER
(Born April 4, 1939)

The Great Gundy meets Big Momma

Some golfers find it tough to make the transition from the amateur to the professional ranks. Not JoAnne Carner. Five times she won the US Women's Amateur (the first three under her maiden name of Gunderson), just one short of Glenna Collett Vare's record. Carner is the only woman to have won that title, the US Girls' Junior Championship and the US Women's Open. She won the latter, the most sought-after honour in women's golf, in both 1971 and 1976.

Her glittering amateur career earned her the nickname of 'the Great Gundy', and in 1969 she became the last amateur to beat the pros on the LPGA Tour. Since she turned professional the following year, her nickname has changed to 'Big Momma', an affectionate reference not only to her less than sylph-like figure but to the prodigious distances she could belt the ball off the tee.

In 1985, Carner won two tour events, taking her career total to 42, but she couldn't add to that during the next seven seasons. In six of those years, frustratingly, her best finish was second, including a playoff loss to Britain's Laura Davies in the 1987 US Women's Open. But, as if to prove that she can't be written off yet, in February 1993 Carner was only denied that 43rd title after a playoff. Victory, at 53, would have taken her past Sam Snead as the oldest player ever to win on the US men's or women's tours. Time hasn't quite run out yet for the woman who will captain the 1994 US Solheim Cup team.

Carner has never been a shrinking violet when it comes to letting her emotions show on the course.

HENRY COTTON

(1907 – 1987)

■ *The first golfer to be awarded a knighthood*

Henry Cotton, 'the Maestro', demonstrated convincingly that the Americans were not invincible when, as a precocious 22 year-old, he secured the critical singles point in Great Britain's victory in the 1929 Ryder Cup match at Leeds.

He went on to win three Open Championships. The first was captured at Sandwich in 1934 and was based on opening rounds of 67 and 65, which permitted him to stumble home in 79 on the last afternoon and still win by five shots. Three years later he fired a closing 71 in atrocious weather at Carnoustie to defy the entire US Ryder Cup team, and in 1948 he recorded his third Open victory at Muirfield. With no Second World War, there would surely have been more Opens for Cotton.

Cotton was blessed with a marvellous hands action, but he didn't just rely on talent. He toiled relentlessly to improve his game, being anxious to learn from the leading Americans of the day, both on and off the course. Like Walter Hagen before him, Cotton refused to accept that the club pro should be treated no better than a servant. He demanded to be accorded privileges and he got them. He was largely responsible for raising the level of tuition fees and, with his erudite and controversial comments in newspaper columns, magazines and books, he increased public awareness and appreciation of the skills of the golf professional. In later life he was involved in course architecture, and his building of Penina did much to popularize Portugal's Algarve coastline as a golfing holiday destination.

In the Queen's New Years Honours List announced at the end of 1987, Cotton became the first golfer to be awarded a knighthood. In the opinion of many supporters of the game, the honour was rather late in coming – in fact, too late. Unintentionally, it proved to be a posthumous tribute. 'Sir Henry' knew of the award but he never had the chance to acknowledge it in public. He had died on December 22, 1987, aged 80. He was buried near Penina, alongside his assertive and flamboyant Argentinian wife Isabel-Maria Estanguet de Moss – known by everyone as 'Toots' – who had been the driving force behind Cotton throughout his career. In that respect, she had been every bit as good a driver as him.

Ever a stylish performer, Cotton adorned magazine covers as well as attracting the admiration of the fans in his heyday.

·GOLF·
ILLUSTRATED
The Weekly Organ of the
Royal and Ancient Game
THE ONLY WEEKLY GOLF JOURNAL IN THE WORLD.
EDITORIAL AND BUSINESS ADDRESS: 18, WOBURN PLACE, LONDON, W.C.1.

No. 1642—VOL. CXXX.   SATURDAY, JULY 17th, 1937

THE NEW CHAMPION
A picture that explains Henry Cotton's astonishing consistency

NICK FALDO

(Born July 18, 1957)

▓ *Totally dedicated world-class champion*

On the night of his 30th birthday, July 18, 1987, Nick Faldo's career had known its ups and downs. After winning 11 times on the European tour, and once in the United States, between 1977 and 1984, Faldo hadn't won at all for three years, until the rot had been halted at the Spanish Open two months previously. Now, he was a shot out of the lead in the Open Championship with 18 holes to play. The next day, Faldo took the title, parring every hole of that final round in the drizzle at Muirfield. The overnight leader, Paul Azinger, bogeyed the last two holes and Faldo had won by a stroke. Since then, it seems he has hardly stopped accumulating majors, even though he lost a US Open playoff in 1988. In 1989, he won the Masters and four tournaments in Europe; in 1990 he won the Masters and the Open; in 1992, he won the Open again and five other tournament titles.

What brought about the transformation? Apart from Faldo's natural athletic ability and single-minded dedication to whatever task he sets himself, the answer is David Leadbetter. Faldo had certainly enjoyed quick success as an amateur after taking up the game at the age of 13 (having watched the 1971 Masters on television). In 1975 he won the British Youths' and the English Amateur. Likewise the early years of his professional career had been rewarding – in 1983, he won five tournaments in Europe and had the best stroke average in the world. By 1985, however, Faldo had convinced himself that he wouldn't win a major championship unless he altered his swing. The swing looked pretty, but at 6'3", he was prone to errors, errors which he realized meant he did not have full control of his game – a lesson he learned in the harshest manner when his challenge for the 1984 Masters subsided while his playing partner, Ben Crenshaw, went on to win. So Faldo entrusted himself fully to Leadbetter, whose glowing reputation as a teacher has been massively assisted by Faldo's subsequent record. They completely rebuilt Faldo's game, a process that would have broken the heart and resolve of a less resilient individual. For two years, the sceptics had said he was mad, but he has emphatically proved the doubters wrong.

The chief accusation against Faldo is that he has almost made the game boring because he has made it predictable. Certainly, at times he seems flawless. Certainly, he is generally the man to beat. And certainly, for Nick Faldo, a new life began at 30.

Whether it be the execution of the golf swing or the meticulousness of his pre-shot preparations, Nick Faldo presently has a matchless talent. The charge of making the game boring that is often levelled against him is the sort of charge previously made against Bjorn Borg in tennis, Steve Davis in snooker, and, latterly, Nigel Mansell in motor racing. It is an allegation that is actually tantamount to an admission of envy.

RAYMOND FLOYD
(Born September 4, 1942)

■ *Golfer for all ages*

Raymond Floyd won his first tournament in 1963, aged 20. In 1992, aged 50, he became the first player to win on the regular and senior US tours in the same season. He has been a golfer for the ages; a golfer for all ages.

When he won his first major, the 1969 US PGA Championship, Floyd was known as Ray in most of the bars and nightclubs where the US tour called a halt. Now he's Raymond, married with a family, and possessor of four major championships – a remarkable effort achieved with what must frankly be described as an ungainly swing, a laboured affair which has nevertheless made him a handsome living.

Floyd won his next two majors – the 1976 Masters and the 1982 PGA – the way he loves best: from the front. He opened with 65-66 at Augusta and eventually equalled the lowest 72-hole score in the tournament's history. Six years later he started with 63-69 at the PGA and that was pretty well that. When he won the 1986 US Open, he was, at 43, the then oldest ever winner of the championship.

In addition to everything else, Floyd was non-playing captain of the US Ryder Cup team in 1989, but back in the side as a player for the seventh time in 1991. In between, he had the 1990 Masters for the taking until he bogeyed the penultimate hole and then lost the ensuing playoff to Nick Faldo at the second hole of sudden-death. He was runner-up again in 1992. A golfer for the ages indeed.

The steel-eyed stare of determination has been as pivotal to Floyd's success as his shot-making.

WALTER HAGEN
(1892 – 1969)

■ *Consummate competitor with dash and elan*

Walter Hagen was golf's first genuine superstar. He was not only capable of outstanding golf but also played the game with dash and elegance, and, off the course, champagne was a regular companion. In truth, the 'Haig' didn't consume half the drinks his reputation suggests, but that didn't stop phrases like "*don't forget to stop and smell the flowers along the way*" and "*I don't want to be a millionaire, just live like one*" coming to represent his outlook on life. It was this philosophy which helped lift his fellow tournament professionals to the level of esteem in which they are regarded today. When he found that pros were refused admission to the clubhouse during the 1920 Open at Deal, he ostentatiously had his Daimler parked outside.

But Hagen wasn't all playboy. He was the consummate competitor. "*Who's gonna be second?*" he would ask on the first tee, and his bravado would regularly be justified. He won the US Open twice, in 1914 and 1919. He won the Open four times between 1922 and 1929, finishing second and third the two times he played and didn't win in those years. He won the US PGA Championship five times from 1921 to 1927, including four in a row. In between, he was runner-up in the only other year he entered.

On the occasions when his tee-to-green game deserted him, which it did quite frequently, he would usually rescue his score with a deft short game and fabulous putting touch. Though past his prime towards the end, Hagen captained the first six US Ryder Cup teams, testimony to his eagerness to cement transatlantic relationships in golf .

While there may have been better golfers than Hagen, there haven't been many, and none with greater charisma.

Not that he was always that amiable towards his British opponents. In 1928, Hagen's agent, Bob Harlow, arranged a 72-hole challenge match at Moor Park between his man and Archie Compston, a leading English professional of the day. Compston demolished Hagen by 18 & 17. "*When you are laid out good and flat, you must not squawk,*" Hagen graciously told the British press.

But as he and Harlow drove away from the humiliation, Hagen declared defiantly:

"*I can beat that sonofabitch on the best day he ever had.*".

From there he went on to Sandwich and won his third Open title. Gene Sarazen was second, Compston third.

HAROLD HILTON

(1869 – 1942)

■ *First golfer to make Amateur Championship double*

Like the great John Ball, Harold Hilton hailed from Liverpool. The first year of Ball's aforementioned break from golf to fight in the Boer War was 1900, and Hilton didn't spurn the opportunity to capitalize while the great man was away. Already three times a beaten finalist, once – in 1892 – at Ball's hands, Hilton took the Amateur Championship for the first time in 1900, at Royal St George's.

He successfully defended it at St Andrews the next year, and won it twice more – in 1911 and 1913. The former was a particularly auspicious triumph. That year, he paired his win at Prestwick with victory in the US Amateur at Apawamis, New York. This made him the first man, and the only Briton, to achieve that double. Three Americans – Bobby Jones, Lawson Little (twice) and Bob Dickson – have also done it. In order to win the US Amateur, Hilton had to survive a tremendous scare in the final. Fred Herreshoff recovered from six down after 22 holes to take him to the 37th, where the Englishman prevailed after his approach shot received a fortunate ricochet on to the green.

Hilton also won the Open Championship twice – in 1892, the year it was extended to 72 holes and first held at Muirfield, and in 1897, at his home course, Royal Liverpool at Hoylake. At 5'7", Hilton may have been short, but his powerful build and competitive temperament meant he wasn't out of his depth in the highest company.

Hilton could reflect that without Ball around, he would have won even more honours.

BEN HOGAN
(Born August 13, 1912)

■ *Indomitable spirit of the 1950s*

Ben Hogan's career did not get off to a fast start. He had to wait seven years for his first win after turning professional in 1931, and he had to wait until after the Second World War to win his first major, the 1946 US PGA Championship. Hogan won the PGA again in 1948, and won his first US Open that summer. Eight months later, he was lucky to be alive.

Hogan was fortunate to survive an appalling car crash in February 1949. He might never walk again, said the doctors, much less play golf. They reckoned without their patient's indomitable spirit; the iron strength that in better times branded him as cold and aloof. By January 1950, he was able to take Sam Snead to a playoff in the Los Angeles Open. By that June, sentimentally, improbably, he was US Open champion again. Most remarkable of all was the fact that he was a more dominant figure after the crash than before it.

Hogan retained his US Open title in 1951, after winning his first Masters. In 1953, he won five of the six tournaments he entered: the Masters for a second time, the US Open for a record-equalling fourth time, and the Open at Carnoustie in his only bid for golf's oldest title. He couldn't play in the PGA because it clashed with the Open, although he never played in it at matchplay after his accident anyway.

The concept of the professional Grand Slam didn't exist at the time. It remains elusive, but it was Hogan's performance in 1953 that helped make it a 'live' subject. That year he won the three majors he could enter and nobody could ask for more. The hours on the practice range – no man has so relentlessly and methodically searched for the perfect swing – paid off to the extent that Hogan is the only 20th-century professional who can claim for a substantial period to have beaten the field more than it beat him. His story was made into a Hollywood film, *Follow The Sun*.

While the early 1950s belonged to Hogan, 1953 was effectively his swansong, though he came agonizingly close to more championships, notably the US Open in 1955 when he was only denied a record fifth crown after a playoff with the almost unknown Jack Fleck. Ben Hogan's name, however, will be known for as long as golf is played. Into his 80s, he is still recognized as epitomizing the closest man has got to attaining perfection in golf.

Hogan with the spoils of victory after completing the final leg of his Triple Slam in 1953 by winning the Open Championship.

HALE IRWIN

(Born June 3, 1945)

■ *Tough guy who's good because he's seldom bad*

The omens look propitious for Hale Irwin. Only four men have won the US Open four times – Willie Anderson, Bobby Jones, Ben Hogan and Jack Nicklaus. Eleven more – Alex Smith, Johnny McDermott, Walter Hagen, Gene Sarazen, Ralph Guldahl, Cary Middlecoff, Julius Boros, Billy Casper, Lee Trevino, Andy North and Curtis Strange – have won it twice. Irwin is the only man to have won it three times. So having moved up into a class of his own with his win at Medinah in 1990, history might suggest that Irwin has one more left in him, although time is not on his side. With that win in 1990, aged 45, Irwin became the oldest US Open champion ever.

Ordinarily, Irwin's quiet, even austere, demeanour indicated what he was – a talented and tough competitor, solid rather than inspirational, who became good by seldom doing anything badly, which was how he won the US Open in 1974 and 1979 over two remorseless layouts. But when in 1990 he sank a putt of around 50 feet for a birdie on the 72nd green that was to earn him a playoff with Mike Donald, which he won, Irwin ran around the green exchanging 'high-fives' with the gallery. It appeared that Irwin had both swapped his spectacles for contact lenses and that he had also undergone a character transplant.

From 1975-78, Irwin didn't miss a cut in 86 starts on the US tour. By 1989, he finished the year 93rd on the Money List. His best days seemed to have gone. His dramatic success at Medinah proved that you just can't keep a tough guy down.

Irwin has been a golfer with an eye for the main chance in the US Open.

TONY JACKLIN

(Born July 7, 1944)

■ *The revitalizer of British golf*

For four seasons – from 1969 to 1972 – there was no brighter star in golf's firmament than Tony Jacklin. He accomplished a great deal. The only regret is that it could have been so much more. Aged 25, he won the Open at Lytham in 1969, the first British champion for 18 years. Watching from the grandstands was a young boy called Sandy Lyle, who would succeed Jacklin as the next home winner. Within a year, Jacklin had added the US Open with no less than seven shots to spare, thus becoming the first Briton for 50 years to win America's national title.

Jacklin revitalized British, and ultimately European, golf with these exploits, but in the

Jacklin's rise to the top coincided, appropriately, with the Swinging Sixties.

ensuing two years he was to suffer cruelly. A month after his US Open triumph he opened his defence of the Open at St Andrews in such blistering fashion that he stood eight under par after 13 holes. Suddenly, a torrential storm halted play. The spell was broken and ultimately he finished fifth. Two summers on, Lee Trevino wickedly chipped him into forlorn submission at Muirfield. Jacklin the golfer was never the same again.

But in 1985, Jacklin was the inspirational non-playing European captain as the United States were beaten in the Ryder Cup for the first time in 28 years. His opposite number on the American side was Trevino. Vengeance was sweet indeed. Two years later, Jacklin skippered Europe to victory again, this time – for the first time – on American soil.

ROBERT TYRE JONES

(1902 – 1971)

■ *Original Grand Slammer & Founder of the Masters*

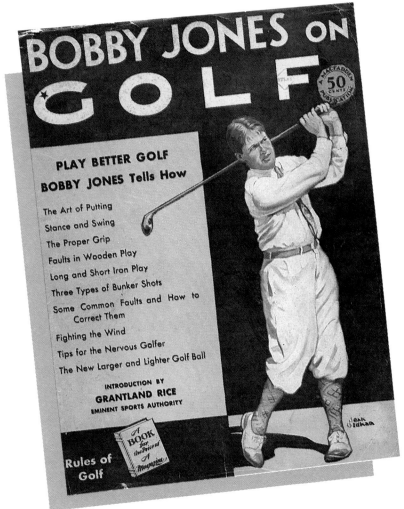

Jones was the most glamorous sporting idol in America in the 1920s, gracing many magazine covers.

Bobby Jones was the greatest amateur golfer ever. It may be that he was the greatest golfer, period. A few facts make the point. From 1922 to 1930, he finished first four times and second four times in the US Open and won on each of his three appearances in the British Open. Outstanding as they were, Walter Hagen and Gene Sarazen each got the better of him only once in either Open from the time that Jones won the American title in 1923. In addition to those seven Opens, Jones won five US Amateurs and one British Amateur. The pinnacle of his achievements came in 1930, when he won all four titles – the 'Impregnable Quadrilateral'. Aged 28, and having no worlds left to conquer, he retired from competitive golf. Jones's feat was the original Grand Slam. It was the realization that nobody could emulate him that ultimately led to the modern Slam bringing in the Masters (founded by Jones) and the US PGA Championship in place of the two Amateurs.

Jones had developed his stylish, rhythmical swing under the tuition of Stewart Maiden, an expatriate Scot, at the East Lake club in Atlanta, but there was much more to him than golf. He was a true amateur. For example, in 1923, 1924 and 1929, the US Open and US Amateur were the only events he entered. "*My wife and children came first, then my profession [law]. Finally, and never in a life by itself, came golf,*" he once said. While winning all those honours, he was studying and ultimately obtaining first-class degrees in mechanical engineering, English literature and law. He was so gifted that such a wealth of talent in one individual might have been a cause for envy had Jones not been the epitome of modesty. His name became such a byword for perfect behaviour that the USGA dedicated its sportsmanship award to him. He was adored on both sides of the Atlantic.

In 1948, Jones played his last round of golf. He was suffering from syringomyelia, a terrible wasting disease which afflicts the spine. He died in 1971, after years of bravely endured agony. The most fitting epitaph has already been written, by the American golf writer, Herbert Warren Wind: "*As a young man, he was able to stand up to just about the best that life can offer, which is not easy, and later he stood up with equal grace to just about the worst.*"

Although an American through and through, Jones had a special affinity for St Andrews. This was the start of his last round there, a friendly game in 1936.

TOM KITE

(Born December 9, 1949)

■ *No longer the best golfer never to win a major*

You won't find many references to prize money in this section, not because it doesn't matter – it is why professional sportsmen are professional sportsmen – but because it is an unworthy, indeed useless, measure of greatness. It cannot reflect the accomplishments of golfers who competed in times when prize money was comparatively meagre, let alone before it had been raised enormously by public interest and inflation; and in any case, the prize-money records of today will be meaningless a decade hence.

Tom Kite has won more prize money than any other golfer in history – nearly $9 million in official earnings on the US tour alone by the spring of 1994.

He had held that honour in June 1992 as well, but then there was a difference. A huge difference. At that point, Kite was known as the best golfer in the world never to have won a major. Talk about a back-handed compliment. He had squandered many excellent opportunities to get rid of that unwanted accolade, notably at the 1984 and 1986 Masters, the 1985 Open and the 1989 US Open. But then came the 1992 US Open at Pebble Beach, and Kite, appropriately, withstood the battering of the wind on the final day better than anyone. At last, he had his major. When everyone had just about given up on him – he hadn't even been invited to the Masters that April – he had come through. That breakthrough having been accomplished, it may be that the best years of Tom Kite belong in the future rather than the past.

A major breakthrough: Kite salutes victory at the 1992 US Open, his first win in a major.

BERNHARD LANGER

(Born August 27, 1957)

■ *Yip yip hooray for the Master*

Bernhard Langer was an obvious beneficiary of the Ballesteros factor: an inheritor of the belief that European golfers could beat the best in the world. In 1985, the German collected the Masters title when, ironically, he outplayed Ballesteros down the stretch. Langer had twice previously topped the European Order of Merit and twice been runner-up in the Open Championship, and the closing 62 that had brought him victory in the 1984 Spanish Open over the gruelling El Saler course had shown what he was capable of. But winning a major was in a different league altogether. In some ways, it was also a major shock. A man who

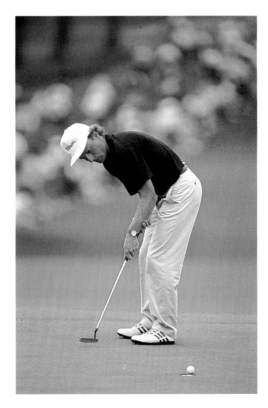

early in his career had been a jabbering wreck on the greens had not only demonstrated that it was possible to conquer the 'yips' but had proved it at Augusta National, arguably the world's most searching examination of putting.

Over the years, Langer has tried everything, from switching putters to holding the club with his left hand below the right, which clasps his left forearm to the upper part of the grip. It's not pretty, but he used the method to make three critical putts in succession over the closing holes of the 1991 Ryder Cup. That he missed the crucial one at the last could not obscure the fact that he can putt when it matters, something he proved in the most emphatic fashion when he won the Masters for a second time, by a convincing four shots, in 1993.

Langer's putting stroke may not look too great, but it can function effectively at the highest level.

BOBBY LOCKE

(1917 – 1987)

■ *The other South African Player*

Christened Arthur D'Arcy Locke but called Bobby throughout his career, this singular South African provided one of golf's classic examples of 'it's not how but how many'. His swing was not the most graceful ever seen but his repetitive hook kept putting the ball on the fairway and then on the green. Once there, 'Old Muffin Face', as the Americans rather unkindly dubbed him, was in his element. He was one of the truly great putters.

Locke even played his putts with a draw, and more often than not that last right-to-left roll took the ball into the cup. His record emphasized the success of his method: four times Open champion and twice runner-up, five times in the top-five at the US Open, and nine times South African Open champion – his first two wins in that, in 1935 and 1937, being years when he was also South African Amateur champion.

Apart from those four Open titles, perhaps Locke's most astonishing feat was winning 11 US tour events from 1947 to 1950; indeed, he won four tournaments in five weeks in 1947 and ended the season second on the US Money List. His performances were received with a sad lack of manners by some Americans, and the jealousy-driven animosity of some of his rivals led to the tour suspending him for a while after a dispute over some contractual technicalities, but their ill-humour only served to underline Locke's achievements in their country as much as it undermined his status.

It may be that though unorthodox, Locke was the greatest putter the game has ever seen.

NANCY LOPEZ

(Born January 6, 1957)

■ *Killer Queen of Golf*

She has been called "*Nancy with the laughing face*", but her sunny disposition cannot disguise the fact that Nancy Lopez has been a killer on the golf course.

Her career started on a high note and has pretty well kept on that way ever since. Aged 15, she won the US Girls' Junior Championship in 1972, and in 1974 she won it again. While still an amateur, she tied for second place in the 1975 US Women's Open. With a pedigree like that, it was no surprise when Lopez turned professional in 1977, and no surprise either that exceptional deeds were expected of her almost immediately. The only surprise may be that she exceeded the expectations.

In her second year on the LPGA Tour, she won nine official events, including the LPGA Championship, one of the women's tour's majors and a title she has now claimed three times. But most remarkably of all, she won five tournaments in succession that summer, a performance that thrust women's golf into prominent places on America's sports pages and inevitably earned the charismatic and ever-pleasant Lopez the tag of being the female Arnold Palmer. The 1978 men's US Open fell during this sequence, but – maybe because it was won by the relatively anonymous and low-key figure of Andy North – Lopez's run was the dominant golf story of the time. She won eight times in 1979, and in 1985, the other year she was leading money-winner, she won five times and had 21 top-10 finishes from 25 outings.

Lopez's unorthodox, looping swing has led to criticisms, but nobody has ever questioned her ability to putt. Above all, her competitive aggression and zest for the game have enabled her not only to supply the results to comprehensively quieten the sceptics but have also helped her to bounce back from the births of three children between 1983 and 1991 and remain a significant force in the game. The only seasons in which she finished outside the top-10 on the Money List, at least until she was 14th in 1993, were those affected by her pregnancies, and she would surely have been the leading money-winner on more than the three occasions she has if she had not been so determined to pursue a normal family life. Going into 1994, she had not won the title she would relish the most – the US Women's Open – but when she won an LPGA event in July 1993, it took her career haul to 47 and showed that the desire to win still burns as brightly as the sparkle in her eyes.

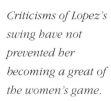

Criticisms of Lopez's swing have not prevented her becoming a great of the women's game.

SANDY LYLE
(Born February 9, 1958)

Precociously talented – uneven form

It may not always look pretty, but Sandy Lyle's swing is one of the most powerful in golf.

After Tony Jacklin, Sandy Lyle. The latter lifted the Open Championship trophy at Royal St George's in July 1985, 16 years after Jacklin had ended an 18-year British drought. Although Lyle was a former double-winner of Europe's Order of Merit – an honour he collected for a third time in 1985 – there were many so-called experts who until then had doubted the inner strength of this massively strong and immensely pleasant man who had shown prodigious talent at a precocious age. It is said that when he hit his first golf shot, at three years old, it went 80 yards. These days, that's a half-wedge.

Subsequent events indicated the cynics should have known better. After a glittering amateur career, Lyle won regularly in Europe before that Open win, and frequently in the United States after it. In 1987, he became the first non-American to win the Tournament Players Championship. In 1988, already having captured two US tour events that year, he became the first Briton to win the Masters. He did it in brilliant style, hitting his approach shot from a fairway bunker to within 10 feet of the flag on the final hole and then sinking the birdie putt. That second shot has been hailed as "*the greatest bunker shot in the history of the game*" by the writer Herb Wind.

Lyle won five times that year, but then went into decline. Although blessed with phenomenal natural talent, his swing has a distinct kink in it, and he sought a plethora of remedies for his inconsistency. Two wins in 1992 suggested he had found the cure, but a winless 1993 indicated that, as ever, Lyle remains an enigma.

JOHNNY MILLER

(Born April 29, 1947)

■ *A brilliant meteor of talent*

Like Tony Jacklin, Johnny Miller spent four years in the limelight. His time immediately followed Jacklin's and has to be acknowledged as even more brilliant.

In the 1970s, Miller set the US tour on fire. In 1974 he won eight events, including the first three of the season. The next January he won the first two tournaments, with a 61 in each, and in 1976 he confirmed himself as the 'Desert King' of American golf by winning the tour's opener for the third consecutive year.

But Miller didn't just leave his best golf for ordinary tournaments. His closing eight-under par 63 at Oakmont in 1973 broke the US Open single-round record and it brought him a fantastic victory. It was, simply, one of the greatest rounds ever played. In the 1975 Masters, he shot 65-66 over the last 36 holes but was pipped by Jack Nicklaus in a tremendous finale. His finishing 66 at Royal Birkdale in 1976 was of the highest class, too, and in thwarting the ambitions of a teenage Seve Ballesteros, it earned Miller the Open Championship. It seemed then as if that would signal further glories but he lost interest, instead devoting himself to his family and to his work for the Mormon church and, latterly, as a TV commentator. But class is a permanent quality. In February 1994, Miller surprised everyone, himself included, by winning the AT&T Pro-Am on the US tour, as if to remind us that Johnny Miller at his best was as good as golf can be.

During the mid-1970s, there wasn't a golfer in the world who swung the club better.

OLD TOM MORRIS

(1821 – 1908)

■ *Pioneer professional and architect*

The face of greatness. Old Tom Morris was the first great golfer after the start of the Open Championship, and the legacy of his talents lives on.

In the last century, the two Tom Morrises, father and son, Old and Young, constituted a golfing dynasty that has never been known before or since. Old Tom won his first Open Championship, the second ever held, in 1861. He defended the title successfully 12 months later by a margin of 13 strokes, which is not only still a record but is likely to remain so forever. He won the Open twice more, in 1864 and 1867. With the latter victory he became, at 47, the oldest winner of the Open – another record that may well never be broken.

By the time of that last triumph Old Tom was Custodian of the Links at St Andrews (effectively greenkeeper to the R & A), a position he retained until 1903. It was he who told a man who wanted to play on a Sunday, *"the Old Course needs a rest on the Sabbath, even if you don't"*. Old Tom formed a link with the romantic days of the pre-Open golfing heroes, like Allan Robertson, who was the best golfer of the 1850s. Great rivals and then foursomes partners, the two men quarrelled bitterly over the introduction of the gutty, which Robertson abhorred. Morris also left a legacy for golfers of all abilities with the work he undertook as a golf course architect, notably at Westward Ho! in England, and also at Muirfield in Scotland and Royal County Down in Ireland, where he pioneered the idea of laying the links out in two loops of nine rather than simply out and back.

YOUNG TOM MORRIS

(1851 – 1875)

Unrivalled young 19th century genius

Old Tom played in the Open until 1896, but by then his even more brilliant son was 21 years dead. How good was Young Tom? In comparing him to Allan Robertson, his father accorded him this posthumous tribute. *"I could cope wi' Allan mysel', but never wi' Tommy."* A vigorous hitter of the ball – it is said that sometimes the strain would cause the shafts of his clubs to snap in mid-swing – Young Tom had an enviably delicate and assured touch with his putter. And, as his record amply underlined, he had a wonderful competitive temperament, too.

Young Tom first played in the Open Championship in 1866, when he finished ninth. The next year he was fourth. In 1868 he won it, as he did the year after and again the year after that. The completion of this incredible hat-trick by a man still a teenager earned him outright possession of the Championship Belt and caused a hiatus of one year before the Open was resumed in 1872.

Young Tom then became the first winner of the replacement trophy, the coveted claret jug which is still contested today. No other golfer has ever won four consecutive Opens. His winning scores of 149 in 1870 and 154 in 1869 were never matched by anyone between 1860 and 1891, after which the championship began to be held over 72 rather than 36 holes. The runner-up in 1869, three strokes behind, was his father, a family one-two that will surely never be matched.

In the Opens of 1873 and 1874, Young Tom finished third and second, respectively. And then he was gone. He died on Christmas Day 1875, aged 24, just three months after his wife and newborn son

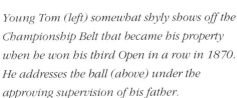

Young Tom (left) somewhat shyly shows off the Championship Belt that became his property when he won his third Open in a row in 1870. He addresses the ball (above) under the approving supervision of his father.

died suddenly while he was away from St Andrews playing an exhibition match with his father. He hurried home after receiving news of their illness, but by the time he got there he was too late. He never recovered from the shock. The popular tale goes that he died of a broken heart but the more prosaic truth is that it was a ruptured lung that caused his death, perhaps brought on by drink and the deprivations he subjected his body to during those few months of mourning. The memorial erected to him by his parents is a much-visited part of St Rule's churchyard in St Andrews; a shrine to a genius.

BYRON NELSON

(Born February 4, 1912)

■ *Iron Byron – superlative ball striker*

If John Ball's total of eight Amateur Championships and Bobby Jones's remarkable Grand Slam will never be matched, then surely neither will the phenomenal exploits of Byron Nelson in 1945. He won 18 of the 30 US tour events he entered, was second in another seven and was never worse than ninth. Included in this *annus mirabilis* was a streak of 11 consecutive tournament victories. He smashed pretty well all the circuit's scoring records. For example, he had a stroke average of 68.33 shots and was a cumulative 320 under par for the season. He earned the equivalent of $63,335 in War Bonds, a staggering 14.5 per cent of the total prize money on offer. That would translate to around $8.7 million on the 1993 US PGA Tour. Nobody has won that much in an entire career. Nelson's fabulous run through the 1940s created a tour record of 113 consecutive tournaments in the money (without missing a cut) and another record of 19 successive rounds in the 1960s.

It was golf of that calibre that established Nelson's reputation as a superlative ball-striker, a fact which has been confirmed by the USGA naming its repetitive ball-testing machine 'Iron Byron'. Such an unbelievably high standard of sustained performance also explains why Nelson's five major championships – two Masters, two US PGAs and one US Open – are comparatively ignored, even though they were dramatic affairs. He beat Ben Hogan in a playoff for one of his Masters titles and had to endure a two-round playoff for the 1939 US Open after failing to shake off Craig Wood at the first attempt. Had the Second World War not intervened, many more majors would surely have fallen to 'Lord Byron', yet, ironically, he was only free to do what he did in 1945 because he was exempted from National Service as a haemophiliac.

Like Hogan, Nelson was introduced to golf as a caddie at Fort Worth in Texas, so from their earliest days on a golf course they had been keen rivals, and friends. It requires an exceptional talent to have lived one's career with the potentially daunting shadow of Hogan's accomplishments hovering over your every achievement, but Nelson has done that with not only his reputation but also his records intact, and likely to remain so forever.

In an age when sporting records can be quickly eclipsed, Nelson's achievements seem safe forever.

JACK NICKLAUS

(Born January 21, 1940)

◼ *A career that will never be matched*

If one simply looks at the record books, Jack Nicklaus is the greatest golfer of all time. Maybe he is anyway. He is certainly the most successful, in no small part due to the intense thoroughness with which he always prepares himself and the sheer strength which in his prime enabled him to strike the ball as if it were fired from a bazooka. He hit the ball farther than his contemporaries and higher than anyone ever has, especially with the irons.

One could fill a whole chapter merely by listing Nicklaus's achievements, but pride of place goes to his surely unbeatable tally of 20 major championships: two US Amateurs, a record six Masters, a record-equalling four US Opens and five US PGA Championships, and three British Opens. He has thus collected at least three each of professional golf's most important titles. Just three other men – Ben Hogan, Gary Player and Gene Sarazen – have won all four and they have only one complete set each. Nicklaus's tally of seven Opens matches the mark set by Harry Vardon and Bobby Jones.

It could be that the 20th of his 20 majors was Nicklaus's finest hour, because when he won the 1986 Masters by playing the last 10 holes in seven under par he was, at 46, regarded by many as over the hill. As remarkable as the number of tournaments the 'Golden Bear' has won is the frequency with which he has been second or third. Above all, he has always put his wife and family first while simultaneously managing to maintain a balance between his golf on the one hand and business commitments in club and clothing manufacturing and golf course design on the other. His work as a golf course architect in particular, with courses of the calibre of Muirfield Village and Glen Abbey (see Chapter 9) to his

name, has established a fine reputation for himself in another sphere of the game.

Variety of life is part of the reason for his longevity at the highest level. His success has carried on to the (over-50) US Senior tour, where he won on his debut in 1990 and has regularly since – that is, when he can be bothered to play in the 'minor league'.

Nicklaus is today regarded with universal affection and respect. It was not always so. As an overweight, crew-cut kid who ousted Arnold Palmer before the hero's reign had hardly begun, he was subjected to ridicule and venom by overly partisan spectators. The stoical manner in which Jack Nicklaus accepted all that stamped him as a man apart, and stamped him also as a worthy heir to Jones's reputation for graciousness and sportsmanship.

A fierce determination and peerless concentration have made Nicklaus maybe the best golfer of all time. His win at the 1986 Masters (right) may have been his finest hour.

GREG NORMAN

(Born February 10, 1955)

■ *Into the jaws of victory ... and defeat*

The experts had been waiting a long time to hang the label 'champion' around Greg Norman's neck, but going into the 1986 Open Championship at Turnberry it seemed possible that the powerful Australian would keep them waiting forever. He had led both the Masters and the US Open after 54 holes earlier in the season and yet let both slip. Two years previously he had been demolished by Fuzzy Zoeller in an 18-hole playoff for the US Open.

But at Turnberry, he won – convincingly, by five strokes. In a week in which the conditions and the course humbled the greats, Norman was the only man to be level par after four rounds. But within a month, Bob Tway holed a bunker shot on the last hole to deny him in the US PGA Championship. Greg had led all four majors after the third round – the 'Saturday Slam' – and won just one of them. Although he ended the year as leading money-winner on the US tour (something he was to repeat in 1990 and something he had done in Europe in 1980), the heartache Norman suffered as a result of Tway's fortune was subsequently echoed with astonishing regularity.

In 1987, Larry Mize holed a 30-yard chip shot on the second playoff hole to deprive him of the Masters. In 1989, Mark Calcavecchia holed a fluky pitch shot on the 12th hole of the final round in the Open and then beat Norman (and Wayne Grady) under the R & A's new four-hole playoff method. Within five weeks of each other in 1990, Robert Gamez holed a full 7-iron and David Frost holed a bunker shot, both on the last hole, to beat Norman in regular US tour events.

Norman handled this perverse adversity with charm and grace, rarely letting his understandable frustration show, so his demeanour had already been that of a consummate champion before July 1993, when he produced a final round of 64, the lowest ever by a winner, at Royal St George's to beat Nick Faldo and claim his second Open and his second major. In so doing, Norman's total of 267 was a new record low for any major championship. His dazzling golf was typical of the man. So was what happened next. At the US PGA the following month, Paul Azinger beat him in a playoff. That meant Norman had thanklessly emulated Craig Wood by losing a playoff for all four majors - in his case, under three different formats! The way Norman goes at the game, further epic victories and defeats are surely in the pipeline.

With brightly-coloured clothes and distinctive bush hat (left), Norman cuts quite a dash on the course.
Below: One that didn't get away. Norman clutches the trophy after winning the 1986 Open at Turnberry .

ARNOLD PALMER

(Born September 10, 1929)

■ *Catalyst, champion and mass-marketer of the game*

Whether it be by escaping from trouble (left) or in the distinctive manner of his follow-though (below), Palmer's style has thrilled millions of golf fans.

Cometh the hour, cometh the man. Arnold Palmer was the symbol that sold golf to the American public in the television age of the late 1950s and 1960s. He made it exciting for millions of people who knew nothing about the game by making birdies from impossible positions and charging to victory from absolutely nowhere, always watched attentively by the adoring 'Arnie's Army'. Palmer attacked golf courses with brute strength and an angelic putting touch, and he did it all with stylish clan. His rugged all-American good looks, magnetic personality and ready smile made him a hero when he birdied the last two holes to win the 1960 Masters and, two months later, shot a closing 65 to win the US Open; they made him the object of national sympathy when he lost playoffs for three more US Opens and struggled in vain to win the US PGA Championship, which eluded him just as the US Open had eluded Sam Snead.

Palmer's prime years were brief, but spectacular. They ran from 1958 to 1964, but his influence in bringing millions of dollars into the sport lingers on. It is safe to say that the US Senior tour would not have been able to boast a 1994 schedule of 44 tournaments carrying $30 million in prize money if Palmer had not been the catalyst that invigorated it when he turned 50. In addition to his 60 regular tour wins, Palmer won 10 times in senior service between 1981 and 1992.

But it was what Palmer did in those seven glorious seasons that so ignited the public interest in the man and in his sport. He won seven majors to add to his 1954 US Amateur title: four Masters, one US Open and two Opens. He collected those titles from 22 starts, during which time he also managed to lose playoffs for the US Open in 1962 and 1963, throw away the Masters in 1959 and 1961, and finish a shot behind the winner on his debut in the Open in 1960. Palmer resurrected the fortunes of the Open Championship almost single-handedly, by persuading his compatriots to make the pilgrimage to Britain. His best golf probably came at the 1964 Masters when he was 34, an age when Hogan hadn't won his first major. That week, Palmer was remorselessly accurate with his irons and deadly on the greens. Nobody then would have believed it was to be his last major. That was the way fate decreed it should be, but the legacy and legend of Arnold Palmer will surely be enduring facets of professional golf.

GARY PLAYER

(Born November 1, 1935)

■ *A small giant among giants*

This tenacious South African played piggy-in-the-middle to Arnold Palmer and Jack Nicklaus. That is not a flippant or derisory comment but a recognition of how Player, the physically small guy (5' 7") sandwiched between two American giants, came to be regarded as their peer. He was the third link in golf's 'Big Three'. He won the first of his three Opens in 1959, the first of his three Masters in 1961, the first of two PGAs in 1962 and his one US Open in 1965. Even today, he believes he could win a major championship. His strict adherence to a fitness regimen throughout his career has meant he is in enviable condition. He has sometimes suffered from a tendency to overswing, but he is still acknowledged as the master bunker player, and he never gives up. On the way to winning one of his five World Matchplay Championships, in 1965 he beat Tony Lema after being 7 down with 17 holes to play. In 1978, he won his third Masters title, aged 42, by shooting a 64 on the last day to snatch a victory everybody else thought belonged to someone else.

Player has become the international golfer *par excellence*. He had had to overcome the logistical problems imposed by regularly commuting to tournaments from his family home in South Africa, where he has won the national Open 13 times. He was the first overseas golfer to be a dominant force in the United States, where he won 21 official PGA Tour titles. In 1974, he became the first man to break 60 in a national championship when he had a 59 in the Brazilian Open, and that same season he notched up his 100th professional title world-wide.

Player owes much to his unquenchable spirit. That has given him, as it did Palmer, a new competitive life on the US Senior tour, where his successes include

Player's knock-kneed putting stance has enjoyed a high success rate over five different decades.

Despite an impressive past, Player is always looking for new goals to conquer.

what he likes to call the four 'senior majors' – the US Senior Open, PGA Seniors Championship, Senior Players Championship and British Senior Open. Player likes to point out that this makes him the only man in history to have completed the Grand Slam at both the regular and over-50 levels. If nobody else pays much attention to this, that's in part because the official line from the US Senior tour is that a different four events from those designated by Gary constitute the 'Senior Slam' (see Chapter 5) and in part because Player has always been as long on hyperbole as he is short in stature. But nobody has ever been wise to underestimate the man's definitively dogged determination.

GENE SARAZEN

(Born February 27, 1902)

■ *Perpetrator of legends*

Going into the 1922 season, 20-year-old Gene Sarazen (christened Eugenio Saraceni, the son of a New York-Italian carpenter) was the archetypal 'unknown'. His anonymity survived only a matter of months. By July he was US Open champion, making a birdie on the 72nd hole for a closing 68 and thereby becoming the first winner to break 70 in the last round. He won by a shot from John Black and the as yet unfulfilled Bobby Jones. The following month he added the US PGA title to his collection, the second of the seven majors he would win.

In 1923, 'the Squire' beat 'the Haig' (Walter Hagen) at the second extra hole to win the US PGA Championship after 36 holes had failed to separate them. But Sarazen's career then went into comparative decline until he enjoyed a marvellous renaissance in 1932 with victory in both Opens. His revival was helped by his 'invention' of the sand wedge, a feat he performed by the simple expedient of soldering extra metal on to his niblick in order to make its sole heavier and broader. Sarazen took a third PGA the next year, and would surely have retained his Open crown had he not taken triple-bogeys at the short 11th and the long 14th hole during that week at St Andrews. 'The Squire' took a total of five shots in Hill and Hell bunkers and lost by a stroke to Denny Shute. Well, no one ever said this new sand wedge was absolutely foolproof.

Although at 5'4" Sarazen was the shortest of any great golfer, his accomplishments were gargantuan. And they have become the stuff of legend. In 1935 he won the second Masters ever held, thus becoming the first player to win all four professional major championships, and he won it with the invaluable assistance of probably the most famous golf shot in history when he holed out a 4-wood approach to Augusta's 15th green in the last round for an albatross, or double-eagle, two (three under on a par-5 hole). "*That double-eagle wouldn't have meant a thing if I hadn't won the playoff the next day,*" said Sarazen. "*The aspect I cherish most is that both Walter Hagen and Bobby Jones witnessed the shot.*"

That was the most important single stroke of his life, but not the only memorable one. At the age of 71, on the 50th anniversary of his first appearance in Britain, Sarazen holed-in-one at the 'Postage Stamp' 8th hole in the 1973 Open Championship at Troon, where in 1923 – as the coming star of American golf – he had failed to qualify for the championship. Half a century after dominating the headlines, Sarazen was still making news.

A veritable pioneer of bunker play, Sarazen is familiar to modern-day fans in his role as honorary starter of the Masters (above).

SAM SNEAD

(Born May 27, 1912)

■ *The sweetest swinger of all time*

With Ben Hogan and Byron Nelson, Sam Snead might be said to have completed an American version of The Great Triumvirate. They were all born in 1912 and they have all left an indelible mark on the game.

Snead, raised in the backwoods of West Virginia, liked to cultivate his rustic image as the hillbilly boy from mountain country, but he was no bucolic hick when the stakes got serious, whether that be for a private bet – Snead was a notoriously ruthless adversary when his own money was on the line – or when a major title was at stake. He won the Masters and the US PGA Championship three times each, and the Open – at St Andrews in 1946, on one of only three appearances in the championship – once. But he never won the US Open. That latter fact is the one that is eternally recalled in any evaluation of Snead's record, largely because he quite often contrived to squander his chances of victory, and often quite spectacularly. However, it is unfair to dwell on the one blemish in a career which features a record 84 official US tour victories, a figure that the man himself reckons should be doubled to take account of regional events.

Snead has the most natural, fluid swing the game has ever seen. The physical ease with which he could generate immense power enabled him to become the first golfer to break 60 in a significant competition (a 59 at his home course, The Greenbrier, in 1959); to be the oldest winner of a US tournament (52 years 10 months at Greensboro in 1965); to finish tied third when aged 62 in the 1974 US PGA Championship; and to be the first man to beat his age on the US tour (scoring 66 when he was 67 at the Quad Cities Open in 1979). Rather like Hogan, Snead suffered terrible putting problems (the 'yips') as his career progressed, leading to him trying several different techniques on the greens.

Snead's swing is pure and powerful. His 'sidewinder' putting style is less pretty, but it did enable him to cope with the yips.

JOHN HENRY (J.H.) TAYLOR
(1871 – 1963)

▪ *Resolute battler for trophies and underdogs*

The Great Triumvirate began their incomparable reign of collective domination of the Open in 1894, when J. H. Taylor won the first of his five Open Championships and the first of the illustrious trio's 16. The venue was Royal St George's at Sandwich in Kent, which thereby became the first English club to host the championship. Taylor made it a double-Anglo celebration by becoming the first English professional to win it. One didn't have to be an insensitive Sassenach or a partisan Scotsman to detect, amid the cheers for Taylor's triumph, the sound of Allan Robertson vigorously spinning in his grave.

Any Scottish hopes that this was a mere geographical coincidence and one-off aberration were dispelled when Taylor retained the title at St Andrews, no less, the following year. His bid for a hat-trick was a bold one, too. He was only thwarted in a playoff as Harry Vardon emerged victorious after six rounds of Muirfield. (In those days,

playoffs were over 36 holes.) Taylor was to be runner-up in the Open five more times, including four years in a row from 1904, but he also won it three more times – in 1900, 1909 and 1913. When Taylor won, he tended to do it emphatically. None of his five titles were claimed with less than four shots to spare, and in 1900 and 1913 he had an eight-shot margin over the next man. Also in 1900, he was runner-up in the US Open – to Vardon.

Taylor's action was not pretty, and it hasn't been passed down the generations as a model in the same way that Vardon's swing has, but it was certainly effective. He was perhaps a little leaden-footed and sometimes a bit brisk through the ball, but he was a a tremendous bad-weather golfer and a resolute battler. He carried those fighting qualities on into later life, where he assumed the mantle of champion for the lowly artisan golfer, and he was a prime mover in the foundation of the British PGA, which similarly raised the status of the

lowly professional. In 1933, the PGA appointed Taylor non-playing Ryder Cup captain for the match at Southport, where his opposite number was the charismatic Hagen. Britain gained a dramatic last-hole triumph. At 62, Taylor was still capable of outwitting the best.

In either the execution of his swing or its immediate after-effects, Taylor was not the most graceful of golfers. But with a record like his, who can quibble?

PETER THOMSON

(Born August 23, 1929)

■ *Supreme links golfer & five-time Open winner*

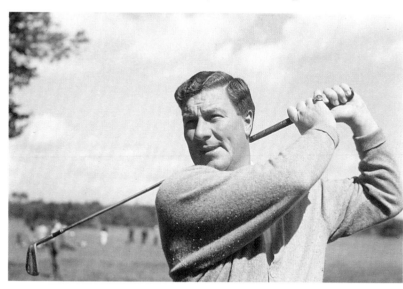

Peter Thomson hardly conforms to type. He is a professional golfer with wide cultural interests outside golf. He is an Australian who prefers discussing politics or listening to classical music rather than drinking beer or surfing. He is a sportsman who has made a successful transition from competitor to writer. Even so, his record stamps him as the most successful Australian golfer ever, and Greg Norman has quite a way to go to usurp him.

Thomson came to Britain in the early 1950s with his enviably simple, orthodox and rhythmical swing, and he made his debut in the Open in 1951. Over the next seven years, he won four championships and was second three times, twice to Bobby Locke, his great rival of the day, and once to Ben Hogan, the greatest golfer of the day. Thomson completed a hat-trick of victories at Hoylake in 1956. Although winning three Opens in succession had been achieved by three men in the 19th century (Young Tom Morris, Jamie Anderson and Bob Ferguson), only Thomson has done it since.

But it was not until Arnold Palmer, with whom Thomson had a respectful but rather frosty rivalry, helped to rejuvenate the Open in the early 1960s that the United States was again represented in force, and so it was not until Thomson won it for the fifth time, at Royal Birkdale in 1965, that he was accorded due credit by his American peers. But when Thomson got the better of the American Tony Lema, the defending champion, in the last round at Southport that year, even the harshest sceptics had to concede that Thomson had proved he was the master of anyone when it came to controlling the small British ball over a demanding links. Those sceptics, of course, had not troubled Thomson unduly. He has always been concerned with more cerebral matters than receiving grudging praise.

Nevertheless, it is always satisfying to silence the doubters and, belatedly, Thomson did that on the flourishing US Senior tour in the 1980s. He won 11 tournaments, 10 of them in 1985, when he amassed nearly $400,000 in official prize money alone. Lately, he has been increasingly involved in course architecture, and he is presently working on the design of a new course at St Andrews. And no one can say he doesn't understand links golf.

In the Open Championship in the 1950s (right), Thomson's hold on the title was only threatened with any regularity by Bobby Locke.

LEE TREVINO

(Born December 1, 1939)

Voluble extrovert with a Midas touch

posterity as a voluble extrovert as well as a formidable golfer.

Trevino's first significant victory could hardly have been more auspicious – the 1968 US Open. Three years later he collected the 'Triple Crown' – the US, Canadian and British Opens – within 20 days, beating Jack Nicklaus in an 18-hole playoff in the former, beating Art Wall in a sudden-death playoff in Canada, and then beating Lu Liang Huan of Taiwan by a stroke at Birkdale. He retained his Open title the following summer when he holed from off the green three times in the last 21 holes at Muirfield to crush the spirit of Tony Jacklin, notably by chipping in when all looked lost to save his par on the 71st hole. Since then Trevino has twice won the US PGA Championship, in 1974 and 1984, but the Masters will now surely elude him. He has never been enamoured with the course at Augusta, where a player who can hit the ball high and from right-to-left, precisely the opposite of what Trevino ordinarily does, has an inestimable advantage. And besides, Trevino's humble roots and impecunious upbringing meant that his relationship with the starchy officials at one of America's most exclusive and conservative institutions was always bound to be strained.

It has been suggested that Trevino's magnificent career would have been still more glittering had he not been struck by lightning during a tournament in Chicago in 1975, an incident which has caused him recurring and severe back problems. On the other hand, his form on the US Senior tour has not been indicative of a man deprived by fate. Since he joined what he calls the fat-bellies circuit full-time in 1990, Trevino had won 20 times by spring 1994 and earned over $4.2 million and rising – and rising fast.

Despite his reputation for instant humour, Trevino is a serious player on the golf course.

Lee Trevino's is a classic story of poor boy made good. Brought up near the United States/Mexico border, this 'Texican' learned his golf with a bottle in hand – to hit the ball with, not to drink from. He developed what was termed an 'agricultural' swing, but whatever it looked like, then and now, it has earned Trevino a fortune. He is a magical shot-maker and has a fast wit with which he has entertained crowds all over the globe. The private Trevino is a very different character, as withdrawn and wary as one might expect of someone who has more than once been ripped off by so-called friends and advisers, but this enigmatic individual will be remembered by

HARRY VARDON

(1870 – 1937)

■ *An example for all generations*

From the unlikely birthplace of the island of Jersey, Harry Vardon rose to become one of the greatest golfers in the history of the game, and also one of the most influential. His role in the development of contemporary golf techniques, especially with regard to the grip and the swing, was discussed in the previous chapter. It was both the consistency and the majesty of Vardon's striking – he seldom took a divot, instead almost brushing the ball away, even with the irons – that led to his methods being so imitated.

Vardon won the first of his record six Open Championships in 1896 when he got the better of J. H. Taylor after a 36-hole playoff at Muirfield. Regulation play had reached a climax with Vardon needing a four at the last to win. The question was: should he go for broke with his second shot in the hope of making four, but thus run the risk of finding the pernicious bunker that guarded the green and then maybe taking six? Vardon played safe. He made a solid five and the next day denied Taylor in his bid for a third consecutive Open. Instead, he was embarked on a record-breaking run of his own.

Vardon won again in 1898 and 1899, and in between an endless stream of tournament victories and lucrative exhibition matches, he found time to go to America for more of the same in 1900. While there, he became the first transatlantic traveller to win either Open when he captured the US Open in Chicago. Vardon then took his fourth Open, his first with the gutty, in 1903. His brother, Tom, was second. Harry's health had been shaky and he had been advised by his doctor not to play at Prestwick. As it was, during the last round he almost fainted several times. Shortly afterwards, he found he had contracted tuberculosis. This weakened him considerably, some say irreparably, but he recovered sufficiently to win the Open for a fifth time in 1911 and a sixth time in 1914. And he was close to two more US Opens. In 1913 he and Ted Ray were defeated by Francis Ouimet in a momentous playoff, while in 1920 Vardon dropped seven shots in the last seven holes, a fierce storm having sapped his stamina and shredded his putting stroke, and Ray beat him by a stroke.

His frail health meant that Vardon did not build as many golf courses as he might have done, but Ganton and Little Aston are among the excellent English courses he bequeathed to the game. Harry Vardon gave a lot to golf and he remains, for the moment at least, the greatest non-American golfer of all time.

In close up or in full shot, Vardon's swing was one to watch. The painting below is 'The Champions', showing Vardon and his companions of the Great Triumvirate, Braid and Taylor.

ROBERTO DE VICENZO

(Born April 14, 1923)

■ *South American supremo with over 240 trophies*

To borrow a clumsy but accurate American word, Roberto de Vicenzo is the 'winningest' golfer in history, having won about 240 tournaments. Record-keeping is not the strongest suit of golf in South America, from where de Vicenzo is the only world-class golfer to emerge, but that total is a good estimate. Most of those wins were in his native Argentina and elsewhere in South America, but he also won throughout Europe and on the US tour. He won the US Senior Open in 1980, 36 years after winning his first Argentinian Open. But his place in golfing lore is not so much due to his longevity as to the events that occurred at two major championships within 12 months; one an occasion of unbounded joy, the other an edifying example of dignity in despair.

At Royal Liverpool in 1967, in one of the most popular triumphs ever, Roberto, as he was universally known, at last won the Open Championship after several heartbreaking near-misses. Down the stretch, only one man stood between him and the destiny he craved for. Formidably, that man was Jack Nicklaus. De Vicenzo knew that pars on the last three holes would do the job. On the long 16th, he fired a typically powerful 3-wood to the heart of the green and walked off with a birdie. Two pars later he had won by two shots.

From the sublime to the disastrous. On his 45th birthday the following April, de Vicenzo appeared to have tied Bob Goalby for the Masters. They had produced some breathtaking golf, de Vicenzo making an eagle two at the first. At one particularly thrilling moment late in the afternoon, Goalby rolled in an eagle putt from eight feet on the 15th at exactly the same moment as de Vicenzo holed from three feet to birdie the

De Vicenzo's longevity can partly be ascribed to the excellence of his swing (above). At Hoylake in 1967 (left), Roberto celebrates his triumph in the Open.

17th. Both players were at 12 under par. But it was what happened at the 17th that proved pivotal. De Vicenzo made that birdie three to stay level with Goalby all right, but when he bogeyed the last he thought he had thrown it all away, and he signed his card with only a cursory check. At about that time, Goalby was bogeying the 17th. It then transpired that de Vicenzo's playing partner, Tommy Aaron, had inadvertently marked Roberto down for a four on the 17th. Signing for that score meant de Vicenzo was beaten by a shot. His reaction was typical – he attributed his error to the pressure exerted by Goalby. "*What a stupid I am to be wrong in this wonderful tournament,*" he told the press. Later, privately, he apologised to the relevant rules official: "*I sorry I cause you so much trouble.*" De Vicenzo lost that Masters, but sportsmanship, as on some 240 other occasions, was a winner.

TOM WATSON

(Born September 4, 1949)

■ *Glory days and grim years*

By July 1975, Tom Watson was called a 'choker', a cruel label applied to this articulate Kansan because of the manner in which he had wasted opportunities to win the US Open in 1974 and 1975.

Subsequently, nobody could have more vehemently made the point that he was a champion rather than a chicken.

Watson won his first Open Championship that July of 1975. By 1983 he had won his fifth. Only Harry Vardon, with six, has won more; only Braid, Taylor and Thomson have won as many. Furthermore, by 1983 Watson had also won the Masters twice and the US Open once, and still found time to lose playoffs for the Masters and the US PGA Championship. Like Palmer, the lack of the PGA title may eternally frustrate Watson in his attempt to complete a personal Grand Slam. By 1984, Watson had taken

Watson's economical, repeating swing enabled him to lift the Open Championship trophy five times between 1975 and 1983.

over from Jack Nicklaus as the best golfer in the world, and he cemented that position by topping the US Money List for the fifth time, although at St Andrews Ballesteros had denied him that coveted sixth Open. And then...crash! Between the end of 1984 and the spring of 1994, Watson won just once on the US tour (in 1987) plus the Hong Kong Open in 1992, a year after he came to the last hole of the Masters needing a par to force a playoff but instead finished with a double-bogey.

If he could putt anything like he used to, Watson would win again. Maybe he will anyway. But, undeniably, the glory days were glorious indeed. Two of Watson's triumphs will be remembered forever. His head-to-head confrontation with Nicklaus at Turnberry for the 1977 Open may have been the greatest major championship in history. The Young Pretender, then aged 27, prevailed with a final two rounds of 65-65 to Nicklaus's 65-66. In 1982 he got the better of Nicklaus at the US Open, largely because he holed an outrageous chip shot on the penultimate hole. In those days, Watson's short game was magical, and never did he show it off to better effect than on the last nine holes that day at Pebble Beach, as he sank several lengthy putts and one monster, from 60 feet at the 14th. When, just a month later, he won the Open Championship for a fourth time, he became only the fifth man to win both major Opens in the same year, the others being Jones (twice), Sarazen, Hogan and Trevino. Which makes it one more thing that Watson has over the great Nicklaus.

JOYCE WETHERED

(Born November 17, 1901)

◼ *The definitively charming champion*

Just as it's hard to better Herb Wind's tribute to Bobby Jones that I quoted earlier, so it is impossible to be more flattering about Joyce Wethered than was Jones himself. And remember, Jones didn't go in for empty flattery, so one has to assume that when he called her the best golfer, man or woman, he had ever seen, he meant it. And given his credentials, he certainly knew what he was talking about. His compliment is akin to Shakespeare saying that someone was a better playwright than him. Just as with the men it is invidious to claim that anyone has ever been better than Jones, so it would be unwise to say there has ever been a better woman golfer than Miss Wethered. And like Jones, she earned a matchless reputation for courtesy, charm and sportsmanship.

Although she was English, Miss Wethered learned the game at Royal Dornoch in Scotland, where her parents had a holiday home. There she developed her languid, powerful swing. It was a weapon that would serve her well. In the 1920s, when Jones was at his peak, Miss Wethered was similarly dominant in the British amateur game. She entered the English Ladies' Amateur Championship five times and won it five times. You can't be more dominant than that. Between 1921 and 1925, she won the Ladies' British Amateur three times from five attempts. And then she retired.

Four years later, she made the comeback of all comebacks. At St Andrews in 1929, she played in the British Amateur one last time and reached the final, where she found herself up against Glenna Collett, the American champion. Miss Wethered was 5 down after nine holes but she rallied with some fabulous golf to win by 3 & 1. And then she retired again, except for her annual outings in the Worplesdon Mixed Foursomes and her one-off appearance as captain in the first Curtis Cup match between Britain and the United States, at Wentworth in 1932, when she reminded Glenna Collett (then still America's best woman golfer)

exactly who was boss by beating her 6 & 4.

Miss Wethered became Lady Heathcoat-Amory on her marriage in 1937 and later retired to tend to her extensive gardens in Devon, leaving her substantial golfing records behind her. As with Jones's records, they will not be forgotten.

Bobby Jones was only the most eminent among many golfers who paid fulsome tribute to the qualities of Miss Wethered's swing.

IAN WOOSNAM

(Born March 2, 1958)

■ *Small but powerful swinger*

Although he's as short as Gene Sarazen, Ian Woosnam is one of the longest hitters in the modern game. With just two flicks and a swish, it seems, the ball is dispatched out of sight. When he's at his best, no one can make power golf look achievable with so little effort. His 'Popeye' forearms and an innate sense of timing are gifts he has used to devastating effect since he broke through with his first win on the European tour in 1982, after six lean years of struggling to make a living.

But 'Woosie' had to wait until 1987 to establish himself as not only the best Welsh golfer in history but as something harder – one of the best golfers in the game. That year, he won five tournaments in Europe and three elsewhere, amounting to $1.8 million in prize-money, led Wales to victory in the World Cup, and teamed with Nick Faldo to play a crucial role in Europe's retention of the Ryder Cup. He topped the European Order of Merit for a second time in 1990, again with five wins, but for all his protests to the contrary, inside he knew there was one thing he hadn't done to lay a claim to greatness. Despite a couple of solid efforts, notably finishing one shot out of a playoff at the 1989 US Open, he hadn't won a major championship. Woosnam put that right at the Masters in 1991. Needing a par to win, he got it by nervelessly rolling in a six-foot putt on the last green. With that, he really had arrived as a champion.

At last: Woosnam exults as he makes the putt that won the 1991 Masters and with it his first major championship.

MARY 'MICKEY' WRIGHT

(Born February 14, 1935)

■ *All-conquering heroine of the women's circuit*

Chalking up another win, a familiar pastime for Wright.

At around the time that Arnold Palmer was revitalizing the image of the US PGA Tour, Mickey Wright was encouraging people to take an interest in what was happening on the women's circuit. *"Mickey got the outside world to take a second look at women's golf, and when they looked, they discovered the rest of us,"* was how Judy Rankin, an LPGA Tour stalwart, put it. When anyone looked at women's golf in the 1960s, what they generally saw was Mickey Wright winning a tournament. She won 82 of them between 1956 and 1973, and although Kathy Whitworth has since extended her mark to 88 – an American tour record for men or women – she has never been the force that Wright was. With a swing that was eulogized by her rivals, she dominated the women's game for over a decade while Arnold Palmer and JackNicklaus were hogging the limelight on the men's tour. That swing was still good enough for her to be pounding out 270-yard drives in an LPGA event she entered in 1993.

Wright won 13 women's majors, an outright record, including four US Women's Opens, a joint record. In five years from 1960, she won 50 of the 130 LPGA tournaments she entered; twice she won four back-to-back victories; in six seasons she was the leading tournament-winner; five times she led the stroke averages; in four years she was the leading money-winner. Wright's greatest year was 1963, when she won 13 times from 32 starts. The 62 she shot in the Tall City Open in 1964 is still a tour record.

In 1979, six years after her last win, Wright was only denied victory No. 83 after a playoff for the Coca-Cola Classic. At least the dream was spoilt by a worthy winner. Wright's conqueror that day was Nancy Lopez, but even she will never conquer Wright's records.

MILDRED 'BABE' ZAHARIAS

(1914 –1956)

■ *Multi-talented athlete who took naturally to golf*

In a chapter crammed with references to outstanding sportsmen and women, it is fitting to close it with perhaps the finest athlete of the lot. There was almost no sport that young Mildred Didriksen wasn't good at. She acquired the nickname 'Babe' after Babe Ruth, the American baseball idol, because baseball was just one sport at which she excelled. And then there was athletics. At one time, she held outright or shared world records in the javelin, 80-metre hurdles, high jump and long jump. At the 1932 Olympic Games in Los Angeles, she won two gold medals and one silver. Grantland Rice, the legendary American sportswriter, was so impressed by her natural talent that he suggested she try her hand at golf. In 1935, she won the second event she ever entered. Nothing to it!

Things couldn't go on like that, and they didn't. The USGA declared the money she had earned from her sporting endeavours made her a professional, and since there wasn't a women's professional tour around in those days, that put a halt to her competitive career. But by 1945, the Second World War was over, she was married, and her amateur status had been restored. As if desperate to make up for lost time, the now Mrs Zaharias won 17 consecutive amateur events, including the US Women's Amateur in 1946 and the British Amateur in 1947. She was the first American to win the latter

title, but she didn't hang around to try and retain it. By 1948 Zaharias was a professional again, this time by choice and as a founder-member of the LPGA Tour.

The calibre of her golf helped to establish the nascent circuit. Stories about her long-hitting are legion: she could drive the ball 280 yards under normal conditions, and on par-5s where everyone else was taking three good blows to get home, she would be on in two. Thus she aroused attention in the women's game, and she delivered the goods. From 1948 to 1954, she won 10 major championships – three US Women's Opens, three Titleholders' Championships and four Western Opens. She saved the best till last. In 1954, she won five tournaments, including the US Open by a record 12 shots, less than a year after having surgery for cancer. She won twice more in 1955 but died from the cancer the following September. Time had at last caught up with the Babe.

Her powerful swing was one of the most astonishing aspects of Zaharias's all-round astonishing talent.

CHAPTER FOUR

THE MAJORS

In 1930, there were four major championships in golf – the four Bobby Jones had just won to complete the romantically styled 'Impregnable Quadrilateral'. They were the two Open Championships and the two Amateur Championships of the world's two foremost golfing nations. But as times moved on, it became increasingly clear that the notion of the British and US Amateurs remaining an integral part of the package was redundant. The world's best golfers were all pros, which had not been the case in Jones's day, and two alternative tournaments were needed to complete the set.

Gradually, after a haphazard process involving the golfing establishment, the players and the media, the Masters and the US PGA Championship were drafted in to plug the gap. It is impossible to pinpoint exactly the year in which this occurred, although in 1960 Arnold Palmer was quoted as saying: "*What if a guy were to win the Masters, the US and British Opens, and the PGA? That would be a Grand Slam.*" The Masters and the PGA invariably had the strongest fields in the world outside the two Opens, and both had a rich catalogue of outstanding past winners.

Viewed from a historical perspective, this whole area is riddled with anomalies. Thus we say that Horton Smith won two majors: the Masters in 1934 and 1936, even though the Masters wasn't even called the Masters at the time, let alone regarded as an event with anything close to the prestige of either the British or US Opens. Again, Jack Nicklaus is credited with 20 majors, including his two US Amateur titles, which means he is using five majors in his total. On the other hand, Walter Hagen's 11 takes in only three championships – there was no Masters when he was in his prime, which has led some savants to say the Western Open, as a kind of pseudo-major between the wars, should count towards Hagen's total, which would give him 16. As I said, the topic is potentially a statistical minefield.

Today, one thing is certain: the two Opens, the Masters and the US PGA are the four tournaments that constitute the modern 'Grand Slam'. Tennis, too, has its Grand Slam, and though golf isn't tennis, there is a fairly good comparison to be made between the two sports.

OLYMPIAN SETTING *Golf's greatest drama is provided by the major championships. Here the crowds watch the action unfold in the natural amphitheatre around the 18th green at the Olympic Club in San Francisco during the 1987 US Open.*

Tennis's Grand Slam is played on four different surfaces, and so, in a way, are three of golf's four legs. The British Open is played on a links (typically, firm sand-based turf that lies on land long ago reclaimed from the sea) where the main hazards are often the elements; the US Open puts a premium on heavy rough and well-protected target areas; while the Masters offers almost no rough but is unremitting in its demands on the player's strategy and putting stroke. The PGA, since it abandoned its matchplay format in favour of strokeplay in 1958, has been a bit like a second-rate US Open, but more of that later.

There is sporadic talk, sometimes engendered by the PGA's comparative loss of lustre, about which tournament would be the most deserving candidate to be regarded as a fifth major. The US tour's Players Championship is the most frequently cited example, but one thing that is clear is that the United States is the last place that should have another major championship.

Finally, this chapter also incorporates the Ryder Cup, the greatest team event in golf. Unlike the Grand Slam majors, the Ryder Cup is played at matchplay, and so tends to provide the most compelling action of the season when it is contested in the odd-numbered years. Twelve professional golfers from both Europe and the United States do battle over three days, each man representing his side with nothing more at stake than pride, honour, reputation and the weight of media and public expectancy. In other words, the sorts of pressures that Jones had to endure. And there is no prize-money. Jones could have related to that, too.

PORTRAIT OF A CHAMPION *No one has ever emulated Bobby Jones and won all four 'Grand Slam' majors in a single season, and it's highly unlikely that anyone ever will. Jones was also responsible for establishing Augusta National and the Masters.*

THE OPEN CHAMPIONSHIP

To foreigners, it perhaps sounds like an emblematic example of British arrogance that the Open Championship is called just that, as if it were the only Open in the world. When it began in 1860, it was.

THE PRE-OPEN PRE-EMINENCE *Allan Robertson, who was considered the finest golfer of his day (below). When he died in 1859 it was decided to hold a tournament to identify his successor. Thus was born the Open Championship.*

Today the Open is regularly referred to as the 'British Open' to distinguish it from the Opens of every other golf-playing nation, and especially from its co-major, the US Open. But 'British' is technically a superfluous addition that gained currency in the l960s, when the fortunes of the championship were revived by Arnold Palmer and other Americans who, understandably, used the single word 'Open' to mean the national championship of their country. Ironically, in the 1990s, the simple, unencumbered title 'Open Championship' is more justified than it has ever been. No golf tournament in the world can match the quality of its international field.

Having said that, the first Open was a closed affair. Only professionals were permitted to enter and only eight of them did. Willie Park won by two strokes from Old Tom Morris with a score of 174 for three circuits of Prestwick's 12-hole layout on Wednesday October 17, 1860. He received a red Moroccan leather belt, an unusual memento of victory in the days when a medal was invariably the prize. Park was to win the title three more times. His son, Willie Jnr, won it twice and his brother, Mungo, once.

Park's total in 1860 did not represent good scoring, even in the early days of the gutty, and there was discontent among several leading amateurs that they had been excluded. Accordingly, Major J. O. Fairlie, the Prestwick member who proposed the competition in the first place, acceded to their wishes. He was initially inclined to restrict the invitation to the "gentlemen" of eight prominent clubs but, after being persuaded at the 11th hour to be more generous and extend the offer, on the eve of the competition Major Fairlie declared that the "*Belt to be played for tomorrow and on all other occasions until it be otherwise resolved shall be open to all the world*". Seldom can the intentions of such a grandiose statement have been so impressively fulfilled.

The championship had been inaugurated in 1860 to determine who was Scotland's – and perforce the world's – best golfer following the death the previous year of Allan Robertson, who was recognized to be supreme. Robertson had covered the Old Course at St Andrews in 79 strokes in 1858. It was the first time 80 had been broken and, given the equipment of the day and the unkempt condition of the links, it has to be considered a more formidable feat than many a 62 in a modern tournament. It was golf of that quality that led to one R & A member commenting, after Robertson had succumbed to hepatitis at the age of 44: "*They may shut up their shops and toll their bells, for the greatest among them is gone.*"

In fact, Old Tom Morris was such a keen rival and near-equal that Robertson had shied away from further matches against him after two defeats, taking him on instead as his foursomes partner. With Robertson's death, Morris came into his own and, like Willie Park, he won the Open four times. When Morris won for the last time in 1867, aged 46 years and 99 days, he became, and still remains, the oldest winner. The next year his son was, and is ever likely to be, the youngest champion at 17 years and 161 days.

Prize money had been introduced in 1863 but by 1870 there was no belt left to dispute. Young Tom had claimed ownership of it by completing a hat-trick of victories. His winning totals in 1869 and 1870 added up to 303 for 72 holes: not until Harry Vardon shot 300 round the same course, Prestwick, in 1903 was that bettered. Obviously, such comparisons are invidious and take no account of different conditions, but it has

to be pointed out that Vardon's score was achieved after the demise of the gutty in favour of the rubber-cored ball. To play Prestwick's first hole of over 500 yards in three, as Morris did in 1870, was remarkable, but then Young Tom was a prodigy. Apart from his other prodigious feats, he is also assured of one footnote in Open history. In 1868 he recorded the championship's first hole-in-one.

With Young Tom perhaps fondly gazing at the belt resting on his mantelpiece, there was no tournament in 1871. When hostilities were resumed in 1872, the Championship Trophy had replaced it· a silver claret jug which had been jointly donated by the Prestwick Club, the R & A at St Andrews and the Honourable Company, then at Musselburgh. The three agreed to host the Open on a rota basis, a system which in essence still exists, although it now involves more clubs and has a much less strict order of rotation. There was no renewal of the clause about three wins in succession earning the victor outright possession of the trophy, and just as well. Jamie Anderson (1877-1879) and Bob Ferguson (1880-1882) both accomplished the hat-trick, though not before Young Tom had emulated his father and won a fourth championship, in 1872, before his untimely death in 1875.

The following year, 1876, Bob Martin tied with

David Strath, but the latter refused to enter a playoff after a protracted and acrimonious debate following allegations that he had contravened the conventions of etiquette by hitting to the green on the infamous 'Road Hole', the 17th at St Andrews, before it was clear, thus ensuring that his ball was prevented from going on to the dreaded road. Martin won again in 1885 and this time he was indebted to the notorious Road Bunker as well as the road. Davie Ayton ran up an 11 by flitting between the two hazards. He finished two shots behind Martin. By then, overtime had actually been contested for the first time, over 36 holes in 1883, when Willie Fernie had made a two at the last to beat Bob Ferguson by a stroke and thereby deny him the chance to equal Young Tom's four consecutive triumphs.

The Open has always been a byword for constancy, but in the 1890s several of the earliest traditions were cast aside and barriers were broken. John Ball won at Prestwick in 1890 – the first English champion, the first amateur winner. Victories by amateurs have not become commonplace (just Ball once, Harold Hilton twice and Bobby Jones three times) but Ball's success did signal the end of the Scottish stranglehold on the Open.

A veritable revolution occurred in 1892. Prize-

MARQUEE NAME *James Braid holing out (above) for the first of his five Open Championships, at Muirfield in 1901. Clearly, the tented village isn't entirely a modern phenomenon.*

GETTING A GRIP *Harry Vardon (above), in many ways the pioneer of modern golf technique, on the tee during the Open of 1900 at St Andrews.*

money soared, from £28/10 (£28.50) to £110. An entry fee was imposed. The championship was doubled to 72 holes and played over two days. The Honourable Company had just quit Musselburgh and settled in at Muirfield, so the Open broke fresh ground since it was their turn to stage it. With a distinct echo of the old feud between the R & A and the Honourable Company, a disgusted Andrew Kirkaldy from St Andrews said of the new course: "*It's an auld water meadie. I'm glad I'm gaun home.*" His temper was not improved by the victory of Hilton, Ball's amateur colleague from the Royal Liverpool Club at Hoylake; and no doubt his humour got no better 12 months later when that course and St George's at Sandwich were added to the rota. First the English won the Open, now they were staging it. In 1894, they did both.

J.H. Taylor's win at St George's that year ushered in the era of the Great Triumvirate of Taylor, Harry Vardon and James Braid. They would dominate matters at the expense of the artisans – the plasterers, slaters, stonemasons, bakers – who had prevailed as part-time professional golfers for the preceding 15 years or so. But although the earlier pros might have been additionally attracted to the Open by the prospect of a little betting action on the side, even late into the 19th century it was not the be-all and end-all of tournament golf. After having tied for the 1896 Open, Vardon and Taylor had to wait an extra day to play off because there was another tournament scheduled between times at North Berwick.

Into this century, more courses have come on to the championship roster while others have fallen from favour. Royal Cinque Ports at Deal (1909), Troon (1923), Royal Lytham & St Annes (1926), Carnoustie (1931), Prince's (1932) and Royal Portrush (1951) – the

two latter playing host just once – Royal Birkdale (1954) and Turnberry (1977) have joined the list of courses which have enjoyed the highest accolade in British golf. All are links, and it is probably the most revered element of Open tradition that the championship should retain this connection with its roots. The truth is rather more prosaic, or at least rather more commercial, in that the wide open spaces adjoining links courses are perfect for erecting the vast tented village and the rest of the paraphernalia associated with the Open today. Few, if any, inland courses could cope with these extensive trimmings, and indeed venues like Hoylake and Carnoustie have been rendered redundant by the importance of essential frills such as hotel accommodation, road access and other commercial considerations. Whether their absence from Open duty will be temporary or permanent is hard to say, especially in view of Sandwich's successful resurrection in 1981 after 32 years in the metaphorical wilderness. At present, St Andrews, Muirfield, Troon and Turnberry in Scotland, plus Birkdale, Lytham and St George's in England, are the only seven courses to have hosted the Open since 1975 or scheduled to do so before 1997. Prestwick, incidentally, was retired in 1925. The course, now regarded as a delightful anachronism, was even by then outdated as a genuine test of ability. The Open was held there 24 times in all, a tally which St Andrews will pass in 1995.

But back to the past. The 20 years preceding the First World War were monopolized by the Great Triumvirate, which explains why Sandy Herd's one-shot triumph over Braid and Vardon in the 1902 Open was such a potent advertisement for the Haskell ball.

Standards were improving rapidly. Vardon's win at Prestwick in 1898 represented the first occasion 80 had been beaten in all four rounds. When the Open returned there in 1903, Vardon won again with a record total of 300, beating his brother Tom by six shots. At St George's the following season, a number of new marks were set as Jack White shot 296 and three players (White, Braid and Vardon) became the first Open competitors to shoot a round in the 60s. In 1907, the year that qualifying rounds were introduced, Arnaud Massy of France became the first overseas player to grasp the coveted silver jug.

Vardon edged ahead of Braid and Taylor in the immortality stakes with his record sixth and last victory in 1914, and the war in Europe meant it was 1920 before he had to relinquish the trophy to George Duncan. At Deal, Duncan opened with consecutive rounds of 80 (the last champion to return a score over 79) and was 13 shots adrift, but by closing with rounds of 71-72 he made up the deficit with two shots to spare.

That was the first championship held under the auspices of the R & A, the result of an accord between the six hosting clubs of the time who decided it would be good for golf, as well as for the Open, for there to be just one ruling body. The R & A has since instigated a massive increase in the popularity and scope of the championship. The number of entrants has multiplied hugely, but nothing makes the point more clearly than a glance at the rising prize fund over the years. In 1920, the purse was £225, of which the winner received £75. The former didn't breach the four-figure barrier until 1946, the latter until 1955. As recently as 1975, total prize money was a modest £75,000 and Tom Watson collected 10 per cent of that. In 1993, the purse was over £1 million and Greg Norman, the champion, won £100,000. Even allowing for inflation, these statistics are nothing short of astonishing. In financial terms, the Open used to be the poor relation. Today, despite the vagaries of the pound's international value, it is invariably among the ten richest tournaments in the world, and surely the richest in terms of prestige.

If the traditionalists of the 1920s were hoping the formal acknowledgement of St Andrews' predominance

GOLF ILLUSTRATED

The Weekly Organ of the "Royal and Ancient" Game.
THE ONLY WEEKLY GOLF JOURNAL IN THE WORLD. Established in 1890
No. 1416.—Vol. XCVII. FRIDAY, MAY 17th, 1929. Price Ninepence.

WALTER HAGEN.
Who gained his second successive victory in the British Open Championship at Muirfield last week, and his fourth in all.
Copies of the above exclusive picture may be purchased from "Golf Illustrated."

would coincide with a return to the days of Scottish domination, they were in for a devastating shock. The 1921 champion was Jock Hutchison, a Scotsman by birth but an American by residence, who prevented Roger Wethered becoming the third amateur winner by thrashing him by nine strokes in a 36-hole playoff. Thus the trophy went across the Atlantic for the first time. It was to become a very familiar journey, for until 1934 only Arthur Havers (in 1923) was able to stem the inexorable shift of power to the west.

In the vanguard of the transatlantic assault was Walter Hagen. He pioneered the idea of Americans contesting golf's oldest honour, much as Arnold Palmer was to resuscitate the notion in the 1960s. Hagen made his first appearance in the Open in 1920 when, to quote the American writer Herbert Warren Wind, he had been *"press-agented as the golfer who would show the British a thing or two. Walter had showed them four rounds in the 80s and finished a lurid 55th."*

But 'the Haig' turned the tables on George Duncan in 1922, and won for a second time in 1924, having to hole from eight feet at the last to beat Ernie Whitcombe. He sank it with aplomb. *"You seemed to treat that putt very casually,"* somebody remarked afterwards. *"Did you know you had it to win?"* Hagen's response was typical. *"Sure, I knew I had it to win, but no man ever beat me in a playoff."*

The answer wasn't so much an example of cool confidence as of an outright lie. Gene Sarazen had nipped him in a playoff for the US PGA Championship less than a year beforehand, but Hagen was never inclined to let a small matter of fact bother him. He was content in the knowledge of his own capabilities,

COVER GUY *Walter Hagen adorns the cover of Golf Illustrated magazine in 1929 after winning the Open for the fourth and final time.*

which were such that Bernard Darwin, the doyen of all golf writers, was moved to comment of Whitcombe's gallant but ultimately futile challenge that *"there is this difference between the two, as so often between Hagen and the other man. Hagen just won and the other man just didn't"*.

Hagen stories are always good value. They are even better for being true rather than apocryphal. He was audacious – in 1926 he ordered the flagstick to be removed while he attempted to hole out from 150 yards to tie Bobby Jones at Lytham. He was generous – he presented his winner's cheque in 1928 to his caddie. He was arrogant – while out partying the night before the final two rounds at Muirfield in 1929, he was reminded that the leader, Leo Diegel, was already in bed. *"Yeah, but he ain't sleeping,"* was the snappy riposte. Walter Hagen won,

and Leo Diegel was third.

The other American stars of this glorious, vintage stretch were Sarazen and Jones. Sarazen arrived at Troon in 1923 as the reigning US Open champion but he left without striking a blow in the championship proper. Like everybody in those days, however mighty or humble, he had to play two qualifying rounds to get in (a situation not remedied until 1963, when specified categories of leading players were exempted from the ordeal). Sarazen drew the worst of some atrocious weather and failed to qualify. Nine years later he was triumphant at Prince's, and he might well have won in 1928 and 1933 as well.

Jones was the winner in 1926, 1927 and 1930. In the first, victory at Royal Lytham was rescued from apparent defeat in the final round when he struck a tremendous long-iron shot from a sand bunker to the heart of the 17th green. Jones later called it the greatest shot he ever hit when it really mattered. Jones's bunker shot so startled his closest rival, Al Watrous, that he three-putted. The Lytham members later erected a

TRANSATLANTIC LEGENDS *Hagen wasn't the only American star to plunder the Open between the wars. Gene Sarazen (above) won in 1932, after being denied by Hagen in 1928, while Bobby Jones is shown (right) putting on the final green at Royal Lytham & St Annes in 1926, the first of his three Open Championship victories.*

plaque to commemorate the spot from where Jones played the stroke. His win in 1930, of course, led to the Impregnable Quadrilateral.

In between times, two more exiled Britons – Jim Barnes (1925) and Tommy Armour (1931) – emulated Jock Hutchison, and in 1933 Denny Shute was consistency personified with four 73s. That got him into a playoff with another American, Craig Wood, which he won comfortably .

Shute and his compatriots only took part at St Andrews because they had been in Britain anyway for the fourth Ryder Cup match at Southport. From 1934 until Palmer took up Hagen's cause in 1960, a lot of the gloss was stripped from the Open. The Americans came in force just once more, in 1937, when the Ryder Cup was again scheduled close to the Open.

It isn't hard to discover the reasons for the championship being discarded like last year's fashions. In the 1930s, the United States was suffering from the Great Depression and travel was prohibitively expensive. The Second World War came next, which

depressed everybody. When that ended in 1945, the British economy was hopelessly ravaged while happy American golfers were finding themselves deluged by dollars at home. There was simply insufficient incentive to make a long sea journey, at colossal cost which even the first prize could not cover, on the off-chance of winning a trophy, however important. And until Arnold Palmer arrived the importance of the Open came to be greatly diminished in American circles.

That is not to suggest there were no worthy winners for 25 years. In 1934 Henry Cotton began a sequence of six successive British victories, against largely domestic opposition, with a stylish triumph at Sandwich. His record 65 in the second round was used to name the Dunlop 65 ball and it was not bettered until Mark Hayes shot 63 at Turnberry in 1977. Three years later, in 1937, Cotton, in his finest hour, repulsed the heavy American threat in terrible conditions at Carnoustie.

The immediate post-war years were dominated by Bobby Locke and Peter Thomson with four wins each. Locke's first is invariably remembered for a bizarre incident on the 5th hole during the second round when Harry Bradshaw's ball got lodged in a broken bottle. The genial Irishman double-bogeyed the hole and the fact that the episode led to a change in the rules was scant consolation to him. He ended the tournament tied with Locke and lost the playoff. It has often been argued that the bottle cost him the championship, but that is to ignore the truth that one cannot alter one fact in a sequence and assume all the others would have remained constant. The same was to be the case in 1983, when Hale Irwin 'whiffed' a putt – took an air shot – in the third round and by the conclusion of the fourth found himself just one stroke behind the winner.

Locke's farewell appearance on the victory rostrum in 1957 was also touched by controversy. It was an odd week anyway. The venue had been switched from Muirfield to St Andrews at short notice because of the petrol shortage afflicting Britain in the wake of the Suez crisis. Locke caused something of a crisis within

THEY HAD A LOCK ON THE OPEN *Bobby Locke (above) shared the domination of the championship in the 1950s with Peter Thomson (far left). But Thomson is shown here in 1965, sinking the short putt that would claim the last and sweetest of his five Opens, when he beat the cream of American golf at Royal Birkdale.*

TOO HOT TO HANDLE

*A magical – almost
supernatural – short game
enabled Lee Trevino to
retain his title at Tony
Jacklin's expense at
Muirfield in 1972.*

the R & A when it was
realized after he had received
the trophy and his cheque
that he had not replaced his
ball properly before holing
out on the last green. He had
marked it a putter-head away
from its spot in order not to
interfere with his partner's
line, but had then forgotten
to allow for that when
replacing it. Since he had
won by three strokes, the
championship committee felt
it safe to deduct a theoretical
two-shot penalty (but didn't
actually do so) without
affecting the outcome. Locke
might, indeed, have been
disqualified, but such a
decision would really have
been a travesty.

There were three British
winners, an increasingly
endangered species, in this
period: Fred Daly (1947), Cotton (1948) and Max
Faulkner (1951), the latter on the only occasion the
Open has been held in Ireland. The hard-luck stories
of the other leading home players of the 1940s and
1950s were legion. Charlie Ward, Dai Rees, Eric Brown,
Dave Thomas, Christy O'Connor and many more were
near-miss experts.

Not so the top American professionals. Sam Snead
won in 1946 on the second of only three attempts. In
1953, Ben Hogan – chasing a third major of the year –
memorably came, saw and conquered Carnoustie. He
hadn't been before and he never returned. Otherwise it
was Locke or Thomson (whose hat-trick from 1954 to
1956 is unique this century) until a young South
African called Gary Player survived a double-bogey at
the 72nd hole in a final round of 68 to win at Muirfield
in 1959. And then came Palmer.

The great man lost by a shot to Kel Nagle on his
debut appearance in 1960, at the Centenary Open at St
Andrews. In 1961 and 1962 he won it. That he did so

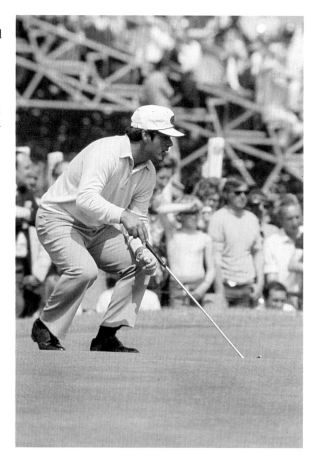

impressed his fellow
Americans; that he could be
bothered to make the trip
influenced them. Suddenly,
the Open was back in
business. Soon it was to be
big business.

In 1966 Jack Nicklaus
completed his collection of
the four majors with a
victory at a rough-strewn
Muirfield. This proved
conclusively to himself and
to his dwindling band of
doubters that he could cope
with the wind and the fast-
running turf of British links
golf. That same year, the
traditional Friday double-
round was abandoned.
Instead the Open was
played over four days and
ended on Saturday, a
belated acknowledgement
that there were regular
tournament professionals who did not have to be back
behind the counters of their pro shops for the
weekend. Saturday play obviously made commercial
sense, as did the earlier decision to replace the 36-hole
playoff with one of just 18 holes in the event of a tie.
This move followed the one-sided battle between Bob
Charles and Phil Rodgers in 1963 when the former, the
best putter in the world for a decade, became the only
left-hander to win a major championship.

In 1967, the ABC TV company bought the
American television rights for the championship and in
1968 Keith Mackenzie, who was to be a marvellous
salesman and entrepreneur for the Open, was
appointed secretary of the R & A. These two apparently
quite diverse occurrences were connected by
subsequent developments.

The television deal presaged the broadcasting of
the Open to Japan, Australia and all points of the
compass. It is reckoned that tens of millions fans now
watch it from their armchairs. Mackenzie presided over

DRIVEN TO DISTRACTION
Tony Jacklin won the Open in 1969, and might have won it again in 1970 and 1972. He is seen here on the last, fateful day of the 1972 Open, when Trevino's luck and his own impetuosity conspired to deprive him of the title.

the physical and financial flourishing of the Open – unquestionably assisted by the enthusiasm generated by Tony Jacklin's exhilarating triumph at Lytham in 1969 – before retiring to make way for Michael Bonallack in 1983. Mackenzie made endless visits to the United States to cajole that country's leading players into competing. He encouraged the creation of the tented village complex containing banks, bars, a champagne tent, eating facilities, hospitality units, golf equipment and merchandise stalls, and an enormous press centre. In 1980, he moved the finish of the championship to Sunday. On the course, he arranged dozens of fixed and mobile scoreboards, and huge grandstands around the final hole and at other strategic locations to cope with the crowds. And all this is forgetting necessities like course preparation, administration and ancillary services.

Bonallack has maintained the trend. It seems odd, even ironic, that in the marketing and meticulous organization of its championship, an august British institution like the R & A should have been an inspiration to, rather than the pupil of, the Americans at the USGA. Critics allege it's not so much marketing as manipulation; witness the late starting times on the

last day of the Open and the decision, taken in 1984, to hold any future playoffs over just four or five selected holes, even though the USGA has retained the 18-hole playoff. These steps are seen in some quarters as acts of appeasement to the great god TV, though that is not to suggest that the R & A has wantonly forsaken its grand traditions and heritage. The financial proceeds generated by the Open are applied to a host of worthy and indigent golfing causes in Britain and overseas – from turf research to the purchase of equipment, from encouraging junior golf programmes to funding amateur competitions – and the R & A remains ever-eager to promote its championship internationally. In February 1994, it announced three new qualification categories, embracing the European, US and Japanese tours, that ensured exemption from qualifying for in-form players.

While the Open has moved with the times, the drama has never lessened. From its saviour, Palmer, in the 1960s through to Nick Faldo's current domination of the scene, the Open has assuredly retained that link with its past.

If the losing of a golf tournament can ever justify being called a tragedy, then that is what happened to

WANING INFLUENCE

Americans dominated the Open for over 20 years until the early 1980s, never more so than when Tom Watson gloriously beat Jack Nicklaus in 1977 (below). But after Watson's win in 1983, Mark Calcavecchia, in 1989 (right) was the only American champion for the next 10 years.

Doug Sanders at St Andrews in 1970. He had brilliantly saved his par on the Road Hole with the most gorgeous bunker shot imaginable. That should have been the stroke that won the Open. He needed only to par the 18th, surely the most straightforward closing hole in championship golf, to be the winner. Horribly, he three-putted, missing from three feet for the title, and he had to return the next day to face Jack Nicklaus. That he put up a brave fight was commendable; that he would lose the playoff was almost inevitable.

At Muirfield in 1972, Tony Jacklin suffered as badly as Sanders. He had to watch while his playing partner and rival, the defending champion Lee Trevino, thinned a bunker shot against the flagstick and then into the hole for a birdie at the 16th in the third round, and then trump that by chipping in for another on the 18th. Yet, with two holes of the championship remaining on the Saturday, Jacklin's star seemed to be in the ascendancy. Trevino volubly conceded he had lost his chance when he lay four over the back of the 17th green. Instead, his 'give-up' chip went into the hole. Jacklin, shocked into misguided aggression, charged his birdie putt, missed the short one back and took six. He would never again have the chance to repeat his triumph of 1969.

Turnberry made its championship debut in 1977 and instantly produced an epic, arguably the greatest golf tournament ever played. Only two men were involved: Tom Watson and Jack Nicklaus. Watson played the last 36 holes in 65-65, Nicklaus in 65-66. It was virtually matchplay. So emphatically did they trounce the pack that third place went to Hubert Green, who was 11 shots off the pace. Watson birdied four of the last six holes in the most breathtaking fashion to make up three shots on Nicklaus and win by one. Nicklaus, who has been runner-up in the Open a record seven times, won it for a third time the next summer, while Watson got his fifth in 1983.

At Turnberry, the leading non-American had been Tommy Horton of England, who tied for ninth. That represented the nadir for non-American golf. The rest of the world were about to demonstrate to the Americans that they could play, too.

Following Watson's win in 1983, Mark Calcavecchia (in 1989) was the only American winner in the next 10 years, and he had to beat two Australians – Greg Norman and Wayne Grady – in a playoff to do that.

Seve Ballesteros, champion in 1979, the first continental winner since 1907, collected his second title at St Andrews in 1984. This was the best Open since Turnberry, not least because it also involved the then two best golfers in the world. Level with Watson playing the 17th – yes, that hole again! – Ballesteros made his first par of the week there. Behind him, Watson, who was aiming for his sixth Open on a fifth different Scottish course, misjudged his approach shot

went on the road and took five. While he was doing
that, Ballesteros appeared to be impersonating a
matador on the 18th green, where he had just holed
from 12 feet for a birdie. The Spaniard's celebrations as
the winning putt disappeared were among the
most exuberant displays of pleasure spectators at
the Old Course have ever witnessed.

At Sandwich the next year, Sandy Lyle succeeded
Ballesteros and became the first British winner since
Jacklin. Greg Norman won in 1986 in rough weather
and over one of the most stringently set up major
championship courses in history. Someone called it the
US Open with wind. Norman's remarkable 63 on the
Friday at Turnberry comprised one eagle, eight birdies
and three bogeys, a stark contrast to Nick Faldo's
performance at Muirfield 12 months later where 18 pars
on Sunday gave him the title after Paul Azinger had
bogeyed the last two holes.

BACK-TO-BACK EUROPEANS *Seve Ballesteros (right)
indulges his delight after holing what proved to be the winning
putt on the last green of the 1984 Open at St Andrews. Sandy
Lyle (below) also seems to be pretty happy about succeeding
the Spaniard as champion after his win at Sandwich in 1985.*

DOOM AT TROON *Greg Norman won the Open in 1986 and seemed likely to in 1989. But despite here acknowledging the applause that greeted his opening six birdies on the Sunday that year, the afternoon turned into one of bitter distress for the Australian.*

In 1988, it was a case of happy returns to Lytham for Ballesteros, who won there for a second time with a blistering final round of 65. And still the drama persisted. At Royal Troon in 1989, Norman fired a stunning closing round of 64, eight under par, that had begun with six birdies. That got him into a playoff, the first to be contested via the R & A's four-hole system. Greg birdied the first hole and the second. Surely the Australian would win it now? But he bogeyed the third hole, thoughtlessly drove into a bunker at the last, and

from the next bunker he was in, he thinned his ball out-of-bounds. Calcavecchia, who had birdied the 18th hole to make the playoff, birdied it again to beat Grady by three strokes.

At St Andrews in 1990, Norman's aspirations were doomed after Faldo demolished him with a 67 to his 76 in the third round. By Saturday evening, Faldo had a five-shot lead, as he had come Sunday night.

Ian Baker-Finch at last struck a blow for Australia by winning in 1991, before Faldo regained his title at

Muirfield in 1992. He had seen a four-shot lead at the start of Sunday become a two-shot deficit with four holes to play, but courageous birdies at the 15th and 17th and an imperious 3-iron to set up his par at the last rescued him from ignominy, admittedly with a little help from John Cook's missed two-foot birdie putt on the 17th and wild bogey on the 18th. The Open champion was again, as he has so often been down the ages, genuinely the champion golfer of the world.

That week, Faldo broke the 36-hole and 54-hole scoring records, joined Ballesteros as a five-time major winner, and extended to 21 his astonishing run of consecutive top-30 finishes in the major championships. One day, some or all of those distinctions may be eclipsed, but Faldo knows that his Open victories are recorded for posterity.

He was near to retaining his crown at Royal St George's the following summer, but this time the records were set by Greg Norman. Faldo was tied for the lead with Corey Pavin going into the last round and shot a three-under-par 67. That should have been enough to win, but it wasn't. Norman shot 64, a stunning round only marred by a missed 14-inch putt at the 17th. All the best golfers in the world were on the leaderboard – Faldo, Langer, Pavin, Price, Couples – and Norman destroyed them and the course.

His total of 267 set a record for any major. Faldo shot 269. At Turnberry in 1977, Watson had shot 268 to Nicklaus's 269. No one else has ever broken 270 in any major championship. No one had ever broken 70 in all four rounds of the Open before, but at Sandwich both

Norman and the young South African prodigy, Ernie Els, did it.

Britons, Spaniards, Americans, Australians and South Africans – the Open is not only the oldest but also the most cosmopolitan of Opens. And from Tom Morris to Tom Watson, Sandy Herd to Sandy Lyle, all its champion have felt, for 12 months at least, that they have followed in the footsteps of Allan Robertson as "*the greatest among them*".

DRAMATIC THEATRE
Greg Norman and Bernhard Langer amid the amphitheatre of spectators at the conclusion of the magnificent 1993 Open Championship.

THE US OPEN CHAMPIONSHIP

When Harry Vardon entered the US Open in 1900, it was partly as a break from a series of promotional outings and exhibitions he was conducting in the United States. Although exhibitions are regarded with some scorn these days, they used to be the professional golfer's major means of making money. When Walter Hagen won all his championships in the 1920s, he said they were welcome not only for the glory but also as invaluable meal tickets he could take on the road. Hagen used to manage a gruelling schedule of anything up to ten exhibition matches per week.

TREND SETTER *The flamboyant follow-though (far right) of Johnny McDermott , the first American-born golfer to win his country's national Open.*

Thus it was that Harry Vardon incidentally won the sixth US Open while in the country for some lucrative extra-curricular remuneration. His triumph was a fillip for his own golf days and also for American golf. By the time he returned in 1913, the championship was well established and had even been won by a home-bred player.

The early days of the US Open were dominated by displaced Britons – Horace Rawlins, James Foulis, Joe Lloyd, Fred Herd, Willie Smith, Willie Anderson, Laurie Auchterlonie, Alex Smith, Alec Ross, Fred McLeod and George Sargent. Vardon was the only champion to have made a transatlantic journey to win but, with the exception of Anderson, the rest had honed their games in the old country, usually Scotland, and brought their skills over to America with them.

Willie Anderson was exceptional in many ways. He won the title four times: in 1901 and then from 1903 to 1905. Nobody else has ever accomplished the hat-trick, and his record of four victories is shared by Bobby Jones, Ben Hogan and Jack Nicklaus but bettered by nobody. Those three are impressive company. In the 1950s, several people who saw Anderson, Jones and Hogan in their respective primes vouched that Anderson was superior. He was indeed a marvellous striker and a fearsome competitor (he won his first two Opens in playoffs) but one is tempted to suggest that the evidence of those eyewitnesses is flawed by nostalgia, frequently the enemy of truth. Jones and

Hogan were the best players in the world in their eras; Anderson was the best in America in his. It is hard to believe that he would have been so successful had Vardon, Taylor and Braid bothered to compete during the years of his brief reign. Whatever their comparative merits, it was a sad loss when Anderson, aged just 32, died of arteriosclerosis in 1910.

The US Open matured quickly, picking up the habits of its British cousin with alacrity. Prize money was instituted straight away rather than after a three-year wait. It took only four years rather than 32 to be extended to 72 holes. Standards of scoring soon caught up, too. It was in 1898 that 80 was first broken on all four days of the Open; four years later Auchterlonie did it in the US Open. A total below 300 and a single round below 70 were not achieved in Britain until

1904; in the United States the first of those hurdles fell in 1906 and the second in 1909. The most emphatic margins of victory in both Opens were set in their formative years: in Britain it remains the 13 shots by which Old Tom Morris swamped the rest in 1862; in the United States the 11 by which Willie Smith prevailed in 1899. Neither is likely to be increased, not least because the fields these days are rather larger.

By 1911, the championship had been staged 16 times and a native had yet to win. It was all about to change. Johnny McDermott took the title at Chicago in 1911, at 19 the youngest-ever winner. He won again in 1912, in the process becoming the first man to record a sub-par total. And he was close to matching Anderson's hat-trick. In 1910, both McDermott and Macdonald Smith had been beaten in a playoff by the latter's brother, Alex Smith.

Despite McDermott's heroics, the big breakthrough was still 12 months away. In 1913, the US Open was won by 20-year-old Francis Ouimet (pronounced, in cumbersome franglais, as 'We-met').

A good but hardly spectacular amateur, Ouimet nearly withdrew from the tournament a week beforehand and rather wished he had when he struggled to a pair of 88s in two late practice rounds. But play he did, and play himself into the history books.

The weather that week at The Country Club in Brookline, Massachusetts, was uniformly awful. It had either just rained, was doing so or was about to, but the conditions did not stop the cream of British golf, Harry Vardon and Ted Ray, rising to the top with the lowest totals of 304. Out on the course, an unknown pro called Walter Hagen needed to par the last five holes to tie them but nobody was surprised when he blew up with a seven. He had to wait 12 months to win the title, Ouimet just another 24 hours.

Ouimet was a regular caddie at The Country Club.

Carrying his bag in the Open was a 10-year-old boy, Eddie Lowery, who repeatedly and tersely reminded his man: "*Keep your eye on the ball.*" Sound advice, but it didn't seem likely to be sufficient when Ouimet, having astonished and delighted the damp gallery by being in contention for so long, needed to birdie two of the last six holes to catch the Englishmen. He not only did it but then routed his rivals in the playoff; Vardon by five shots – though Ouimet led him by only one with two holes to play – and Ray by six. Romantically, Ouimet permitted Lowery to keep the bag for the playoff after the boy had tearfully pleaded

GIANT SLAYERS *The 20-year-old Francis Ouimet and his 10-year-old caddie Eddie Lowery (above), who were too good for British titans Harry Vardon and Ted Ray in a drama-packed playoff for the 1913 US Open. Americans were usually winning the US Open by the time Hogan won his second in 1950 (inset) after his horrific car crash.*

with him to reverse his decision to have a friend take it over. The kindness had its due reward.

It is often stated that, overnight, Ouimet's phenomenal performance converted a hitherto arcane pastime derided as *"cow-pasture pool"* into the biggest thing since hash browns. It did not, but Ouimet's relatively humble social status and engaging, pleasant manner did help to diminish golf's upper-crust image and broaden its appeal. One may argue that after the First World War the United States would have taken to golf anyway, as it did to many other sports. Maybe, but the fact that Ouimet had convincingly and dramatically beaten the world's best players head-to-head did wonders for the confidence of American golfers. It is a reflection of the significance attached to the events of September 20, 1913 by the USGA that few years ago The Country Club was awarded the 1988 US Open – the 75th anniversary of the occasion, the centenary celebration of John Reid's game in his cow pasture.

HERO OF THE ERA *The most acceptable face of golf. Bobby Jones (inset) was not only the greatest golfer of the 1920s, and maybe of all time, he was a modest, unassuming man whose competitive grace was only matched by his talent.*

Just as John Ball had severed the Scots' grip on the game, so Ouimet broke that of the British. Coincidentally, both were the first amateurs to win their respective national Opens, but whereas Ball's success did not herald a decline in the influence of the professionals in Britain, Ouimet's victory was the precursor of two glorious decades of amateur achievement. Nineteen US Opens took place between 1913 and 1933 (the war caused cancellations in 1917 and 1918) and amateurs won eight of them: Ouimet (1913), Jerome Travers (1915), Chick Evans (1916), Bobby Jones (1923, 1926, 1929 and 1930) and Johnny Goodman (1933), the last amateur to win one of the four major championships. In addition, Jones was second four times, twice losing playoffs.

The period between the wars was crammed with marvellous championships. After Hagen had won his second, and surprisingly last, US Open in an ill-tempered playoff with Mike Brady in 1919, Ted Ray took the trophy back to Britain from Inverness, Ohio, in 1920. That was a watershed year.

It was the first time the clubhouse had been completely opened up to the professionals. Once this giant step had been taken other clubs soon followed suit and the old prejudices were swept away; in the United States, it must be said, before Britain. The professionals, duly grateful, donated a grand clock, which still graces the clubhouse, in recognition of the Inverness members' emancipatory attitude.

Inverness also witnessed the Open debut of men like Bobby Jones, Gene Sarazen, Johnny Farrell, Tommy Armour and Leo Diegel, and the unhappy farewell of Harry Vardon. The great man, seeking a second US Open 20 years after his first, led by five shots after 11 holes of the final round but a sudden and severe storm off Lake Erie destroyed his game, especially his putting touch which was by then quite delicate anyway, and he stumbled home in level fives for the last seven holes. Ray beat Vardon and three others with a stroke to spare to become the then oldest winner of the championship. Vardon's record in the three US Opens he played in was won one, lost one playoff and lost by one stroke.

One anecdote from that week is priceless. Vardon was paired with Jones in a qualifying round when the latter thinned a shot terribly. *"Mr. Vardon,"* he asked, *"did you ever see a worse shot than that?"* *"No,"* came the reply. But Vardon's day was done. The 'twenties' roared for Bobby Jones. He won the first of his 13 majors at the 1923 US Open, despite a double-bogey on the 72nd hole which enabled Bobby Cruickshank to catch him with a birdie. In what was to be the first of six US Open playoffs in nine years, Jones clinched the title by two strokes.

Jones was involved in four of those extended Opens, but curiously, in view of his superb matchplay record in amateur competition, he could claim only a

50 per cent success rate. He lost to Willie Macfarlane in 1925 and to Johnny Farrell in 1928, both times by one shot over 36 holes, though in the first instance that was because an extra 18 had not been enough to separate them.

The second round of normal play in 1925 threw up a famous incident. Jones called a shot penalty on himself when his ball moved fractionally as he was addressing it. Nobody else saw it happen but when Jones was later congratulated for his sportsmanship he responded: "*You might as well praise a man for not robbing a bank.*" Jones knew only one way to play and it is golf's great good fortune that this mode of behaviour has been adopted by the vast majority of those who chase the rich rewards available in the contemporary professional game.

One cannot say that Jones would have won that Open had his ball not budged: one can say that he would have beaten Macfarlane in their second playoff had he not frittered away a four-shot lead over the last nine holes. In any event, he only had to rue his mistake for a year. By winning the title at Scioto, Jones became the first player to hold simultaneously the British and US Opens (in those days the American event was held second of the two). He repeated the feat in his Grand Slam year of 1930, and to date just Sarazen (1932), Hogan (1953), Trevino (1971) and Watson (1982) have emulated him. Jones's third US Open victory, in 1929, was also noteworthy. He faced the most treacherous 12-footer conceivable on the last green at Winged Foot but he sank it to tie Al Espinosa. He demolished his opponent by 23 strokes in a 36-hole massacre the next day, but not before he had graciously asked the USGA to delay the playoff to allow his opponent, a devout Catholic, to attend Mass.

Bobby Jones was not the only man then playing decent golf in the US Open. Tommy Armour, a transplanted Scot like Cruickshank and Macfarlane, won in 1927 at Oakmont, with Jones down in 11th place. Armour knew he had to birdie the last hole, a formidable par-4, to catch Harry Cooper. As the 'Silver Scot' surveyed the 3-iron shot he had left, a club member, so the legend goes, called out: "*I've been reading that you're a great iron player. Let's see you hit one now.*" Armour hit it 10 feet from the hole. "*Will*

that do?*" he asked. He made the putt and defeated Cooper the following day.

Following Jones's retirement, Inverness in 1931 was the setting for a marathon. George von Elm, who had beaten Jones in the final of the 1926 US Amateur, finished on the wrong end of the 144-hole Open (72 holes of regulation play plus two 36-hole playoffs). He and Billy Burke tied on 292 after four rounds. They were still level on 149 after another day's battle, and Burke finally nipped it 148-149 the next afternoon. With that the 36-hole playoff, which had only been introduced in 1928 yet had already been used once previously, was abolished in favour of a return to 18 holes. The USGA probably felt that while stamina is an integral part of any sport, this was going a bit far.

In 1932, Gene Sarazen played the last 28 holes at Fresh Meadow in exactly 100 strokes – the last 18 in 66, a record that stood until 1960 – to win by three. Two years later he took a triple-bogey seven at Merion's 11th hole in the final round and lost to Olin Dutra by one. Such is tournament golf – win some, lose some. But for Sam Snead, there were to be no US Open wins to offset the losses, and some of those were horribly hard to bear.

Snead made his debut in 1937 and finished runner-up, two strokes adrift of Ralph Guldahl. It was surely

A WINNING CENTURY
Gene Sarazen uses the last of the 100 shots he needed to cover the final 28 holes of the 1932 US Open at Fresh Meadow, thereby adding his native title to the British Open he had already secured that year.

NO SMALL ACHIEVEMENT
Lawson Little (far right), whose amateur career was crowned by the unique distinction of completing the British and US Amateur double in consecutive years, had a win in the 1940 US Open as the highlight of his professional career.

just a matter of time, the sages said. In 1939, in one of the most infamous blow-ups in golf lore, Snead made an eight on the last hole at Philadelphia when a par-5 was all he needed to win. The wise men changed their minds. Snead is one of the game's great players but fate treated him cruelly in the US Open.

Another man to be jinxed in the major championships was Craig Wood. Snead's munificence meant that Wood, Byron Nelson and Denny Shute played off for the title in 1939. Shute was eliminated on the first 18 while Nelson stayed alive by dint of a birdie at the last. On the fourth hole of the second playoff, Nelson holed a 1-iron for an eagle two and was never caught. Wood's defeat gave him a place in the record books – a playoff loser in all four major championships. It's an exclusive club whose membership was doubled in 1993 when Greg Norman joined it. Happily, by all that's right, Wood eventually went on to win two majors, the Masters and US Open, both in 1941.

In 1940, yet another playoff was won by Lawson Little. (One wonders what modern-day union leaders would have made of all this overtime, though at least it was paid.) Poor 'Porky' Oliver returned a score of 287, which appeared to tie Little and Sarazen until it was learned that he and five others had been disqualified for teeing off in advance of their starting times for the last round because they were worried about a brewing storm – a case of safety-first not being safe.

The war halted the golf action between 1942 and 1945. If anyone bothered to reflect on the respective status of the two Opens at this time there was only one conclusion to be drawn: the US Open had moved past its British counterpart in a very few years. The decline of the latter could be traced to the moment Jones quit the competitive arena. Apart from Cotton's victory in 1937, the Americans won it if they went over – Armour in 1931, Sarazen in 1932 and Shute in 1933 – but generally they were losing interest. They already knew they were the best players in the world; to them their national Open, as the premier tournament of the world's premier golfing nation, was *per se* the game's most prestigious title. Why waste time and money, they thought, and ruin a good swing in the sea winds off the British coast?

This attitude hardened after the war when the

Ryder Cup matches between the professionals of the two countries were seldom worthy of the name contest. It was reinforced when Snead won the Open at St Andrews in 1946 and Locke won it four times in eight years. Americans knew that Snead could win everything except the US Open and that Locke could win US tour events but not the US Open. When Hogan decided to have one attempt at the British Open and won it in 1953, that settled it. A great champion like Hogan could walk over and win in Britain at will, but even he couldn't win the US Open every year (though he wasn't far off for a time). The British Open was a nice link with history but the US Open was *the* championship. It was perhaps inevitable that it took an American – Palmer – to tip the scales back towards equilibrium, or even beyond as many would argue with some justification today.

Back in 1946, the Germans and the Japanese had been seen off but the Americans were not rid of their penchant for playoffs. Lloyd Mangrum, Byron Nelson and Vic Ghezzi were in this one but, after another in the long chain of golfs bizarre occurrences, Nelson had every right to feel hard done by. His caddie had inadvertently trodden on Byron's ball in the third round, costing him a one-shot penalty and possibly a second US Open. In another protracted drama,

Mangrum took the playoff at the second attempt after all three had shot 72s for the first 18 holes. Even Snead got into the playoff act in 1947, thanks to a six-yard putt on the last hole. Just 24 hours later, however, Snead missed from a yard on the same green to lose to Lew Worsham. Snead's last chance had gone. Enter Ben Hogan.

From 1948 to 1953, Hogan won the US Open four times and was third once. He didn't play in 1949 because he couldn't walk, a legacy of his near-fatal car crash that February. In 1948 at Riviera he set an aggregate scoring record of 276, which was five better than anything before and lasted until 1967. At Merion in 1950 he was so pained by cramps in his still sore legs that with a few holes left he contemplated quitting, but he stoically soldiered on and tied Mangrum and George Fazio. It had been a whole three years since the last playoff and Hogan took this one by four strokes, a margin exaggerated because Mangrum literally blew away his chance on the 16th green by thoughtlessly picking up his ball, which was at that time against the rules, to blow off a bug.

The following year, Hogan manufactured a masterly winning last round of 67 – "*the greatest round I have ever played*" – at Oakland Hills, a course stringently doctored by Robert Trent Jones who was appointed by a committee which, in the words of one member, wanted a layout "*so tough that nobody can win*". At the prize-giving ceremony, Hogan remarked: "*I am glad to have brought this monster to its knees.*"

Two years later he won for a fourth time at Oakmont with a consummate display of shot-making that leant support to the apparently absurd theory that what should have been a debilitating accident had actually been the catalyst which led to an improved technique. The runner-up, six shots in his wake, courtesy of Hogan's birdie-birdie finish, was Sam Snead, the eternal bridesmaid.

Hogan made three strong bids for an unprecedented fifth title, notably in 1955. He had finished with a total of 287 at Olympic and, though he refused to acknowledge victory in public, he was confident enough to proffer the ball with which he had holed out for display in the USGA's museum. His challengers wilted until only Jack Fleck remained, and hardly anyone had heard of him before, let alone considered him a threat to Hogan. He needed two birdies in the last four holes to tie (leaders then did not necessarily go out last) and improbably – shades of Ouimet – he got them, in his case with a birdie at the last. Like Ouimet, he beat his fancied rival in the playoff. Hogan was second again in 1956 but there were to be no more major championships for him after 1953. However, Hoganites will forever allege that the Hale America Open that Hogan won in 1942, when regular competition was suspended because of the war, should count as that fifth US Open. The history books are against them, but they remain doggedly undeterred despite that.

Cary Middlecoff was the man who denied Hogan

TAMING OF THE MONSTER *Ben Hogan on the 17th hole at Oakland Hills in 1951 on his way to a closing 67 over the 'monster'. Hogan said: "I haven't played all the courses in the world, but I don't want to if there are any tougher than this one."*

THE ONE AND ONLY

Arnold Palmer celebrates the conclusion of one of the greatest closing rounds in major championship history, the one that won him the US Open for the only time, at Cherry Hills in 1960.

in 1956. It was Middlecoff's second Open (he had won in 1949) and he came as close as is possible to retaining the title in 1957 but was beaten – in a playoff, of course – by Dick Mayer. Hogan was also in the thick of things in 1960 until he uncharacteristically gambled everything on a nervy pitch shot over water to the 17th green in the final round. He felt his legs wouldn't carry him comfortably for the 18 holes of a playoff and he had to try to make a winning birdie. When the ball toppled back into the hazard, that chance had gone. It was all he could do to walk up the hill to the final green, hitting the ball seven times on his way to the clubhouse. Shortly afterwards, Arnold Palmer, who had begun the afternoon seven shots behind the leader, came home with a 65 to win in fantastic style.

The manner in which Palmer began that round is one of the most famous episodes in championship golf. He drove the first green, a par-4, and two-putted for a three. This kind of stuff – no holds barred, smash the course into submission – was typically Palmer. Never mind that the same aggressive policy in the first three rounds had led to him dropping three strokes to par on

what was really an innocuous opening hole, this was Palmer's hallmark. After his perfect start, he birdied five of the next six holes and the foundations for one of the most memorable days' golf ever seen were solidly and spectacularly laid.

It was as well Palmer won that Open. He wasn't to win another. There were four playoffs in the 1960s (a good vintage) and Palmer lost three of them: in 1962 to Jack Nicklaus, the first professional win for the rookie who had been second to Palmer as an amateur in 1960 and who was to bring Palmer's era to a close not long after it had begun; in 1963 to Julius Boros, who had also won in 1952; and in 1966 to Billy Casper (the 1959 champion) when Palmer let slip a seven-shot lead with nine holes of regulation play remaining because he foolishly forgot about his rival and instead mounted a vain assault on Hogan's record total of 276. Ironically, the following summer Nicklaus produced a series of magnificent iron shots towards the finish at Baltusrol and, in relegating Palmer into second place, shot 275.

The third member of the Big Three, South African Gary Player, became the first overseas winner of the US Open since Ted Ray when he captured the 1965 championship in a playoff with Kel Nagle of Australia. The previous June the tournament had reached an emotional high not experienced since Ouimet's sensational win when Ken Venturi triumphed at Congressional.

Triumphed is the correct description. Venturi was a peerless iron player at his best, but he had lost three Masters in heartbreaking fashion and in the preceding few years had been plagued by back injuries, pneumonia, and a circulatory problem in his hands which impaired his sense of feel. In the 1964 Open Venturi also suffered from heat exhaustion and intense dehydration caused by the oppressive humidity that hung over Washington that week; indeed, he was so badly affected that a doctor had to accompany him for the final round. In spite of it all, he made birdies and pars while those around him faltered. As he walked down the hill to the last green, with victory secure, he was cheered home a hero by the fans massed along the sides of the fairway, many of whom had tears in their eyes. When Venturi holed the final putt to win by four strokes, he raised his eyes to the heavens and cried out: "*My God. I've won the Open.*"

Even the Lord may have been surprised at some of those who succeeded him, such as Orville Moody (1969), Lou Graham (1975) and Andy North (1978 and 1985). Lee Trevino looked likely to be a freak winner when he won in 1968, but he has proved to be right out of the top drawer. With hindsight, we should have known it then. At Oak Hill, he became the first man to break 70 in all four rounds of the championship, a feat matched by Lee Janzen at Baltusrol in 1993.

Trevino had first come to public attention in the 1967 championship, not so much for finishing fifth but because he wore scuba goggles in the dry air of New Jersey. He explained that was how he dressed for golf in El Paso, Texas: goggles were essential to protect his eyes from the sand and dirt whipped up by the wind. But any suggestions that Trevino had been a fluke champion in 1968 were dispelled when he did it again in 1971, this time in a playoff. He quoted Hagen: "*Anyone can win the Open once. It takes a great player to win it twice.*" That, of course, was before the days of Andy North, who has only won one other tour event in his life. Trevino's pedigree was further enhanced by the identity of the runner-up to him on both occasions – Jack Nicklaus.

Between Trevino's double act were Moody and Tony Jacklin, the latter winning by seven strokes in 1970 and in so doing being the first Briton to steal the opposite Open since Ray had precisely 50 years before. Three years on, Johnny Miller set fire to a rain-sodden

TOUR DE FORCE *Thirty years on from Palmer's US Open win, Hale Irwin circles the gallery in celebration of one of the greatest putts in major championship history, the 50-footer that got him into a playoff which he went on to win, at Medinah in 1990.*

WHEN THE CHIPS ARE DOWN: *Another 'greatest' moment. Tom Watson holes one of the greatest chip shots in major championship history, on the penultimate hole of the 1982 US Open at Pebble Beach. He beat Jack Nicklaus by two shots.*

Oakmont with a 63, the lowest winning finale in major championship history, to take the title by a shot. A further three years elapsed before Jerry Pate, needing a par for victory, struck a glorious 5-iron to within two feet of the last hole at Atlanta for an easy birdie and his first success as a pro. The Atlanta Athletic Club was the 47th different US Open venue but the first in the Deep South. The club was awarded the honour at the behest of Bobby Jones, who died in 1971, and the people of Georgia responded by setting new attendance records.

The roll-call of recent champions is impressive and each has an extraordinary tale to tell. Hubert Green defied a death threat in 1977. Hale Irwin overcame the jitters in 1979 as effectively as he had in 1974. Jack Nicklaus turned back the years and a Japanese putting machine called Isao Aoki to receive that record-equalling fourth trophy in 1980 with a record low total of 272, beating the old mark that he had set over the same course, Baltusrol, in 1967. Twelve months later David Graham struck so many wonderful shots on the Sunday at Merion that even Ben Hogan would have been

envious. The Australian was the first overseas winner since Tony Jacklin, and he remains the last to date.

Tom Watson won in 1982 at Pebble Beach, thwarting Jack Nicklaus as dramatically as he had done at Turnberry five years previously. He holed consecutive putts of 25 feet on the 10th and 11th holes in the final round, made a monster of 60 feet on the 14th, and then chipped in from a hanging lie for the crucial birdie at the 17th. "*Try to get it close,*" his caddie Bruce Edwards had suggested, a trifle unnecessarily but also, it appeared, optimistically in view of the lie of the ball and the speed of the green between Watson and the hole, 20 feet away. "*Close?*" replied Watson. "*I'm going to hole it.*" When he did, he toured the green, arms aloft, in a lap of honour, before calming himself sufficiently to sink another putt of 20 feet at the last for a closing birdie which widened the gap between himself and Nicklaus to two shots. In the most devastating manner, Watson thus denied Nicklaus a fifth US Open and ensured that he himself would not have to carry forever the stigma borne by Sam Snead. The US Open was already threatening to become a psychological hurdle. At Pebble Beach, Watson laid the bogey with a blitz of birdies.

He might well have won the next year, too, but Larry Nelson played the last two rounds in 65-67 (10 under par), the best-ever aggregate for the second half of the championship. A thunderstorm delayed the finale until the Monday, when Nelson had three holes to play, but though the torrential rain had interrupted his flow it couldn't disrupt it. He holed a birdie putt of fully 60 feet on the 16th in the eerie atmosphere of the morning after and he was on his way again.

If in this chapter the exploits of Byron Nelson and other names from the past have been accorded more space than those of Larry Nelson and other contemporary players, that is not to denigrate the skills of the latter group. It is simply an acknowledgement that the deeds of the former are perhaps less familiar than the better chronicled occurrences of recent times. But however far back one goes, no tournament (let alone the US Open) has ever seen a man make three more miraculous pars than did Greg Norman on the last three holes at Winged Foot in 1984. The putt of 30 feet he holed at the 18th, as slippery as a snake, seemed well nigh impossible. As Norman exulted at yet another escape, Fuzzy Zoeller stood back down the fairway waving a white towel in mock surrender at his rival's unfailing ability to extricate himself from trouble. That gesture of supreme sportsmanship will be spoken of for as long as people care about the game.

Zoeller parred the hole in Norman's wake and went on to win an anti-climactic playoff by eight shots, a shattering defeat which Norman bore with laughter and grace. The following summer, Tze-Chung Chen of Taiwan demonstrated that orientals are not necessarily inscrutable by smiling in adversity as Andy North won for a second time, and adversity in golf does not come any tougher than taking an eight on a par-4 to lose a major championship by a stroke.

In June 1986 Shinnecock Hills hosted the US Open after a hiatus of 90 years. The old layout had been interfered with somewhat in the meantime, but the major change was in the preparation of the course. Shinnecock underwent the kind of surgery which the USGA routinely performs on all Open venues these days. This operation creates narrow but immaculately groomed fairways lined with thick rough, and lightning-fast greens surrounded by lush, tufty grass; the speed of the greens themselves being determined by a ball-rolling device known as a Stimpmeter which enables a quick, uniform pace to be established and maintained for all 18 holes.

Critics complain these measures mean that the US Open isn't a test of driving (because no player dare use a driver off the tee) or chipping (because once in the heavy stuff it requires brute strength rather than finesse to get out). The USGA responds that its methods are designed to identify the best golfer in the world, not to penalize him, while simultaneously trying to protect the integrity of the course. The latter job was so well done in 1986 that Raymond Floyd was the only man to break par, and he was only one under.

Shinnecock proved itself to be old but not old-fashioned, although Floyd became the oldest-ever winner of the title, a distinction he kept for only four years. Hale Irwin topped that by winning in 1990 at the age of 45. He had to endure a gruelling time of it, too, having to survive an 18-hole playoff with Mike Donald, who bogeyed the 90th hole of the week, before beating him with a birdie at the first extra hole, the 91st. Irwin had only got into the championship thanks to a special invitation from the USGA, and he celebrated by sinking a 50-footer on the 72nd green which later proved good enough to force the tie. Irwin

SAND SAVER *Curtis Strange got up and down from this bunker on the final hole of the 1988 championship to make his par and tie Nick Faldo before beating the Englishman in a playoff.*

LEADERS	TODAY	HOLE	TOTAL
MORGAN	5	10	1
WOOSNAM	5	10	2
AZINGER	6	16	3
KITE	0	11	3
SINDELAR	7	12	5
SLUMAN	6	15	4
FALD	6	12	4

ALMOST THERE *Tom Kite sinks a 40-foot birdie putt on the 12th hole of the final round of the 1992 US Open. His win ended a miserable sequence of near-misses in the majors.*

may have been fortunate in one other respect. Nick Faldo's 15-foot birdie putt on the last green that would have got him into the playoff somehow stayed above ground, thus preventing him from adding the US Open to the Masters he had won two months previously and to the British Open he would win the next month.

Between the victories of the two oldies, Curtis Strange was the dominant figure in the championship, although not before Scott Simpson had ruined the chance of a popular triumph for Tom Watson at Olympic in 1987 with birdies at 14, 15 and 16 in the final round.

Strange won in 1988 and 1989. First he beat Faldo

by four strokes in a playoff that never lived up to the drama of the evening before, when Strange had played a brilliant bunker shot to salvage his par at the last hole. Faldo's defeat maintained a remarkable coincidence. On the three occasions that The Country Club at Brookline has hosted the US Open (1913, 1963 and 1988), the British Open champion of the previous year – Ted Ray, Palmer and Faldo – has been vanquished in a playoff. Strange retained his title at Oak Hill, although Tom Kite had seemed the likely winner until he blew a three-shot lead with a triple-bogey seven at the 5th hole on Sunday on his way to a 78. He had to wait three years for redemption.

The US Open reached playoff No. 30 at Hazeltine in 1991, where Payne Stewart won the title largely because Scott Simpson couldn't play the controversially remodelled 16th hole. This was a tragic week in a real sense, with a spectator being killed in a vicious lightning storm that hit the course on the first day, and it was a sad one for Simpson, who not only threw this US Open away but had to reflect that if he had played the last 18 holes in level par in 1988 and 1989 he would, respectively, have been in a playoff and been the winner. And in 1990 he would have been in a playoff for the title he had won in 1987 if he had managed to play the last 21 holes in level par. In other words, at Hazeltine, Simpson could have been going for his fifth consecutive US Open.

In fact, Stewart either had a share of or the outright lead every day, thereby making him the first wire-to-wire winner since Nicklaus in 1980, but Simpson should have won it. On Saturday he bogeyed the 16th and then the 17th to blow a two-shot lead. On Sunday he bogeyed the 16th and then the 18th to do the same. In Monday's playoff he took a two-shot lead to the 16th, three-putted for a bogey while Stewart made his first birdie in 31 holes, and then Simpson bogeyed the last two holes. US Open champions aren't supposed to finish like that.

They are supposed to finish like Tom Kite did at Pebble Beach in 1992. At the 3rd hole on Saturday, Gil Morgan had become the first man in US Open history to get to 10 under par. Indeed, he was 12 under after 43 holes of the championship, but he played the last 29 in 17 over as his nerves took over as venomously as the wind off the Pacific.

Kite effectively wrapped matters up much as Watson had done at the same venue 10 years before – by holing a preposterous shot on a par-3. This one came on the 7th, a downhill hole of 107 yards that required a 6-iron tee shot into the teeth of the gale. Kite missed the green left but his pitch from 30 yards hit the hole dead centre. That day, Kite only seemed to have to pick up his putter to hole out, and bogeys on the 16th and 17th merely trimmed his margin to two shots. He shot level-par 72 on a day when only four

men, the earlier starters, broke par. Payne Stewart almost claimed his second title at Baltusrol in 1993, but he had to give second best to his 28-year-old countryman, Lee Janzen, whose total of 272 equalled the championship record established by Jack Nicklaus over the same course in 1980.

As the US Open looks forward to its centenary staging at, appositely, Shinnecock Hills in 1995, the USGA has lately taken steps to upgrade the international stature of the championship, as if aware that the British equivalent has gained in prestige by having a greater representation of golfers from all over the world. For 1994, it invited the top-15 players on the 1993 European Order of Merit, a welcome first, and in general it has recently ensured the presence of other talented foreigners from elsewhere, like Vijay Singh from Fiji, Ernie Els from South Africa and Robert Allenby from Australia. At this rate, some foreigner may even win the thing again one of these years.

KILLER THRUST *This holed chip shot for a birdie two at the 16th hole on Sunday gave Lee Janzen a decisive two-shot lead in the 1993 US Open.*

THE MASTERS TOURNAMENT

If the Open Championships of Great Britain and the United States are the two most important and prestigious events in golf, the next in line is the Masters Tournament, held at Augusta National Golf Club in Georgia each April. It is remarkable that something which isn't the championship of anywhere or anything, and which was only inaugurated in 1934, is held in such high esteem, but the origins of that respect and affection can be traced to one man: Bobby Jones.

Jones was the greatest amateur golfer in history; some would simply say the greatest golfer in history. He retired from competition in 1930 having, at the age of 28, completed the Impregnable Quadrilateral – or Grand Slam in modern parlance – by winning the Open and Amateur Championships of Britain and the United States in the same season. He quit because there was nothing left for him to prove and, it has to be confessed, because his constitution had been tormented by the strain of contending for major championships. He followed the advice of that popular sporting aphorism and got out when he was on top.

But Jones was not about to become totally divorced from the game to which he had given so much and derived such pleasure. He and Clifford Roberts, a New York banker who combined with Jones to establish Augusta National and the Masters and was later to rule the tournament with an iron hand, learned of an old horticultural nursery at Augusta, Georgia, about 140 miles from Jones's hometown of Atlanta, which would make an ideal site for the golf course of their dreams. Jones called in an expatriate Scotsman, Dr Alister Mackenzie, who was responsible for the creation of fine British

LUCKY HAT-TRICK *Forget Royal Ascot! This spectator's headgear boasts its owner's good luck by displaying a collection of the coveted series badges that are the only means for fans to gain entry to the Masters.*

courses like Alwoodley and Moortown at Leeds and the spectacular Cypress Point in California. By 1934 the course was ready to host its 'First Annual Invitation Tournament'; a gathering of several of Jones's friends (the field comprised 72 players) who also happened to be the best golfers in the world. Jones actually played, too, as he did on 12 occasions altogether, but it was always more out of a sense of politeness to his guests than with any hope or desire to win.

Horton Smith won the first event but the press and other admirers of Jones were not prepared to tolerate the modest and innocuous title he had bestowed upon his tournament. It became known as the Masters, despite Jones's initial protestations that such a name was pretentious, because the masters of golf were all in attendance. The label stuck more readily the following year when one of those masters, Gene Sarazen, holed a full 4-wood shot on the par-5 15th hole of the final round for an albatross, or double-eagle, two. It enabled him to catch Craig Wood and Sarazen won the ensuing playoff. Thus was the Masters endowed with what can only be termed 'instant tradition'.

It would not have been possible for Sarazen to make this devastating challenge to Wood at such a crucial moment in the round had Augusta National been designed in the order it had been the year before. Then the 15th was the 6th, but in 1935 the order of the two loops of nine was reversed and that is the way the course has remained ever since, even though some holes have changed over the years. For example, Mackenzie would not recognize the famous 16th, a testing par-3 over water which has witnessed many dramatic moments. It was built after the last war by Robert Trent Jones, the renowned American golf course architect, and it bears no resemblance at all to the original.

The golf course is an integral part of the Masters for the obvious reason that the tournament is the only one of golf's four major championships to be played at the same venue every year. That is one unique feature. Another is the complete absence of billboards and advertising slogans which are to be found everywhere else in the increasingly commercial world of golf. Yet a third is the system of series badges operated by the club for the four days of competition. There is no admission to the course on a normal daily basis so these coveted season tickets are treated as family heirlooms, passed down through the generations. The American commentators who describe the Masters as "the toughest ticket in sport" are not exaggerating, but then nothing is easy to get into at Augusta.

It is one of the world's most exclusive clubs; not only are invitations to join precious and rare but it isn't even a simple matter to play the course as a member's guest. It has been suggested that the easiest way to join Augusta National is via the honorary membership given to all Masters champions, and that the easiest way to get a game over the hallowed fairways is to play in the championship. The latter remark is greeted with scepticism in some quarters because getting into the tournament is hard enough, even for good players.

One doesn't enter the Masters. To this day it remains a relatively small-field, select event. (In 1994, there were 86 competitors, not counting the honorary starters, Sarazen, Sam Snead and Byron Nelson.) There are no pre-qualifying competitions as there are at the major Open Championships. Criteria are laid down which mean that a native player who fulfils a certain requirement knows he is in – for instance, by finishing in the top-24 at the preceding Masters – but these only apply to Americans and represent their only avenue into the tournament. Some foreigners may happen to fall into one of the categories, such as being a past champion, but strictly speaking they have to rely on an invitation for their place.

There have been criticisms that the Masters officials are too parsimonious with these, and that they fail to take sufficient account of the rapidly rising standards of golfers elsewhere in the world. This is a fair point, but not as convincing a gripe as it used to be. (In 1994, there were 28 non-Americans in the line-up.) Another

common complaint – that there are comparatively too many amateurs cluttering up the field – again is less true than it was, and in any case it demonstrates a failure to acknowledge and understand a tradition which owes its existence to Jones's roots. But tradition and controversy are no strangers to the Masters.

The traditions include the previous year's champion helping his successor into a club member's green jacket, a ritual performed once for the benefit of the TV audience in a closed room (Jones and Roberts were not unaware of the power of television) and then again at the prize-giving ceremony. Just twice has the neatness of this formality been upset – in 1966 and 1990, when Jack Nicklaus and Nick Faldo, respectively, retained the title. There are formal pre-tournament dinners for the past champions (when the defending champion picks up the bill), the international players and the amateurs. On the eve of the championship, a nine-hole par-3 competition is held over the club's beautiful short course, but it isn't taken too seriously. All the entrants are aware that nobody has ever won the big event after winning the little one.

Controversy may seem an odd companion for such a smooth operation as the Masters but it is never easy to make everything look perfect. Both in public and behind the scenes there have been enough sensational

MAJOR CONTROVERSY

Arnold Palmer's first major championship victory was tinged with controversy. Palmer (in the light shirt) is pictured at the critical moment in the 1958 Masters, discussing a ruling with Masters officials. He had holed out for a double-bogey five on the 12th but believed himself to be entitled to a free drop for an embedded ball. He had accordingly played another ball and made a par with it. As he was playing the 15th, he was told that he was right and his score for the 12th was duly altered to a three. Listening to the debate is Palmer's playing partner, Ken Venturi (seen in the white cap, above).

stories at Augusta to satisfy any soap-opera buff.

In 1968, Roberto de Vicenzo and Bob Goalby appeared to have tied for the championship after some scintillating golf on the final afternoon (65 by de Vicenzo, 66 for Goalby). The assembled multitude had barely gathered its collective breath when it was learned that de Vicenzo had mistakenly signed for a four on the 17th when he had actually taken a three. His 65 became a 66. He was 'beaten by the pencil' and there was to be no playoff. Under the rules, there was no choice. Goalby was declared the champion. Jones would have loved to have bent the laws of the game but he would have been the last man to do so.

Jones was inevitably involved in that sad decision but his crippling illness was annually taking a greater toll and Roberts – who in later life dispensed with the 'benevolent' bit before 'dictator', a label often applied behind his back – arranged for Jones to take no part in any of the post-tournament formalities. Such ruthless behaviour towards a sick man, an old friend, is indicative of the autocratic manner in which Roberts ordered affairs at Augusta. Television commentators were not allowed to mention prize-money during the tournament: nor were the cameras permitted to show

the usually immaculate course when it was flooded so severely in 1973 that play had to be postponed. The Masters has an enviable image of beauty, serenity and efficiency and Roberts would not allow anything to besmirch that. As someone aptly remarked: *"At Augusta, dogs do not bark and babies do not cry."*

But perfection had a high price. Roberts so distressed Jones with his authoritarian rebuff in 1968 that the two never spoke to each other again before Jones died in December 1971. By then the Masters was embroiled in a heated debate.

Georgia is in America's Deep South. By the beginning of the 1970s, no black golfer had ever qualified to play at Augusta. Civil rights' campaigners called it a scandal and complained that the club was pursuing a racist policy. This was arrant nonsense. It was just that no black player had made the grade demanded of American golfers under the criteria for entry. But rather than permit the issue to escalate, in 1971 Roberts expanded the qualification categories and announced that henceforth any winner of a US tour event would automatically qualify for the Masters.

Two years later, no black golfer had yet fulfilled this new requirement and a deputation from Congress

THE MAGNIFICENT SEVEN
Some of the earlier Masters champions. From left to right: Horton Smith (1934 and 1936), Byron Nelson (1937 and 1942), Henry Picard (1938), Jimmy Demaret (1940, 1947 and 1950), Craig Wood (1941), the diminutive Gene Sarazen (1935) and Herman Keiser (1946).

alleged that the Masters was still a discriminatory institution. Roberts was now on firmer ground and replied that having changed the rules he wasn't going to invite a player just because he was black. He added: "*We are a little surprised as well as being flattered that 18 Congressmen should be able to take time out to help us operate a golf tournament.*" The row ended when Lee Elder won the Monsanto Open and thereby secured an invitation to the 1975 Masters.

Roberts, to the surprise of many expert Augusta-watchers, resigned as chairman in 1976 and handed over the reins to Bill Lane – but in name only. Roberts didn't actually relinquish power until one evening the next year he walked out on to the club grounds and shot himself. No one knows for sure, but it is presumed that he realized he was becoming increasingly ill and that, unlike Jones, he was not prepared to suffer the consequences.

Lane died in 1980 and was succeeded by Hord Hardin, who in return was replaced by Jackson Stephens in 1991. This was a year after the composition of Augusta's membership – one black, no women – had come under hostile scrutiny in the wake of the row that erupted at Shoal Creek (see page 111) prior to the 1990 US PGA Championship, where the host club practised a similarly segregationist policy. Augusta has subsequently enrolled a black member, though as yet there are no women members.

Stephens generated quite a controversy of his own in 1992 by offering the club to the city of Atlanta as the site of the putative golf tournament in the 1996 Olympic Games. That would have meant opening the course in August – when it is usually in the middle of a five-month closure – and allowing women to compete there. However, in January 1993 the attempt to include golf in the Olympics for the first time since 1904 was abandoned, Augusta's membership policy having been a factor in attracting vociferous opposition to the idea.

As I said, controversy and tradition seem to go hand in hand at Augusta, and one of the traditions is that the shape of the course changes. Some alterations have been major, such as the wholesale restructuring of the 16th hole, as mentioned previously; the relocating of the 10th green to create one of the most majestic par-4s in the world; and the moving of the tee

on the 11th which, together with the building of a pond to the left of the green, converted a mundane drive-and pitch hole into a formidable test which demands length and accuracy off the tee and considerable nerve with the approach shot. Ben Hogan, perhaps the most remorselessly accurate striker in history, once said: "*If you ever see me on the 11th green in two, you'll know I missed my second shot.*" He always elected to play safe to the right with his iron, generally saving par with a chip and a putt.

Every year at Augusta something is added or altered: a new bunker on the 1st fairway, mounds inserted in the driving zone on the 3rd and 15th, more humps put in to protect the entrance to the 8th, a swale over the back of the 13th green, and so on. Some players at the Masters, usually after they have dropped a shot as a result of tangling with one of these modifications, protest that the course should be left alone. They are neglecting the fact that Augusta is a living memorial to Jones, not a mausoleum. Jones approved many amendments to the design on which he and Mackenzie had collaborated.

In 1980, the club decided to kill off the old Bermuda and rye grasses and re-seed the greens with bent grass. The result has been to speed them up even more and, by cutting the holes in the trickiest places for Masters week, Augusta National can be turned from a gentle giant into a magnificent monster.

It is the magnificence of the scenery at Augusta which has, over the years, attracted and awed millions of golf fans, whether they be fortunate enough to have attended in person or been forced to settle for watching the Masters on television. To golfers, spring-time is Masters time, when the legacy of the old Fruitlands nursery is in glorious evidence, with azalea, dogwood, redbud, wisteria and a score of other blooms in a host of vivid colours, all set against a marvellous backdrop of tall pines, emerald fairways and deep blue water hazards. Even the sand used to fill in the divots is dyed green, and the ponds and streams are given an artificial tint of blue.

There is nothing false about the water within, as hundreds of golfers have discovered during the Masters. From the 11th to the 16th holes at Augusta, only the 14th is devoid of water. The most notorious of

THE MASTER OF THE MASTERS *Clifford Roberts ruled Augusta with an iron hand until one night in 1977 when he wandered out to the club's par-3 course and committed suicide.*

PERFECT TORTURE *The 12th hole at Augusta National is protected by an unfathomable breeze that capriciously twirls the tree-tops behind the green, and by the all-too-apparent blue depths of Rae's Creek. Many Masters have been lost, and some won, on this hole.*

these hazards is Rae's Creek, which takes the form of a pond in front of the 12th green. A meandering stream then takes over down the left-hand side of the fairway of the dogleg 13th, the archetypal short par-5 at 485 yards. The stream finishes its journey with a flourish by skirting the front edge and right side of the 13th green. As their balls have plummeted into either this creek or Rae's, or into the little lakes protecting the 15th and 16th greens, several notable names have waved a deep blue goodbye to their aspirations of winning the Masters for at least one more year.

In 1937, Ralph Guldahl sampled damp misery beside both the 12th and 13th greens in the final round. He took five on the 12th, a par-3 of only 155 yards but such a severe test of accuracy and

temperament that Jack Nicklaus has called it "*the most demanding tournament hole in the world*", and six on the 13th. Byron Nelson came along behind him and played them in 2-3. Having made up six shots on the leader in just two holes, Nelson beat Guldahl for the title by two strokes. Two years later, Guldahl got his revenge. He eagled the 13th and jumped into a one-shot lead over Sam Snead which he carried to the end.

There have been many similar stories of heartache and happiness. In 1954, Billy Joe Patton, an eminent amateur golfer from North Carolina, had a hole-in-one at the 6th on the Sunday and led the field as he played the 13th. But then courage got the better of him. He went for the green with his second shot, found the creek and walked off with a seven. He made the same decision on the 15th and took six. He finished a shot adrift of Hogan and Snead. Two subsequent horror stories graphically illustrate the perils of the water. Tsuneyuki (Tommy) Nakajima of Japan had a 13 on the 13th in 1978, while Tom Weiskopf carded the same score at the 12th in 1980.

The stretch from the 11th to the 13th at Augusta is known as 'Amen Corner', a nickname apparently derived from an old jazz song and justified by the number of times that golfers' prayers have been answered, kindly or otherwise, over that fiendish three-hole spell. Arnold Palmer got the nod in 1958 when he made a fortunate par on the 12th after being awarded a free drop from a plugged lie, and he followed that with an eagle on the 13th. An hour or so later, he had won the first of his four Masters by a stroke. One year later, Palmer got the thumbs down. He was cruising home until the sirens protecting the 12th green lured his ball into the creek. He took a triple-bogey six and was left floundering in the wake of Art Wall, who birdied five of the last six holes.

George Archer (1969), Seve Ballesteros (1980) – in his case twice – Tom Watson (1981), Sandy Lyle (1988) and Ian Woosnam (1991) are among those who have hung on to win despite last-round visits to the waters of Augusta's back nine, but proving that one's ball does not have amphibious properties tends to be an extremely painful experience. Conversely, those devilish holes also tend to be where someone else's heroics effectively wrap matters up.

In 1984, Ben Crenshaw struck a marvellous 6-iron to within four yards of the flag at the 12th and, as one expects of him, the putt went down for a two. Just before Crenshaw played the hole, Larry Nelson had found the water there with a weak tee shot; a few minutes after Crenshaw left the green, Tom Kite did likewise. Nelson took five, Kite six. Crenshaw played the 13th and 15th conservatively, laying up short of each green in two, but he still birdied the latter. That, coming on top of putts of 60 feet and 20 feet for birdie and par, respectively, on the 10th and 14th, gave him a couple of shots to spare in one of the most popular of major championship victories.

The next year, Curtis Strange seemed poised to overcome the burden of an 80 in the first round and earn an improbable triumph. Then he found the water on the 13th and 15th on the last day and bogeyed both holes. Bernhard Langer birdied them and won by two strokes. In 1986, for all Jack Nicklaus's glorious golf on Sunday – birdies on 9, 10, 11, 13, 16 and 17 and an eagle on 15 – it was Seve Ballesteros who looked a certain champion until he hit what, in the circumstances, has to be considered the worst shot of his career when his 4-iron to the 15th fell feebly into the pond. He eventually holed out for a six and was thus hopelessly vulnerable to Nicklaus's charge.

Nicklaus has won more Masters than anyone else. The 1986 victory was his sixth and made him, at 46, the oldest winner. His longevity is such that his

WHO NEEDS A PUTTER?
Seve Ballesteros holed this chip shot on the last hole to win the 1980 Masters by four shots.

MAGIC FROM MIZE *Native Augustan Larry Mize jumps for joy as he unexpectedly sinks a 30-yard chip shot at the second playoff hole (the 11th) to clinch victory from Greg Norman in the 1987 Masters' playoff. Seve Ballesteros had already dropped out after the first extra hole.*

successes have spanned 23 years, but before him several other players enjoyed brief spells of dominance in the Masters, even if these sometimes overlapped. From 1940 to 1954, for instance, Jimmy Demaret, Sam Snead and Ben Hogan won it eight of the 12 times it was played.

Demaret was the first three-time winner, his years being 1940, 1947 and 1950. The latter was gained at some psychological cost to the Australian Jim Ferrier, who bogeyed five of the last six holes to lose by two shots.

Sam Snead captured the title on three occasions in six years: in 1949 (with two 67s to close), 1952 and 1954 (when he beat Hogan 70-71 in a playoff). Hogan had also been on the wrong end of a one-stroke margin in the 1942 playoff with Byron Nelson, who played the stretch from the 6th to the 16th in six under par. In 1946, Hogan faced a 12-footer to win on the last green but three-putted to hand the tournament to Herman Keiser. He had to wait until 1951 to break through at Augusta, before winning again in his peerless year of 1953. As late as 1967 he fired a third round of 66, with 30 on the inward half, to bring a glow to the hearts of his admirers and even a smile to his usually stern features. But by then Palmer and Nicklaus had taken over.

Palmer won the Masters in the four even numbered years from 1958. His victories in 1960 and 1962 were classics from the mould that made him synonymous with the word 'charge'. In the first he birdied the last two holes, respectively from 30 and six feet, to pip Ken Venturi by a stroke. (When still an amateur, Venturi had lost the 1956 Masters by a single shot after a disastrous final round of 80 that enabled Jackie Burke to come back from a record nine-shot deficit after 54 holes.) That magnificent finale, and the uproarious reaction of Palmer's gallery to it, led to his fans being

christened 'Arnie's Army'. They cheered him home just as tumultuously in 1962 when he chipped in on the 16th and holed from 12 feet on the 17th to catch Gary Player and Dow Finsterwald. In the playoff, Palmer gave Player a three-shot start and then thrashed him with a devastating burst of birdies early on the back nine. That gave Palmer special pleasure since the previous year he had ceded the championship to Player by contriving a six on the last hole, thus enabling the South African to become the first overseas winner.

Nicklaus won for the first time in 1963 but his *tour de force* came in 1965. He equalled the course record of eight-under-par 64 in the third round, a mark only bettered by Nick Price's 63 in 1986. Nicklaus's total of 271 left him nine shots ahead of his great adversaries, Palmer and Player, and has only been matched once, by Ray Floyd in 1976. At the presentation ceremony, Bobby Jones famously remarked of Nicklaus's stunning power golf: "*Jack is playing an entirely different game, one which I'm not even familiar with.*"

In 1966, Nicklaus retained the title after a playoff with Gay Brewer (who was to win the next year) and Tommy Jacobs, and he regained it in a dull tournament in 1972. His fifth victory, in 1975, was a spectacular affair as he, Johnny Miller and Tom Weiskopf produced blazing golf to match the weather, ultimately being separated by a putt of fully 40 feet which Nicklaus sank on the 70th hole. Many experts claim 1975 to be at least the equal of any Masters. Nicklaus might have won again a number of times, such as in 1971 when he surprisingly let in Charles Coody and in 1977 when Tom Watson, as so often against the Golden Bear, got the upper hand in a keen duel.

Until 1980, Gary Player was the sole non-American Masters champion. He was victorious for a third time in 1978, capping a marvellous homeward nine of 30 with a birdie putt of 15 feet at the last for a round of 64, which proved to be good enough when Hubert Green fluffed a short putt on the last green that would have forced a playoff. There was overtime in 1979, however. The hapless Ed Sneed squandered a five-shot lead on the Sunday afternoon, a calamity climaxed with bogeys at the last three holes. Fuzzy Zoeller took advantage by stealing the first 'sudden-death' Masters at the second extra hole with a birdie to beat Sneed and Watson, thereby becoming the first man since Sarazen in 1935 to win on his debut.

In recent years, Player has had plenty of company as an overseas winner. In 1980, Seve Ballesteros became, at 23 years and 4 days, the youngest-ever champion, but he had to settle for a four-shot triumph after dissipating the 10-shot lead he had held with nine holes to play by going in the water on the 12th and 13th. Three years later he opened the final round with a brilliant salvo of birdie-eagle-par-birdie which destroyed his immediate rivals, Watson, Floyd and Craig Stadler, the 1982 champion.

Ballesteros was the favourite to win entering the last round in 1985, but instead Bernhard Langer prevailed as Curtis Strange faltered. It was the German rather than the Spaniard who scorched the back nine, garnering four birdies to his rival's one. As we have seen, Ballesteros should have won in 1986 and he nearly won in 1987, when he made it into a playoff with Greg Norman and Larry Mize.

Just about everybody but the unheralded Mize, a native of Augusta, fancied Ballesteros or Norman to win, but Ballesteros three-putted the first extra hole to drop out of the playoff, and at the next, Augusta's 11th, Mize holed a 30-yard chip shot for an extravagant birdie and victory.

Having gone for so long with only Player breaking the American monopoly, we were now approaching the middle of an era when European golfers would win eight out of twelve Masters, and heading into a stretch where they would win

A PUTT TOO FAR *Scott Hoch (below) agonizes after missing a winning putt from less than a yard at the first playoff hole in 1989.*

PUTTING INTO THE RECORD BOOKS *Sandy Lyle (left) holes from 10 feet on the last green to deny Mark Calcavecchia in 1988, and secure the honour of being the first British player to win the Masters.*

ELEVENTH HEAVEN *In two straight years, Nick Faldo won the Masters at the 11th. This is his moment of victory (above) against Raymond Floyd on the second playoff hole in 1990, which made him the only man apart from Jack Nicklaus to retain the title.*

HOME AND DRY *Fred Couples may well have won the 1992 Masters at the 12th (left), where after an indifferent tee shot his ball somehow stayed dry on the bank above Rae's Creek. Again, Floyd was the runner-up.*

six out of seven. Even more remarkably, the next four all fell to Britons. If any one fact could be held up as a demonstration of how far European golf has progressed since Ballesteros won the Open in 1979, this period of supremacy in the Masters is surely it.

Sandy Lyle led the tournament for 40 holes in 1988 until he dumped his tee shot into Rae's Creek at the 12th hole on Sunday. He took five, and did likewise on the two par-5s, the 13th and 15th. Just as it seemed that Mark Calcavecchia would profit from these lapses, Lyle birdied the 16th and then, having hit a prodigious 1-iron into a fairway bunker from the 18th tee, he hit his 7-iron from the sand to 10 feet above the cup and sank the putt for a winning birdie. It was arguably the

FOUR UP WITH THREE TO PLAY *With this birdie putt on the 15th, Bernhard Langer (left) took a four-shot lead and effectively an unassailable grip on the 1993 Masters.*

greatest bunker shot in history.

The next year Scott Hoch perpetrated one of the worst putts in history. Nick Faldo had holed two monsters for birdies on the 16th and 17th to take Hoch into a playoff; a playoff Hoch should have finished at the first extra hole. But he missed from less than a yard and Faldo holed from 30 feet for a birdie at the next to win. That same hole, the 11th, was the scene of the denouement for the third time in four years in 1990 when Faldo, who had again clawed his way back into contention with some tenacious golf on the back nine of regulation play, beat Raymond Floyd in a playoff. In part, Floyd beat himself. He hit his approach shot into the pond to the left of the 11th green and that was that. Floyd had been tempting fate anyway. He had made the mistake of winning the par-3 tournament.

In 1991, Ian Woosnam made it a case of the Scotsman, the Englishman and the Welshman. Playing the last hole, he was tied with Tom Watson and Jose Maria Olazabal of Spain. Olazabal made a bogey after visiting two bunkers; Watson a double-bogey after visiting the woods and a bunker and then compounding his problems by taking three putts.

Amid this carnage, Woosnam carried his drive 270 yards through the air into a safe area miles left of the fairway. His 8-iron got him to the edge of the green and he got down in two putts – the second one from six feet – to secure victory and his first major.

Any fear that the tournament was in danger of becoming known as the British Masters was curbed by America's Fred Couples in 1992. There was no denying that Couples was a worthy winner. At the time, he was the best player in the game.

But Europe prevailed again in 1993 and 1994. First, Bernhard Langer won for the second time. As ever, the back nine settled it. Langer eagled the 13th to take a three-shot lead that he never looked in danger of relinquishing, especially once his closest pursuer, Chip Beck, had decided against going for the 15th green in two. Twelve months later, Jose Maria Olazabal did go for it in two. His ball barely cleared the pond, but his 30-foot putt for an eagle never looked like going anywhere but the centre of the hole. That gave him a two-shot lead over Tom Lehman, and that was the margin of his triumph. Following upon the victories of Woosnam and Couples at Augusta, and of Tom Kite (1992 US Open), Nick Price (1992 US PGA) and Paul Azinger (1993 US PGA), Olazabal thus became the latest golfer in the '90s to rid himself of the label 'best player not to have won a major'.

And in 1994, not for the first time and surely not for the last, the destiny of the green jacket had been decided amid the intimidating majesty of Augusta's notorious water holes.

You could say it's traditional.

THE EAGLE HAS LANDED
This 30-foot putt for a three at the 15th gave Jose Maria Olazabal a winning lead in the 1994 Masters.

THE US PGA CHAMPIONSHIP

Although there have been some changes to the dates down the ages, these days golf's four major championships each occupy a different month. The Masters is in April, the US Open in June and the Open Championship in July. The United States Professional Golfers' Association Championship (US PGA) is held in August, and it is not only the last chronologically.

A TRIO OF CHAMPIONS

Early 20th-century US pros pose for posterity: Horace Rawlins sits in front of Willie Anderson, who has his arm round Alex Smith's shoulder. They were all winners of the US Open, Anderson four times and Smith twice.

The US PGA is indisputably fourth of the four, bottom of an admittedly exalted class. It has been that way since 1953, perhaps, when Ben Hogan completed the Triple Crown by playing in the Open at Carnoustie but not in the US PGA, which he had skipped since 1949; or 1958, when the organizers ditched the matchplay format for strokeplay; or 1968, when the tour players broke away from the PGA of America to form their own division and in 1974, in a

logical consequence of the split, launched the Tournament Players' Championship (TPC), now the Players Championship, which undermined the original still further.

The political in-fighting involved in the dispute of 1968, an acrimonious affair, is best left until the next chapter, but it is pertinent to point out here that the US PGA Championship is run by the PGA of America. This organization primarily represents the interests of club professionals, so it is no shock to learn that many tour people feel that the Players Championship's sometime-nickname of 'the fifth major' should be upgraded a notch. However, most people not associated with the tour would not agree.

In recent years the US PGA Championship has recaptured something of its former glory. It might lack the kudos of the other three majors, but the PGA of America has largely realized that if the battered flagship

of its operations is to improve its tarnished image, it needs to be held on superior golf courses which are worthy of a major championship, rather than on poorly maintained and averagely designed layouts which were sometimes selected for dubious motives.

That is one significant factor which has helped the tournament to retain, if at times tenuously, its status. The other is something neither the Players Championship nor anything else can easily acquire – and that is history.

The US PGA goes back to 1916 and has champions of bygone generations like Hagen (five times), Sarazen and Snead (three times each) and Hogan and Nelson (twice each). In the modern era Jack Nicklaus has equalled Hagen's mark, while Gary Player, Lee Trevino and Raymond Floyd each have two wins to their credit. Arnold Palmer has never won it.

That is a sad omission from his record because, if the idea of the professional Grand Slam in part grew out of Hogan's hat-trick year of 1953, it was Palmer who first made it seem feasible that a professional could come as close as is possible to emulating what Bobby Jones did in 1930 and win the four most important tournaments open to him. Palmer gave credence to the notion by winning the Masters and the US Open in 1960. The US PGA, as the next most esteemed event on the American golf calendar, was to be the fourth leg of the Grand Slam after Palmer had gone to St Andrews and brought back the British Open. Instead, Kel Nagle ruined everything when he foiled Palmer by a shot in the Centenary Open.

Twelve years later, Jack Nicklaus also won the Masters and the US Open but went down by a stroke in the British Open. His defeat came at the hands of the mercurial Trevino, who destroyed Tony Jacklin and denied Nicklaus by literally as well as metaphorically proving what it means to win when the chips are down. Thus was the US PGA twice narrowly deprived of the climax to the season that would have been its ultimate *raison d'être*.

The tournament had no pretensions to being the fourth anything when it began life in 1916 as a matchplay competition for the championship of the United States' fledgling Professional Golfers' Association. It was won by Jim Barnes, a Cornishman who had left England for America some time before. With hindsight, it was typical of the event's chequered existence that no sooner had it been started than it was stopped. The First World War called a halt in 1917 and 1918, before Barnes retained possession of the trophy by winning again in 1919.

Barnes was a fine golfer. He went on to win the 1921 US Open by nine strokes (a record margin this century) and the 1925 Open at Prestwick, the last hurrah for the original Open venue. He was succeeded as US PGA champion in 1920 by Jock Hutchison, another British expatriate and the losing finalist in the tournament's inaugural year.

The following decade was dominated by one man, Walter Hagen, although two others, Gene Sarazen and Leo Diegel, each found room to fit in a couple of wins. Hagen beat Barnes by 3 & 2 in the 1921 final, thus becoming the first native American champion. Sarazen took over in 1922 but it was something of a hollow victory as Hagen was not present to defend the title. It was thus apposite that in 1923 the two men met in the final at the Pelham Country Club, New York.

The event was, as ever until matchplay was abandoned in 1958, contested over 36 holes, and Hagen stood 2 down with only three to play. He won

THE DEBUTANT *Jim Barnes won the first two US PGA Championships and then lost to Walter Hagen in two other finals.*

THE DOMINATOR *Walter Hagen was the undisputed supremo of professional matchplay golf. His domination of the US PGA in the 1920s has never been matched by any other professional in any other major championship this century.*

the next two holes to square matters and, after the 36th had been halved, the match went into sudden death. At the second extra hole, Sarazen conjured up a miraculous recovery shot after a wayward drive, putting the ball within two feet of the pin. Hagen, for once flabbergasted rather than flamboyant, fluffed an easy pitch into a bunker and with that went his hopes of the championship.

He made amends with no half measures, winning the US PGA from 1924 to 1927, a sequence beginning with a second triumph over Barnes. Hagen is the only 20th-century golfer to have won the same major championship in four consecutive years, and it is a safe bet that the distinction will remain unique. He appears to have been less than enthusiastic about bidding for a fifth title in a row. Tournament officials only lured him to Baltimore at the eleventh hour, Hagen either having forgotten about his defence or being more concerned about raking in more dollars from yet another exhibition match.

He needn't have turned up. Diegel beat him in the semi-finals, thus avenging his defeat in the final of 1926, and then dispatched Al Espinosa by 6 & 5. When Hagen was asked for the trophy so that it could be presented to Diegel, he announced that he had lost it. He had apparently left it in a taxi. The cup materialised a few months later when it was discovered in the Chicago offices of Hagen's clubmakers.

Diegel retained the title – and this time had a trophy to show for it – in 1929, trouncing the reigning US Open champion Johnny Farrell by 6 & 4 in the final. Diegel employed a singular putting stance, with feet spread, elbows locked and the top of the putter shaft brushing against his stomach. It looked terribly ungainly and uncomfortable but it certainly worked.

He was a shade unlucky to win no more than two major championships, but that was the price of reaching one's peak during the age of Jones and Hagen. Jones won at least one major championship – if one includes the US Amateur – every year between 1923 and 1930, while Hagen had a similar unbroken six-year span from 1924. Jack Nicklaus, who won five majors in four years from 1970, is the only other golfer this century to have maintained such a run for longer than three seasons.

Neither Hagen nor Diegel were factors in the US PGA after the 1920s. Gene Sarazen was, however. He lost an epic final to Tommy Armour in 1930 but he was back three years later to win for a third time, beating Willie Goggin with just seven clubs in his bag. Densmore Shute won twice and was runner-up once during this period; Paul Runyan also won twice, including an 8 & 7 hammering of Sam Snead in 1938, the most emphatic margin of victory in any final. Runyan produced marvellous golf that day, but nothing so astounding as the performance of Bobby Cruickshank against Al Watrous in the first round in 1932. He rallied to win from being 9 down with 12 holes to play – the biggest recovery known in an important matchplay competition – only to be eliminated in the quarter-finals.

While the war was raging in Europe, Byron Nelson was on the rampage in the US PGA Championship. From 1939 to 1945, he was thrice the beaten finalist (losing once on the 36th green, once on the 37th and once at the 38th) and twice the winner. He beat Sam Snead in 1940 and Sam Byrd in 1945, the latter being part of his incredible stretch of 11 consecutive tournament victories (see page 52).

(see page 52)

After the war, Ben Hogan won in 1946 and 1948. Snead, who had taken the title in 1942 in Nelson's rare absence from the final, picked it up again in 1949 and 1951 but Hogan was no longer in the field. His car accident in February 1949 meant his legs could not withstand the arduous chore of walking for a series of 36-hole matches. He didn't enter the US PGA again until 1960, when it had switched to a strokeplay format and he was well past his prime.

But the fact that in 1953 Hogan, unquestionably the best golfer in the world, was playing elsewhere was not good for the morale of the US PGA. Nor were champions like Walter Burkemo what was wanted: journeyman club professionals who happened to hit the jackpot that week. Not that Burkemo didn't deserve to win against Felice Torza in the 1953 final. Any man who can make up a seven-hole deficit in 18 holes is a worthy winner, and Burkemo went all the way to the last hurdle in 1954 as well before he was stopped by Chick Harbert, the last club pro, as opposed to tour player, to lift the trophy.

APPEARANCES CAN BE DECEPTIVE *And you thought Bernhard Langer's putting style was idiosyncratic? Leo Diegel won two US PGA Championships by doing it this way.*

The US PGA was losing its lustre. Doug Ford won in 1955 but nobody remembers him for that; instead, he's the man who holed out from a bunker at the 72nd green to clinch the Masters two years later. Jack Burke took the US PGA in 1956 but his victory was already overshadowed by his sensational come-from-nowhere triumph at Augusta that spring. Lionel Hebert followed them in 1957 and his 2 & 1 defeat of Dow Finsterwald was matchplay's last fling.

Television has a long history of antipathy towards matchplay, with its inherent risk of a final between two relative nonentities (Walter Burkemo and Chick Harbert, perhaps) and the chance that even a potentially mouth-watering tussle between Nick Faldo and Greg Norman could be ended well before the 18th green – that is, out of convenient camera range and with no respect for the niceties of programme scheduling.

It was the desire to pander to the small screen that led the PGA of America to make the move to strokeplay. It was pointed out to no avail both then and since that by doing this the PGA of America was digging its own grave; that one of the attractions of the tournament was its valid claim to be the most important matchplay event in the world. It wasn't the format that was wrong but the cluttering up of the field with club pros to the exclusion of the regular tour players. The number of spots these no-hopers filled was not cut drastically for another 13 years – and that was a costly prevarication.

Today, despite the recent revival in its fortunes, the US PGA is paying the penalty for that step taken back in 1958. Look at it this way. The British and US Opens are without doubt the two most prestigious championships in the world and they welcome, either through exemptions or via qualifying competitions, all professional golfers plus any amateurs who can fulfil the stipulated handicap requirements. The Masters is invitational, with specified categories of player gaining entry as of right but with absolutely no qualifying procedures. But the US PGA's qualifying competitions are regional affairs from which a few club pros emerge, usually to provide cannon fodder for the big boys in the main event. At this rarefied level, they don't so much sort out the wheat from the chaff as the chaff from the dirt. The championship itself may be the fourth most coveted in the world but, as a strokeplay tournament, it can never rank higher than last of a small elite. Although the US PGA's recent policy of inviting more international players has helped the championship's cause, it is at best a sort of inferior version of the US Open, played on similar courses set up in similar fashion. At matchplay, it would unquestionably come out top of its class.

Nevertheless, for better or worse, the changes were rung in 1958, but the conversion to strokeplay did not reveal itself to be an instant panacea for the US PGA's ills. Just as the British Open laboured in a slough of despond in the 1950s, and only recovered in the next decade after receiving a life-saving injection of Palmer serum, the US PGA suffered for 10 years and didn't receive medicine appropriate to its malady until the 1970s.

It wasn't wholly deprived in the meantime, however. It had sentiment – Jay Hebert emulated his brother Lionel and won in 1960. It had drama – Bob Rosburg closed with a 66 to win by a stroke in 1959, and it would be hard to envisage anything more remarkable than Jerry Barber holing putts of 18, 35 and 60 feet on the last three greens in 1961 to tie the leader; hard, too, to imagine what poor Don January must have thought when he lost the playoff with a 68 to a 67. The US PGA even had champions of calibre – like Gary Player in 1962 and Jack Nicklaus in 1963.

What it did lack was vision. The row between the tournament players and the officials of the PGA of America had turned so nasty by 1967 that a fortnight before play was to begin the players were openly talking of mutiny and threatening to pull out of the championship. In the end it was all so much hot air, but what Jack Nicklaus – who is invariably as articulate with his words as he is with his clubs – had to say on the eve of the competition was not.

"*The US PGA is killing its own tournament. The British Open is a major tournament and scheduling the US PGA right behind it in July is not very smart.*" It was also selfish. Palmer, the saviour of the Open, had opted to give it a miss in 1967 in order to acclimatize to the altitude and summer heat of Denver for what

SHUTING FOR GLORY
Denny Shute was a winner of the US PGA Championship in 1936 and 1937, at Pinehurst and Pittsburgh respectively.

transpired to be another futile assault on the US PGA.

Nicklaus continued: "*All the players would like to see the US PGA be a better tournament than it is, but it won't be if it is going to be scheduled this way and if we continue to try to make golf courses famous by playing the US PGA on them instead of playing the US PGA on famous courses.*"

Curing the two faults Nicklaus highlighted has enabled the US PGA to re-establish itself, though the point that it would be stronger still if it reverted to matchplay remains in the suggestion box.

The 1968 US PGA, the last under the old regime, illustrated the championship's flaws perfectly. For a start, over 60 per cent of the field of 168 were club pros. Once again, the tournament was held immediately after the British Open, this time in the

DOUBLE TAKE *Lee Trevino (not wearing a silly blazer) won the title for a second time at Shoal Creek in 1984, ten years after his first win in the championship. When Shoal Creek hosted the PGA again in 1990, most of the news was created by unsavoury off-course activities.*

save a difficult par at the final hole to edge out the luckless Palmer and Bob Charles by a shot and thus become, at 48 years and 140 days, the oldest winner of a major championship.

The shake-up affecting the organization of professional golf in America, to which I referred earlier, came soon afterwards. In 1969, the PGA Championship was moved to a new August slot, which (except for 1971) it has kept. Ray Floyd won that one by a stroke from a plucky Gary Player, who had to endure several upsetting disturbances from anti-apartheid demonstrators which were timed and guaranteed to harm his golf.

In 1970, the championship went to Southern Hills in Tulsa, another notable landmark because it indicated that the PGA of America was anxious to promote the status of its most prized possession. Southern Hills was only the fourth course to be used for the championship since the war which had previously been considered fit to host the US Open; in contrast, between 1970 and 1994 the authorities selected only nine venues which had not already received the ultimate endorsement from the USGA, although the least said about some of those, like Kemper Lakes in 1989, the better.

Dave Stockton won the first of his two titles in 1970 (Palmer was runner-up) but he held it for just six months. The 1971 championship graced the PGA of America's own course at headquarters in Florida, the Sunshine State's debut as home to a major golf championship.

The tournament was temporarily moved to February to avoid the unpleasant humidity of summer, although this precaution was evidently considered unnecessary when the PGA of America, having shifted offices, brought its championship back to Palm Beach Gardens in 1987. Then the weather was unbearable, the course in awful condition, and the fact that Larry Nelson won the event for the second time was overshadowed by this latest display of PGA of America incompetence.

The early 1970s were vintage days for the US PGA, especially as regards the calibre of its champions. Nicklaus won in the three odd-numbered years; Player and Trevino filled in the gaps. The latter half of the decade, before Nicklaus claimed his record-equalling

stifling, inhospitable heat of San Antonio, Texas, on a five-year-old condominium-lined course which had been awarded the honour because at the time of the nomination a former President of the US PGA had a financial interest in the development of the Pecan Valley Country Club. It is only fair to mention that the course was better than the sceptics expected and so was the tournament. Julius Boros got up and down to

fifth triumph in 1980, could not boast winners like that, but from 1976-79 the US PGA Championship provided a series of cliff-hanging finishes.

Dave Stockton holed a par putt of 15 feet on the final green at Congressional to win in 1976, probably the longest putt ever made on the 72nd hole to win a major when its maker knew he needed it. Ecstasy for Stockton was followed by agony for Gene Littler. He had bravely overcome cancer of the lymph glands in the early 1970s and at Pebble Beach it looked as though the 1961 US Open champion was about to collect another big one. He led by five strokes with nine holes to play but bogeys on five of the first six holes on the back nine dumped him into a playoff with Lanny Wadkins. It was the first instance of sudden death resolving any major championship and Wadkins, having saved his skin with an almost impossible 20-foot putt at the first extra hole, sank one of six feet at the third to take it.

The unlikely victim of a collapse in the 1978 championship was Tom Watson. He held a four-stroke advantage as he turned for home on the Sunday afternoon but he was caught by Jerry Pate and John Mahaffey. The latter had lost a playoff for the 1975 US Open and it was his errors which paved the way for Pate to snatch his glorious victory at Atlanta the next summer, but at Oakmont there were no mistakes. Mahaffey birdied the second hole of overtime and, as he put it, "*went bananas*". Like Palmer, Watson is still missing the US PGA from his major collection.

And the decade closed with a playoff. David Graham needed a par at the last hole at Oakland Hills to break Bobby Nichols' championship record of 271 (established in 1964) and to match fellow-Australian Bruce Crampton's US PGA single-round record of 63 (set in 1975 and subsequently equalled by Ray Floyd in 1982, Gary Player in 1984 and Vijay Singh in 1993). Instead, he took a double-bogey six and opened the door for Ben Crenshaw. To Graham's eternal credit, he made a putt to stay alive at the first extra hole which was reminiscent of the one Wadkins had canned two years before. Like Wadkins, he prevailed two holes later.

There was a savage sting in the tail for Crenshaw. His total of 272 was made up of four rounds below 70.

Arnold Palmer had accomplished the same feat in the 1964 US PGA and discovered it wasn't good enough. The same fate also awaited Greg Norman and Nick Faldo in 1993, when Paul Azinger joined Lee Trevino (1984) as the only men to shoot in the 60s on all four days of the championship and win it.

It was appropriate that in 1986 it should be at the Inverness Golf Club in Toledo, Ohio – the place where the tour pros were first welcomed into the clubhouse at the 1920 US Open – that the reputation of the US PGA was boosted further. The PGA of America invited all 12 members of the European Ryder Cup team who in 1985 had caused the Americans to suffer their first defeat in the competition for 28 years. Not all of them accepted and only two made the halfway cut, but

MOON MAN *Bob Tway bids to become the first golfer into orbit (with due deference to Alan Shepard) after holing a bunker shot on the final hole to pinch the 1986 PGA from Greg Norman.*

neither of those things detracted from a gesture which was widely applauded and seen in a favourable light when compared to the earlier refusal of the officials at Augusta to do likewise in respect of the 1986 Masters.

The 1986 US PGA also provided a classic championship. After the third day Greg Norman completed an unprecedented 'Saturday Slam' by leading all the year's four majors going into Sunday's final round. In fact, at Inverness a colossal and prolonged thunderstorm meant Sunday dragged into Monday, and for the third time that season Norman let slip his advantage. He was four shots clear of Bob Tway with eight holes to play but when they reached the 18th they were level. There Tway produced a shot destined to be remembered forever. He holed out from a bunker for a birdie three and a mortified Norman had to settle for second again. By the end of October he had beaten Tway in their race to top the US PGA Tour Money List, but that was

THE NO-NAME WITH THE HUGE GAME *John Daly's win at Crooked Stick in 1991 was one of golf's greatest fairy-tale victories (above).*

HAPPINESS AND PAYNE *This birdie (right) at the last hole capped a fantastic back nine for Payne Stewart in 1989. When Mike Reid went to pieces, it proved to be a winning combination.*

small satisfaction.

Talking of small, the 5' 7" Jeff Sluman won in 1988 for his first – and so far only – tour victory. In 1989, Payne Stewart played the last nine in 31 while Mike Reid played the par-3 17th in five, taking four shots from within 25 feet of the cup. In 1992, Nick Price of Zimbabwe became the first southern African other than Bobby Locke and Gary Player to win a major, which meant he was no longer the best player in the game not to have one.

Another golfer from the old Commonwealth, Wayne Grady, had won at Shoal Creek in Alabama in 1990, but that US PGA was historic for other reasons. Just before the championship, Hall Thompson, chairman and founder of the club, told a journalist that when it came to membership *"I think we've said we don't discriminate in any other area except blacks."*

His remarks caused a furore. Major corporate sponsors withdrew television advertising, and while the political activists eventually relented in their opposition to Shoal Creek hosting the event, the championship did not get underway until Thompson had formally apologised, the club had offered membership to a prominent local black citizen, and the PGA of America – and soon afterwards the US PGA Tour – had issued guidelines about the necessity for future tournament venues to operate more open membership policies.

The 1991 US PGA was marred, too, when, as at the US Open earlier that summer, a spectator was killed by lightning. The winner generously gave a way a substantial share of his prize-money to the victim's family.

The winner in 1991 was John Daly, the longest driver in the history of serious competitive golf. He humbled Crooked Stick, using a driver and a 9-iron on holes where his rivals needed a 2-iron to get home. A totally obscure journeyman pro, Daly only got into the championship as the ninth alternate, finally owing his place in the field to the withdrawal of Nick Price on the eve of the tournament because his wife was about to give birth. When Price, one of the most popular players in the game, won the title 12 months later, it meant a rare double for his caddie, Jeff 'Squeaky' Medlen, whom Daly had used in 1991.

PAULINE CONVERSION
His win at the 1993 US PGA Championship meant that Azinger was no longer the world's best player not to have won a major.

Since that win, Daly has proved he is no mere big-gun hitter, even though he can be a loose cannon. Having eventually overcome alcohol addiction, he was barred from competing on the US tour for the early part of 1994 after repeatedly walking off the course in mid-competition. By then, under sadder circumstances, Paul Azinger, winner of the US PGA in 1993, was also *hors de combat*, sidelined by cancer.

Azinger collected his first major when he beat Greg Norman at Inverness - not a happy course for him! - at the second playoff hole, where Norman three-putted, after they had emerged from the top of an impressive pile that had almost seen Nick Faldo join them in overtime. By spring 1994, the indications were propitious that Azinger would make a full recovery from his illness. Certainly, the thrilling manner of victories such as his had already helped to restore the health of the US PGA Championship.

THE RYDER CUP

In an age when golf has more cups than the china department at Harrods, the Ryder Cup is something special. The Ryder Cup is played for patriotism: on the one side for Uncle Sam and the American way, on the other for Queen and Country, the Irish Tricolour and assorted continental causes.

A RIGHT RIVETING READ

The programme (below) from the 1933 Ryder Cup match at Southport & Ainsdale – no doubt a bargain at one shilling (five pence in modern money).

What used to be the Great Britain & Ireland team was expanded from 1979 to take in the whole of Europe because the Ryder Cup had become not so much a series of matches as a series of massacres: the British had won only once since the war. (Incidentally, 'British' is acceptable shorthand. The team was not formally called Great Britain & Ireland until 1973, but Irishmen had long been included in it because golf in Ireland is organized without regard for the North/South partition and Irish professionals were registered with the British PGA.)

Accordingly, in 1979 the rest of Europe was drafted in to make the contest a contest again. Any purists who regretted such a fundamental tampering with tradition had their consciences assuaged and their hearts lifted when in 1985 Europe defeated the United States for the first time in 28 years. Europe retained the trophy with a first-ever victory in the United States in 1987, and retained it again after a tied match in 1989. This was one change that was certainly better than the rest.

But all this is rather getting ahead of the story. The Ryder Cup began in 1927. It takes its name from Samuel Ryder, a St Albans businessman who made a fortune from selling penny packets of seed. He was prompted to donate the small solid gold trophy after

KEEPING THE CUP AT HOME *Sam Ryder (left) presents his trophy to the victorious British captain, George Duncan, after the first Ryder Cup match in Britain, at Moortown in 1929.*

attending the second unofficial match between teams of British and American professionals, held at Wentworth in June 1926. Like its forerunner at Gleneagles in 1921, it resulted in a resounding victory for the home team, this time by the almost unbelievable margin of 13 1/2 points to 1 1/2. Abe Mitchell, who was paid a princely annual retainer of £1,000 by Ryder to be his personal professional, thrashed the defending Open champion, Jim Barnes, by 8 & 7, and in the foursomes he and George Duncan routed Barnes and the great Walter Hagen by 9 & 8.

Ryder was so impressed by what he saw and by the camaraderie among the players that he declared some words to the effect *"we must do this more often."* And he did something about it. He had the famous cup made up and engraved, using Mitchell as the model for the little golfer who stands proudly atop the trophy as we see it today.

The first Ryder Cup match took place at Worcester, Massachusetts, the following June. Since Ryder had not endowed the trophy, an appeal for funds was launched by George Philpot, the Editor of *Golf Illustrated*, who also doubled as team manager, and the squad duly embarked from Southampton on a mission with a dual purpose – to return with the Ryder Cup and the US Open trophy. Seldom has optimism been so misplaced. Only once (in 1987) have the Americans failed to win the Ryder Cup on home soil, and Tony Jacklin (in 1970) is the only European golfer to have become US Open champion since Ryder's crusade was waved off in style 60 years ago. And style it unquestionably was.

It is amusing to recall that when Jacklin himself was appointed Ryder Cup captain for the first time in 1983, he insisted his men must make the journey to the United States *"first-class all the way"*. He meant flying on Concorde. Compared to the *Aquitania*, the veritable hotel with a hull which transported the 1927 British team to New York on a leisurely and luxurious five-day voyage, the winged wonder is like a speedboat with hostesses. *"The floating palace"* was how the liner was described by an anonymous author in the contemporary issue of *PGA Journal*. *"Lifts to all decks, lounges, smoke rooms, ballroom, swimming bath and gymnasium were among the outstanding features."*

But old J. H. Taylor, one of the selectors, was at pains to stress *"it is no casual picnic"*. The American domination of the sport was a new, disturbing and totally unacceptable phenomenon to British golfers in the 1920s. Hagen and Bobby Jones were usurpers of the British birthright to rule the world of golf and Taylor and his colleagues were determined that the proper order of things should be reasserted.

Their aspirations suffered an immediate blow when Mitchell went down with appendicitis just after boarding the *Aquitania* and he had to disembark for hospital. Ryder wrote to his friend and mentor: *"Let us hope our team will win, but it is the play without the Prince of Denmark."*

Ted Ray, who had won the US Open in 1920, was nominated captain in Mitchell's absence. His opposite number was Hagen, who was to lead his side in every one of the six pre-war contests, albeit in a non-playing capacity in 1937. Hagen would have approved of the creature comforts enjoyed by his rivals on their Atlantic crossing, but the British were not accustomed to being treated like celebrities and they were further

GETTING SHIP-SHAPE *The British team aboard the* Aquitania *prior to departing for the first Ryder Cup match in 1927. Left to right: George Philpot (team manager), Samuel Ryder (who did not travel), George Gadd, Arthur Havers, George Duncan, Ted Ray, Fred Robson, Archie Compston, Charlie Whitcombe and Abe Mitchell (who was taken ill before the boat sailed). Aubrey Boomer and Herbert Jolly were in the team but not in this picture.*

disorientated when their ship berthed. On landing in America, they were introduced to *"a world of luxury and plenty"*, as Arthur Havers put it. Hagen might have choreographed the whole show – a waiving of customs formalities, a motorcycle escort through Manhattan, limousines permanently at the players' disposal, typically transatlantic hospitality and kindness, and clubhouses equipped with every amenity and furnished to the highest standards. And so on it went.

Totally overawed off the course, the British were overwhelmed on it. They lost 2 1/2–9 1/2. (From 1927 to 1959, the competition consisted of one day of four 36-hole foursomes and another of eight 36-hole singles.) It was generally agreed that the major difference between the teams lay in the short game, especially putting. That has been a familiar refrain down the years.

Although after the war the Ryder Cup often seemed to have degenerated into a grandiose Anglo-American public relations exercise, it was never thus in the 1920s and 1930s. The 1929 match at Moortown, Leeds, brought the British the revenge they had anticipated with what in hindsight can only be regarded as complacency bordering on stupidity. The heroes for the home team were Duncan, who delighted in tearing Hagen apart by the astonishing margin of 10 & 8 – a Ryder Cup singles record – and the 22-year-old Henry

Cotton, who supplied the vital last point by defeating Al Watrous 4 & 3. A month later Hagen cut short any gloating by winning his fourth Open title at Muirfield.

At the end of that year, on December 9, Sam Ryder signed over his trophy to the British PGA under a Deed of Trust, confirming it to be the reward for the winners of a biennial matchplay international *"between two teams of professional golfers, one team representing Great Britain and the other team representing the United States of America"*. From that date, the administration of the Ryder Cup in their respective countries has been undertaken by the British PGA and the PGA of America, although following a rancorous row in 1990 over the venue for the 1993 match, the PGA European Tour has assumed joint responsibility with the British PGA for the match when it is played in Europe every fourth year.

From the cold of a Yorkshire spring in 1929, the scene switched to the enervating heat of an Ohio summer in 1931. The temperature permanently hovered around 100° F and people all over the Columbus area were dying from heat exhaustion and dehydration. Fred Pignon, the British manager, commented: *"In this weather, golf is not a game – it is a form of torture."* He also echoed Havers' remarks about the *"almost embarrassing hospitality"*. Pignon said: *"Until you have been the guest of an American golfer you may think you know something about lavish hospitality, but they begin at the place which we consider the high limit."*

The British started badly and fizzled out altogether in the withering heat. Their hopes were faint anyway, but they were made even more frail by the absence of Cotton, who opted out because he could not resolve his squabbles with the PGA about travelling arrangements and money.

Cotton, despite his late flourish at Moortown, was only ever a sporadic supporter of his country in the Ryder Cup. He didn't play in 1933 or 1935 either, then being precluded by the strict residence clause in the Deed of Trust because he was based in Belgium, and in 1949 he refused to play under the captaincy of Charlie Whitcombe. Nevertheless, he did agree to serve as non-playing captain in 1953.

Cotton was the best British golfer since the Great

Triumvirate but episodes like the above did nothing to boost his popularity, which in some quarters was already jeopardized by his startling self-confidence and habit of saying what he thought. Cotton could only get away with it because he was good, very good, and he worked extraordinarily hard to stay that way. Although his efforts to further his own career and simultaneously raise the status of the professional golfer were not always appreciated at the time (envy of his sophisticated lifestyle, jealousy of his talent and a conservative respect for near-feudal conventions saw to that), the attitudes of his detractors did not worry Cotton, and in later life he was accorded much of the praise that was withheld 50 years before.

His maverick counterpart in America was, of course, the flamboyant Hagen, who adored matchplay and the Ryder Cup. He repaid his 1929 mauling at the hands of George Duncan by pairing up with Densmore Shute to crush Duncan and Arthur Havers by 10 & 9 in the foursomes at Scioto in 1931, the most emphatic margin of victory in any Ryder Cup match. The next

day Hagen faced Charlie Whitcombe in the singles, an occasion prefaced by a classic cameo of vintage Hagen. As the two men stood on the first tee, a waiter sauntered over and handed a martini to the American skipper. Hagen, never one to let golf get in the way of a good time and not averse to drinking and driving, downed the cocktail before cracking a marvellous tee shot down the middle of the fairway. Naturally, like his team, he won.

The 1933 match at Southport & Ainsdale provided a fantastic finish, which for 11th-hour theatre was the equal of the subsequent thrillers like 1969 and 1991. J. H. Taylor was the non-playing British captain, and he ordered his troops out on to the beach at 6.30 each morning to undergo a rigorous training regime. As Red Rum was later to prove in three Grand Nationals, a few gallops on Southport sands is a sound recipe for success, and Taylor's men came out of the stalls like racehorses. They took a foursomes lead for the first time in the four meetings, and therefore they needed only to share the eight singles to regain the Ryder Cup

for Great Britain and Ireland.

There were at least 15,000 people, reckoned then to be the largest attendance on a British golf course, swarming over the sandhills on that second afternoon. Some had come to see the golf, others to see the Prince of Wales, who was among their number. Certainly the Prince was there to see the golf; and, to stretch creative licence to breaking point, it may be that he was instrumental in Britain's famous victory.

The whole issue rested on the final singles. With the contest dead level, Syd Easterbrook and Denny Shute came to the last hole, a par-4, all square. In American eyes, what followed was a tragedy of errors. After three hacks each, both men lay about 15 feet from the cup, with Easterbrook furthest away. He knocked his putt a yard past the hole. At that moment, Hagen, as one might expect, was chatting amiably to the Prince. He contemplated yelling out to Shute not to charge his putt – the Americans only required a half to retain the trophy. Instead, perhaps swayed by respect for the finer points of decorum, he remained silent.

EARLY RYDER CUP FEVER *A huge gallery watches as Walter Hagen gets the better of Arthur Lacey in their singles match at Southport in 1933. But Lacey had the last laugh. The British emerged triumphant for the last time until 1957.*

THE BEST OF BRITISH *Peter Alliss (on the left) congratulates his captain, Dai Rees, after Britain's memorable – and last – win, at Lindrick in 1957. Behind them is Max Faulkner, the 1951 Open champion, who was omitted from the singles at his own suggestion.*

Shute did charge the putt, and then missed the four-footer he had coming back. In the terrible quiet that only thousands of people can generate, Easterbrook sank his putt for the match. For Shute there was the considerable consolation of becoming Open champion a fortnight later.

"*In giving this Cup I am naturally impartial but, of course, we over here are very pleased to have won,*" the Prince wittily observed at the prize-giving ceremony. Sam Ryder never saw Britain do anything else. He never travelled to the United States and by the time the Americans recorded their first of eight away victories in 1937, again at Southport & Ainsdale, he was dead.

That shocking defeat followed the expected drubbing in New Jersey in 1935. The British had been pathetic there and several commentators regarded their performance in 1937 as, with one or two notable exceptions, even more spineless. *Golf Illustrated* queried acidly: "*Is it any use pretending that the Americans are unbeatable when, in point of fact, they threw the foursomes at us, a gift which we, with equal courtesy, refused to accept?*"

At least Cotton went on from Southport to take the

Open Championship at Carnoustie, but otherwise the writing was indelibly on the wall. The Americans had invariably won with ease at home. In Britain they had twice been thwarted narrowly before comfortably confirming their authority in 1937. But the British did have the immense satisfaction of actually having won a couple of times. Nobody knew then, even if many suspected, what a rare occurrence that would become. In those days of pre-war innocence the Ryder Cup was a meaningful sporting battle, hence the attention given to that period here.

In between Britain rescuing Europe in the Second World War and Europe rescuing Britain from golfing annihilation, there were 16 Ryder Cup matches. Only four of them – 1949, 1953, 1957 and 1969 – were close enough to merit much mention here, although a few words are necessary in order to explain how on the whole there came to be such a disparity in the strengths of the teams.

The war exacerbated the differences between the countries. In the United States there was still plenty of cash around to maintain the standards of living experienced briefly by the three visiting pre-war British Ryder Cup teams; quality was attainable. Conversely, in Britain rationing was the order of the day; austerity was the watchword.

In these diverse economic climates the professional tour boomed in America, providing a marvellous means for a man to make a living from tournament golf, whereas in Britain the poor pro spent most of the time in his shop. No wonder he was so regularly outclassed in every department of the game and that Americans could pop over and win the Open Championship almost at will.

In fact, it was at the behest of the Americans that the Ryder Cup was resumed as promptly as 1947, and thanks to the munificence of Bob Hudson, an Oregon fruit packer, that the British could afford to make the long trip to the American north-west. Hudson financed the whole expedition, blazing a trail of sponsorship that was followed by several wealthy individuals and companies, and without which the Ryder Cup may well have died long before it was revived in 1979.

It rained so hard in 1947 at Portland that the match was almost a washout. It was nearly a whitewash, too.

The British lost 1-11. The meeting at Ganton two years later was preceded by Hogan's complaint about the British clubs (see page 30), but this was compensated for by some brilliant golf. The home players snatched a 3-1 foursomes lead and acquitted themselves superbly in the singles, but it wasn't quite sufficient. They couldn't find another gear in the face of a scintillating barrage of birdies from their opponents which caused the scoreboard operators to run out of 3s. The match was lost 5-7.

The Americans held a 3-1 advantage after the first day in 1953 and 1957, but they lost one match and should have lost both. At Wentworth in 1953, Peter Alliss took four to get down from beside the last green; shortly afterwards, Bernard Hunt missed from a yard on the same hole. Had Alliss done the job in three and Hunt made his putt, Britain would have won. Instead the two babes were left to carry the can for a heartbreaking defeat. But they were back in 1957 when, inspired by a vast and enthusiastic Yorkshire crowd at Lindrick and the leadership of Dai Rees, the team stormed home by 6½ -1½ in the singles to earn Britain's third and last victory.

By 1961, though, it was recognized that British triumphs were not likely to be commonplace, so an era of fiddling with the format was ushered in. With spurious logic, the matches were reduced from 36 to 18 holes apiece to create more games, thereby increasing the number of points to fight for. The only impact of this was to increase the number of points won by the Americans. The one glorious exception was at Royal Birkdale in 1969 when the teams finished level on 16 points apiece.

Tony Jacklin was the local hero, as he had been in the Open at Lytham two months previously. Having beaten Jack Nicklaus 4 & 3 in the morning singles, he took him on again in the afternoon. Jacklin holed a 55-foot eagle putt to win the 17th, and the resulting roar led Brian Huggett up ahead to believe he had a five-footer on the 18th to clinch the Ryder Cup. He bravely sank it, only to learn that Jacklin had not won but was level playing the last. So were the teams. The situation was a repeat of 1933 and the finale nearly was, too. Nicklaus eventually lay four feet from the cup, Jacklin a yard away, both in three. Nicklaus knocked in his knee-trembler and, in an unforgettable sporting gesture, conceded Jacklin's putt for the half with the words: "*I don't think that you'd have missed that, Tony, but I'm not going to give you the chance.*" The Americans then graciously agreed that each side would hold the cup for a year.

But by and large, the history of the Ryder Cup from 1947 to 1977 is rather like a mirror image of the Lions v the Christians in Roman times. The lions' supporters (ie. the American spectators) soon got bored with an almost permanent state of no-contest which, apart from inconsequential side-shows like Brian Barnes twice beating Nicklaus in the singles in 1975, is what they got in their home ring. Perversely, the Christians were begging to be thrown in again. Headlines like '*We Can Do It This Time*' and '*Everything Points To Another Lindrick*' were followed by dispiriting tales of another British

HUGGETT AND TIE

Welshman Brian Huggett (above) holes from five feet to halve his crucial singles with Billy Casper in 1969. He mistakenly thought it was a putt to win the Ryder Cup. Ten minutes later, Jack Nicklaus and Tony Jacklin (left) shook hands after Nicklaus had sportingly conceded a short putt that ensured both their match and the team match would be halved.

GENIUS PERSONIFIED *One of golf's great shots from one of its greatest shot-makers. Seve Ballesteros carries a 3-wood some 245 yards from an awkward lie in a sand bunker on to the front edge of the 18th green at PGA National in Florida in 1983. This stroke enabled him to save his par and get a half with Fuzzy Zoeller in the top singles, although Ballesteros had been 3 up at one time.*

IT'S THERE! *By holing a birdie putt on the 18th green, Sam Torrance clinched the 1985 Ryder Cup for Europe. It ended a disastrous run of defeats against the Americans over nearly three decades.*

defeat, usually accompanied by a few caustic barbs aimed at the selectors. At Pinehurst in 1951, the British writer and commentator, Henry Longhurst, was jestingly moved to toast the forthcoming match with the words: *"May the best team lose."*

For more sanguine observers, finding the silver lining was a popular pastime of the day, but the truth is that, for all the optimistic predictions, it was not until the continent reinforced the British challenge in 1979 that post-war victory became a serious possibility, and not until 1985 did it actually become a probability.

The win at Lindrick and the halved match at Birkdale represented remarkable British performances but in many ways they were really flashes in the pan. Occasions like those kept non-Britons out in the cold longer than might otherwise have been the case. They also meant that when reform was introduced it was continental rather than the oft-mooted Commonwealth players who were brought in.

Following Britain's defeat at Lytham in 1977, Jack Nicklaus wrote to Lord Derby, the President of the British PGA, saying he was afraid the Ryder Cup would die unless something was done. He suggested that the British team be expanded to a European one. At a special committee meeting, the PGA decided to vary the Deed of Trust under the powers vested in them and give effect to Nicklaus's wishes.

It was a logical step, given the recent formation of the European Tournament Players' Division. And so Seve Ballesteros and Antonio Garrido of Spain joined 10 Britons at The Greenbrier in 1979, but the new recruits only got one point between them. Larry Nelson was pitched against Ballesteros four times that week and won the lot. At Walton Heath two years later

Nelson extended his personal record in the matches to a unique nine wins from nine starts, but Ballesteros was not among the three Europeans in the home team. He was peevishly omitted because of his recurring rows with the European tour over appearance money, and to nobody's surprise, the Americans won easily.

But Ballesteros was back for the match in Florida in 1983. He replaced his compatriot, Manuel Pinero, while Bernhard Langer and Jose Maria Canizares remained in the squad. The three provided a forceful demonstration of the difference the continentals had made by helping the Europeans hound their opponents down to the line. The United States won by 14½–13½, the closest-ever finish in America, though for much of a thrilling afternoon it seemed Europe would win. In the end, both Ballesteros and Canizares had to regret letting slip three-hole leads and halving matches they seemed to have won.

In 1985, with Tony Jacklin retained as captain, it all came right for Europe. Four Spaniards – Ballesteros, Pinero, Canizares and Jose Rivero – were in a team that included the Masters winner Langer and Open champion Lyle. Victory was likely from the moment Craig Stadler missed a tiny putt on the last green of the second morning's fourballs. That allowed the

Europeans to go into lunch tied at 6-6 and they rammed home this immense psychological boost by running away with the second series of foursomes and the next day's singles. Their 16½–11½ victory, secured when Sam Torrance beat Andy North with an 18-foot birdie putt on the final green of their singles, was the heaviest defeat ever inflicted on the Americans in Ryder Cup history. For Jacklin, vengeance was indeed sweet. The Americans were led by Lee Trevino, his old adversary.

There was more history at Muirfield Village in 1987, at a course designed by the American captain, Jack Nicklaus. The Americans won the first two foursomes matches on the opening morning. In the third match, Lanny Wadkins and Larry Mize had been 4 up after nine holes against Nick Faldo and Ian Woosnam. Normal service, it seemed, was about to be resumed.

But the Europeans hadn't studied the script. Faldo and Woosnam won their match, and behind them the two Spaniards, Ballesteros and Jose Maria Olazabal, beat Larry Nelson (revenge for Ballesteros!) and Payne Stewart. And then Europe won all four of the afternoon's fourballs. From 0-2 to 6-2.

With Faldo and Woosnam only dropping half a point in four outings, and Ballesteros and Olazabal garnering three points from four, the Americans were all but devastated by the time it came to the singles. Europe only won three of those – Howard Clark and Eamonn Darcy both bravely completing their respective tasks on the 18th, and Ballesteros, fittingly, sealing the match by beating Curtis Strange at the 17th – but three halved matches were enough to clinch a marvellous triumph by 15 points to 13.

As it had been in 1969, the 1989 match was tied. This time the Americans took a two-point lead after the opening foursomes but again they got whitewashed in the Friday fourballs. Saturday's matches were evenly split and so Europe needed five wins and a half to be victorious for the third consecutive time.

They got the five wins early, helped by some appalling golf from the Americans. Stewart and Mark Calcavecchia lost at the last to Olazabal and Ronan Rafferty, respectively, because they drove into the water on the 18th; Fred Couples lost there to Christy O'Connor Jnr because he couldn't hit the green with a

9-iron (admittedly having been intimidated by a glorious 2-iron from the Irishman that had nestled down within five feet of the flag on what is surely the most daunting closing hole in matchplay golf); and Ken Green generously took three putts on the final green and then had to watch while a gleeful Canizares sank the four-footer that ensured Europe would tie the match and keep the cup.

Belatedly, the Americans exhibited their pride by winning the last four matches to make the score 14-14. They had rescued a half from a lost cause, although the Ryder Cup was in European hands for another two years. Jacklin, quitting on a high note, resigned from the European captaincy, which was passed on to Bernard Gallacher.

His first campaign was a losing one – to have the 1993 Ryder Cup played in Spain, which was what the PGA European Tour wanted, largely as a tribute to the pivotal role Ballesteros had played in reviving the competition. But a bitter row resulted in a 3-3 tie when the European Ryder Cup committee voted on the issue in May 1990, and Lord Derby, then president of both the PGA and the Tour, used his casting vote in favour of The Belfry, the PGA's choice, which therefore got the match for a third consecutive time in Europe.

However, the Ryder Cup will go to Spain in 1997, having been held at Oak Hill, Rochester, in 1995.

The most recent match in the United States, at Kiawah Island in 1991, was yet another epic. Europe seemed out of it by lunch-time on Saturday, but they won three of the four fourballs that afternoon and halved the other to level matters at eight points each, with the 12 singles to be contested the next day.

Make that eleven singles. America's Steve Pate withdrew because of the after-effects of an injury he had sustained in a car crash on the eve of the match, which meant Gallacher had the thankless task of telling David Gilford that he wouldn't be playing either. That was half a point for each team, and halved points were what it came down to.

Ultimately, Bernhard Langer needed to win his match against Hale Irwin to tie the match at 14-14, which would again have meant that Europe retained the cup. Langer, 2 down with four holes to play, won the 15th and 17th and halved the 16th by making three consecutive putts of between five and eight feet. At the 18th, he faced a six-footer to pull off a remarkable escape, but his putt slid agonizingly past the right lip of the hole. The United States had won the Ryder Cup for the first time in eight years.

Having improved from defeat in 1985 to a draw at The Belfry in 1989, the Americans won there in 1993 after a match that may have hinged upon a captain's decision. Europe led by three points after the second morning's foursomes, but Gallacher acceded to the requests of Ballesteros and Langer to be rested for the afternoon fourballs, respectively on the grounds of poor form and feeling poorly, even though Ballesteros and Olazabal had extended their partnership record to an amazing 11 wins from 15 outings that morning and Langer, the reigning Masters champion, was surely worth playing at better-ball. The Americans duly cut the gap to one point going into the singles.

As two years previously, two players sat out Sunday's play. Sam Torrance withdrew with a foot

THE ONE THAT GOT AWAY *The anguish of Bernhard Langer reflects the importance of the shot. When this putt went past the hole on the final green in 1991, the United States had regained the Ryder Cup.*

injury and Lanny Wadkins asked his captain, Tom Watson, to omit him rather than have a rookie undergo the torment Gilford had experienced. Three Europeans of those who did play had particular reason to lament their performances, with Ballesteros going out in 42 before losing to Jim Gallagher, Barry Lane losing from 3 up with five to play against Chip Beck, and Costantino Rocca, the first Italian to play in the match (in which Joakim Haeggman became Sweden's long-awaited first representative), bogeying the last two holes to go from 1 up to 1 down against Davis Love. The singles victories and week-long heroics of Nick Faldo – who had a hole-in-one at the 14th in his match against Paul Azinger – Colin Montgomerie and debutant Peter Baker were destined to be in vain when Raymond Floyd got the better of Olazabal. The United States won by 15-13.

With the increased interest in the Ryder Cup, in recent years there have been occasional complaints from American players disgruntled at the allegedly overt partisanship of the crowds in Britain. Some fans have certainly left no doubt as to where their sympathies lie, but that is nothing new in matchplay competition.

Back in 1905, Harry Vardon and J. H. Taylor of England were so upset by the behaviour of the spectators at St Andrews during a £400 challenge match against James Braid and Sandy Herd of Scotland that they contemplated quitting. They didn't, and they went on to win. After the 1949 Ryder Cup at Ganton, Henry Longhurst rebuked the crowds: "*It is all right to cheer when your own man puts his ball on the green. It is quite inexcusable to let out a roar when the opposition drives into the woods.*" Dow Finsterwald, the American skipper at Lytham in 1977, said: "*You've got real trouble if those people out there were representative of your normal crowds. There were an awful lot who seemed to think this was a war, not a golf match.*"

Similar sentiments were expressed at The Belfry in

HEAVEN'S ABOVE *Davis Love holes a par putt at the 18th to beat Costantino Rocca in their 1993 Ryder Cup singles match. Love won the last two holes to turn a probable European win into victory for the United States.*

both 1985 and 1989 by American players who felt the audiences in the United States, rendered *blasé* by victory upon victory, would never have behaved as raucously as the British fans. But the 1991 match at Kiawah Island was prefaced by preview stories in the United States under headlines like 'War By The Shore', so the potentially inflammatory hype is not all one way. Some commentators wonder how the American fans might have reacted had Langer holed that putt at Kiawah and thus kept the cup in European hands.

The fact is that matchplay, unlike strokeplay, is about winners and losers, not firsts and seconds. It is blood-and-guts golf. The Ryder Cup stirs these emotions, nowadays mixing them with the kind of commercial trappings found at the Open and adding a large dash of genuinely patriotic fervour, which has no other proper outlet in what is mostly an individual, non-nationalistic sport.

The Ryder Cup offers no prize money, but the best players on either side of the Atlantic are desperate to make their respective teams. Money is not quite everything in sport. In the most important golf international in the world, representative honours count for quite a bit, too.

CHAPTER FIVE

THE MAIN TOURS

Golf has tournament circuits on every continent of the globe bar the Arctic and Antarctic. Before looking at how they have developed, it is important to put the situation into context.

The United States has the most powerful golf tour in the world. And it also has the richest. Those facts are inextricably connected. Part of the reason for this wealth is that members of the US tour cannot, except by fulfilling certain commitments (notably by playing at least 15 tournaments a season), compete abroad without a release from the commissioner. Often this will only be granted if the sponsor of the conflicting American event that week is agreeable, and in this way the interests of those who fund the tour are safeguarded.

The significance of the commissioner's strength has never been more heavily emphasized than in September 1970, when the John Player tobacco company launched a £70,000 tournament in England. To borrow an American expression, that was then big bucks. Christy O'Connor collected the first five-figure cheque ever presented in British golf – a staggering £24,375, nearly five times as much as Jack Nicklaus had earned for winning the Open at St Andrews that summer. The Irishman's prize equalled the biggest on offer in the United States that year, $60,000 in those heady days for sterling.

The tournament is long defunct. Players were sunk almost as soon as they started. Their representative had blithely flown over to the United States with all that money behind him to complete the formalities of signing up the stars. He was told: "No way." It was an expensive lesson, even though O'Connor may have enjoyed it hugely.

While the commissioner's power remains largely untrammelled, a great deal has changed since the day John Players' unfortunate emissary received that rude

awakening. There has been a tremendous growth in the scale of professional golf everywhere, and nowhere more than in Europe, whose golfers have made their presence felt by winning tournaments in the United States. Tony Jacklin showed the way and subsequent major champions in the shape of Seve Ballesteros, Nick Faldo, Bernhard Langer, Sandy Lyle, Ian Woosnam and Jose Maria Olazabal have followed him, which is partly why today the Executive Director of the PGA European Tour, Ken Schofield, is in the position his American counterpart has long been in, of controlling – albeit to a lesser extent – where his top players can play by making them commit to play a minimum number of events (11 in this case) each season in order to remain members of the PGA European Tour.

Those leading European players honed their craft in the United States. Except for Woosnam and Olazabal, they were members of the US tour during the 1980s until familial ties and the increasing commitments demanded by the commissioner, Deane Beman, caused them to resign and, except for appearances in the American major championships and a handful of other tournaments around them, instead base themselves once again in Europe.

November and December are off months in the United States and Europe, which leaves a precious window open for tournament promoters in Japan, Australia and South Africa who wish to entice itinerant professional golfers who are then free from the constraints of their domestic obligations. We will briefly examine those circuits in this chapter, too.

What follows is a passport-free excursion around the cosmopolitan and extraordinarily international world of professional golf.

AN INTERNATIONAL GAME *Greg Norman is an Australian golfer who now plays on the US tour having learned his trade by competing in Europe in the formative years of his career. He, uniquely, has topped the Money List on both sides of the Atlantic as well as in his homeland.*

THE DEANE MACHINE *The Commissioner of the US PGA Tour since 1974, Deane Beman turned professional golf in the United States into a huge commercial enterprise. The announcement of his impending resignation in March 1994 shocked many observers.*

THE US PGA TOUR

The 1993 United States PGA Tour was worth about $55 million. Nick Price won $1,478,557 of that. Both were records, albeit meaningless ones, most likely destined to be obliterated within 12 months. Price's main achievement was in becoming only the third non-American (after Gary Player and Greg Norman) to top the US Money List.

These vast, annually rising sums take no account of the money to be made from 'unofficial' events, such as Skins Games; the $30 million or so available to the 50s-and-over brigade on the burgeoning Senior tour, which carried 44 events in 1994; or the $6 million up for grabs on the 30-tournament secondary circuit, known as the Nike Tour. One cannot ignore either the tens of millions annually raised for charity ('the leading money-winner on the PGA Tour', as the slogan has it, although a series of articles published in the American magazine, *Golf Digest,* in spring 1992 suggested that in reality the tour's munificence was rather less generous than it liked to make out it was).

Whatever the truth of that, the tour is big business, involved in several diverse aspects of the sport, notably – and in some eyes controversially – in the construction of 'stadium golf courses'. The latter are purpose-built tournament sites, designed with such extraneous factors as spectator comfort in mind. As more new venues are opened, so the tour moves another event to one of its facilities.

Whether the tour should find it necessary to have an arm operating under the name PGA Tour Investments, Inc. is a moot point, not least within the membership. What is undeniable is that the tour has become an example of the 20th-century American dream *in excelsis.*

Its origins can be traced to the 1920s, when the United States echoed to the sounds of the motor car and popping champagne corks. Already there was a small nucleus of tournaments in existence: the US Open, of course, founded in 1895, the Western Open (1899), the Canadian Open (1904) and the Texas Open

FACE VALUE *Golf courses on the US tour are invariably immaculate in appearance, and the tour visits some of the most desirable parts of the nation. This is the Bob Hope Classic in Palm Springs.*

(1922). This quartet hardly constituted a quorum for the formation of what might properly be called a tour, but in the Roaring Twenties the circuit's development began in earnest.

Throughout the decade, tournaments sprang up on the West Coast and in Florida, the consequence of professionals moving to the warmer southern climes to escape the rigours of the north-east winter and wanting to keep their games sharp in competition. The Los Angeles Open was launched in 1926, the Pensacola Open in 1929. As the players moved eastwards from California in search of more money in Florida, new tournaments were born in Texas and Louisiana to help them on their way towards the Atlantic. Their sojourn would customarily reach its conclusion at the Pinehurst resort in North Carolina in late March.

Then, as now, the tour theoretically followed the sun, and not just so the golfers could top up their tans. Many of the players would be back in the north during the summer at courses which had been closed while under frost and snow. They would mend clubs, teach the members and perhaps play in occasional events organized by their state golf association. Only the select few – like Walter Hagen and Gene Sarazen – could afford to spurn the regular income of a club job.

These two made money in exhibitions and it was from trips around the country on his personal lucrative circuit that Hagen realized the public would respond to the idea of a winter tour. Shortly afterwards, regional businesses and corporations started to appreciate that supporting the venture represented cheap advertising. Bob Harlow (Hagen's agent) and later Fred Corcoran (who would look after Sam Snead) became early directors of the PGA's Tournament Bureau, and from a schedule of just three events worth around $8,500 in 1921 the little acorn grew into the giant oak we know now, spreading into all four seasons and occupying most weeks of the year. That explains why Sarazen once said of Hagen: "*Golf has never had a showman like him. All the professionals who have a chance to go after the big money today should say a silent thanks to Walter each time they stretch a cheque between their fingers.*"

The tour's expansion continued into the 1930s, despite the Great Depression. If the $7,682 Horton

Smith earned in topping the Money List in 1936 sounds rather paltry in comparison with contemporary hauls, it wasn't a bad reward for playing sport when a quarter of the population was unemployed and scores of golf clubs were filing for bankruptcy. At that time, the game was having to survive not only the tribulations of the American economy but also such factors as the retirement of Bobby Jones and a waning in the influence of Hagen and Sarazen.

As the dominance of these three declined into the past with the coincidental demise of hickory shafts, the circuit was revitalized by Snead, Byron Nelson, Ben Hogan, Ralph Guldahl, Jimmy Demaret and others in the new age of steel. These men took to the road. They liked to play golf and happened to be outstanding at it in an era when the game wasn't readily within reach of the ordinary man's pocket. As the American journalist Ross Goodner put it: "*When Sam Snead won almost $20,000 in 1938 it seemed like all the money in the world to a nation that only recently had trouble finding someone who could spare a dime.*"

Ben Hogan headed the Money List from 1940 to 1942 before golf in the United States was faced with another calamity as America joined the allied forces in the Second World War. There was no tour in 1943 but fund-raising exhibitions and clinics were encouraged, and celebrities like Bing Crosby and Bob Hope raised thousands of dollars for the relief agencies.

Both were confirmed golf nuts. In 1937, Crosby

TALKING HEAD *Walter Hagen doing what came naturally. His love of publicity, allied to his talent, was a distinct boon in launching the professional tour in the United States in the 1920s.*

THE ROAD TO GOLF *Bob Hope (left) and Bing Crosby followed the path to glory with their showbusiness careers but they will always be appreciated in golfing circles for the support and enthusiasm they lavished upon the game.*

had inaugurated his own pro-am tournament in San Diego, which later relocated to three courses on California's Monterey Peninsula – Pebble Beach, Cypress Point and Spyglass Hill. Bob Hope took the same road in 1960 with his Desert Classic, and other entertainers like Glen Campbell, Dean Martin and Andy Williams later amalgamated golf and showbiz on the tour.

Back in the 1940s, though, American golf came cautiously out of its year of enforced abstinence. The powers in Washington came to acknowledge that the pursuit of sport was not unpatriotic but instead provided desirable recreation in a period of stress. The trouble for the professional tour was that a large percentage of its best exponents were in the services and petrol rationing was not exactly conducive to long-distance travelling between venues. It was in this unpromising atmosphere of generally second-rate athletic achievement that Byron Nelson arrived not so much as a breath of fresh air as a hurricane.

In 1944 Nelson practically doubled Snead's money-winning record of 1938 in winning six tournaments, and yet that pales into insignificance compared with what he did in 1945.

The bare bones of his accomplishments have already been outlined on page 52, to which one might add that he also won one other event (non-PGA approved because the purse did not meet the stipulated minimum), making 19 victories in all. It is as safe as anything can be in golf when it comes to discussing the permanence of records to say that Nelson's 11 consecutive wins and several more of his marks will never be bettered. They are immortal. Those who cavil that for much of 1945 Hogan and Snead were not among the opposition have a scintilla of validity on their side, but there is no arguing with Nelson's stroke average of 68.33 on courses which were not short and had the disadvantage of being maintained in inferior condition to those the pros are accustomed to today. And even when Hogan and Snead were in attendance there was nothing they could

do if 'Lord Byron' went about firing scores like 259, as he did in Seattle where the pack was left floundering 13 strokes adrift and Hogan needed a telescope to see Nelson a distant 20 shots away. Bobby Jones, in a tribute that was perhaps a touch too modest but nevertheless genuinely intended, once said: *"At my best, I never came close to the golf that Nelson shoots."*

His record-shattering exploits shattered Nelson. He won five times in 1946, but he had been so wearied by his relentless campaigning – in 1945 he had taken off just one week in 29 – that he effectively retired in 1947, though he still managed to be runner-up in the Masters that year and he emerged to win the French Open as late as 1955.

With Hogan and Snead to the fore, the tour became more structured after the war and professional golf consolidated its public appeal. The two great men clashed in the opening event of the 1950 schedule, the Los Angeles Open, on Hogan's return to the fray after his awful accident. The crowd rooted for him during his brave bid to win first time out but, having tied with Snead, he lost the playoff 76 to 72.

The US golf tour of the 1950s and 1960s spawned many great characters and unlikely anecdotes. Chief buffoon was perhaps Ky Laffoon. He would thump hard objects to punish his hands after he hit a bad shot. His masochism turned to sadism when his putter was to blame. He was once seen trying to strangle it, on another occasion he attempted to drown it in a lake, and he would regularly ride from one tournament to the next with it attached by string to the back of his car so that it would suffer for its recalcitrant behaviour.

He wasn't alone in his eccentricities. Lefty Stackhouse would plunge his right hand into a thorn bush, telling it to *"Take that"*, if its misbehaviour had caused a wayward shot. Sam Snead, who was also known to get fazed now and again, once described Clayton Heafner as *"the most even-tempered player on the tour; he's always angry"*. And then there was Tommy Bolt, inevitably nicknamed 'Thunder'.

Bolt, the 1958 US Open champion, held most of the club-throwing records. His alleged motto was: *"If you are going to throw a club, it is important to throw it ahead of you so you don't waste energy going back to pick it up."* His caddie reputedly once offered him a

PIVOTAL PLAYER *Arnold Palmer was the key figure at a critical moment in US golf history – 1958 – the year when US tour prize money topped $1 million for the first time. Palmer was not only the leading earner that year, he also won the Masters and inspired hero-worship from well outside traditional golf spectators. Ten years later, Palmer's own earnings topped the $1 million mark.*

choice of two clubs for the shot in hand, neither of them being suitable for the purpose, because they were all he had left in his bag. After two drives had found water on the 18th hole in the 1960 US Open, Bolt hurled his driver into the lake in front of the tee. A young boy dived in and retrieved the club, which mollified Bolt until the boy raced past him and made off with his prize over the out-of-bounds fence. They don't make many like Tommy Bolt any more.

The first of three crucial factors which were to inspire the golf boom of the 1960s and its subsequent sustained growth in America occurred in 1953. That was television. The medium which is now often maligned as having too powerful a hold on all sports introduced golf to a TV audience, and hence to millions of the unconverted, at the 1953 George S. May World Championship of Golf at the Tam O'Shanter Club in Chicago. Byron Nelson had captured the then richest title in golf four times in the 1940s but never in the dramatic fashion Lew Worsham won it in 1953. He holed a full wedge shot from over 100 yards out for an eagle two at the last to beat poor Chandler Harper by a

stroke. Isao Aoki did the same thing to Jack Renner at the Hawaiian Open in 1983 to similar acclaim but with considerably less impact. The effect that Worsham's feat had on an uninitiated armchair gallery can be imagined. On its coast-to-coast debut, at a stroke, golf had shown itself to be exciting.

Television coverage has since improved immeasurably, with longer hours, action replays and, above all, colour pictures. But before the advent of these refinements, golf had a second big boost in 1953. Dwight Eisenhower became President of the United States. As the ill-fated Prince of Wales had made golf a subject of conversation for the chattering classes in Britain before the war, Eisenhower popularised golf in America. He was a member of Augusta and had a putting green laid out in the White House grounds. Other presidents – lately Gerald Ford, George Bush and Bill Clinton – have since taken up the torch. Ford's vice-president, Spiro T. Agnew, became the butt of countless jokes as he brought a new meaning to the notion of taking the game to the people. His errant shots regularly inflicted injuries on those who diced

THE MAN BEHIND THE MONEY *Mark McCormack (right, top) began his career in sports management on the basis of a handshake agreement with Palmer. Today he is arguably the most powerful figure in the sport. He could hardly have got off to a more auspicious start. Jack Nicklaus (right) was another early McCormack – client, as was Gary Player (above). They were the original Big Three, although maybe Big Four would have been a more apt description.*

with death while watching him play in pro-ams. Bob Hope used to joke that Agnew didn't decide which course he was playing until after he'd hit his opening tee shot.

The public became hooked on golf in the wake of Eisenhower's example. The tour prospered because of this increased interest and in 1958 the prize fund broke the $1 million barrier. In that year the leading money-winner and Masters champion was one Arnold Daniel Palmer; the third factor, the missing link.

Palmer won tournaments, lots of them, and did so with style. He simultaneously introduced the words 'charge' and 'charisma' into the lexicon of golf. He not only played well but also looked good. He was to post-war golf what Hagen was between the wars; a hero for everyone. Watching him merely hitch up his trousers, the unconscious mannerism that became his trademark, was enough to drive grown men to frenzy. He enthralled women who didn't know the difference

between a duck-hook and duck soup. He was followed religiously by a loyal band of boisterous supporters who acquired the name 'Arnie's Army'. They celebrated raucously when Palmer won his 61 tour events and loved it when he became the first man to take his earnings past $100,000 in a season (in 1963) and $1 million in a career (in 1968).

What the fans did not like was the large shadow of Jack Nicklaus, who was indeed pretty large in those days, which put Palmer in the shade all too frequently. They began to cheer Palmer and jeer Nicklaus; to scream with delight when he hit a rare loose shot. At the 1967 US Open they were even equipped with banners reading 'Right Here, Jack' for display behind a hazard. Palmer himself disdained this behaviour, though there was precious little he could do to dampen the ardour of his fervent supporters. He and Nicklaus remained friends, albeit greater rivals, and they constituted two-thirds of golf's all-powerful Big Three.

The third man was Gary Player, who in 1961 became the first overseas golfer to head the Money List. On November 7 that year Nicklaus gave up chasing the ghost of Jones's record as an amateur and turned pro, with a reluctance surprising for a 21-year-old guaranteed at least $100,000 before he hit a ball in anger. He signed up with Mark McCormack, a Cleveland lawyer who was to make himself and his tremendous trio into exceedingly rich men.

From a famous handshake agreement with Palmer, his first client, McCormack has built up the world's foremost sports marketing and management company. He has had his fingers in more pies than the Queen of Hearts ever baked and in golf alone he has transformed the scene to the point where all the best players have managers, agents or representatives. Many of those players are under the umbrella of his flagship company, the International Management Group (IMG).

McCormack blazed the trail that led to players endorsing products which had nothing to do with their sport and stars being able to demand and receive tens of thousands of dollars in appearance fees from sponsors anxious to have them play in their tournaments. In short, he enabled his clients to capitalise on their skills.

McCormack is undoubtedly one of the most important men to have been involved in golf. His hunch about whom to sign in 1961 was as perceptive as the majority of his moves. The next year Palmer won the Masters and the Open, Nicklaus the US Open and Player the PGA. Palmer and Player remain in McCormack's stable but Nicklaus has long since bolted to set up his own conglomerate, Golden Bear Incorporated. (In January 1994, Greg Norman also flew the coop to set up his own organization, Great White Shark Enterprises, Inc., in what was a huge blow for IMG.)

Although the 1960s belonged to the Big Three, they did not have it all their own way. Billy Casper, who won the US Open twice and the Masters once,

topped the Money List in 1966 and 1968 with his consistent if not spectacular brand of quality golf, and Frank Beard surprisingly succeeded him in 1969. But a decade of expansion on every front was also accompanied by more than a little controversy.

Golf is renowned as a colourful sport but skin-wise there was only one colour on tour going into the 1960s – white. The PGA of America's regulations restricted membership to "*professional golfers of the Caucasian race, residing in North or South America*". In May 1961 this flagrantly racist policy led the state of California to refuse permission for the 1962 PGA Championship to be held in Los Angeles. The PGA removed the offending clause from its constitution later that year. At the Greater Hartford Open in August 1967, Charlie Sifford became the first black golfer to win on tour.

By then the rumblings of discontent about the way the PGA was administering the circuit were getting ominously louder. The tour players had been growing increasingly restless about operating within an organisation whose main base rested on the support of club pros. To cut a very long story short, they said to the PGA: "*We do things our way from now on.*" The PGA replied: "*No chance*", so the players formed a new body, the American Professional Golfers (APG).

The PGA felt it still held the whip hand in view of the courses, sponsors and television rights it had signed up. It was duly horrified to learn that these contracts weren't worth a nickel without the stars. Nobody was going to fork out good money to watch a tournament filled with anonymous sweater salesmen and grip repairers, otherwise known as club pros. On December 1, 1968, the APG announced a 28-event schedule for the new year, with in excess of $3.5 million prize money. The contest was over. In the time-honoured fashion, the PGA's climbdown was hailed as a compromise. The tour players were welcomed back to the fold and their own organization, the Tournament Policy Board, was created. It was the first step towards a full secession.

A BIG FIGURE *Although his portly appearance means that Billy Casper sometimes has to suffer the unkind nickname of Belly Casper, his golf in the 1960s was nothing to laugh at.*

SHARP CARD *In Las Vegas in 1991, Chip Beck became only the second man to shoot in the 50s in an official US PGA Tour event. He collected a $500,000 bonus from a hotel chain but could only finish third in the tournament.*

PRICE IS OFTEN RIGHT
Zimbabwe's Nick Price has become one of the dominant US tour players of the '90s, winning the US PGA Championship in 1992 and topping the Money List in 1993.

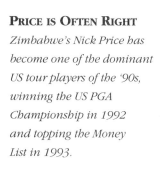

To the delight of the tour pros, in January 1969 Joe Dey agreed to leave his post as Executive Director of the USGA and became the first Commissioner of the Tournament Players' Division (TPD), the forerunner of today's US PGA Tour. Dey, then aged 61, was as respected as any figure in golf and his acceptance of the offer represented a major coup for the players, because it bestowed the Tournament Players' Division with immediate authority and status.

The split caused considerable bitterness among the club pros, who felt they had been kicked in the teeth and treated as second-class citizens by the boys on the glamour side of the game. Perhaps they had, but they had to resign themselves to a *fait accompli*. Dey served until March 1974, when Deane Beman (twice US Amateur and once British Amateur champion, but with only a moderate career as a tour pro behind him) assumed the reins.

On the golf course, Jack Nicklaus and Tom Watson dominated the tour in the 1970s. Only Lee Trevino (1970) and Johnny Miller (1974) were able to break their stranglehold on the title of leading money-winner. Indeed, their grip was not properly broken until Tom Kite took over from Watson in 1981 and ushered in a period of six different winners in as many years.

Also on the course, in 1977 Al Geiberger became the first player to break 60 in an official tour event with his second-round 59 at the Memphis Classic. There was always an asterisk against Geiberger's achievement because preferred lies were in operation when he shot his score, but there were no such question marks about the 59 (also on a par-72 layout) that Chip Beck fired in the third round of the 1991 Las Vegas Invitational. But unlike Geiberger, Beck didn't win the tournament.

In 1974, the year Beman arrived at the tour, the Tournament Players' Championship, American golf's much-vaunted candidate for the honour of being regarded as the 'fifth major', was launched. Jack Nicklaus won its first staging, and three of the first five, which helped its claims, but not sufficiently for it to be that highly regarded by anyone not involved in the tour's propaganda machine.

Since 1982, the tournament – now restyled as simply the Players Championship – has had a permanent home at the tour's headquarters in Ponte

Vedra, Florida, but the $2.5 million purse it offered in 1994 – when Greg Norman compiled an astonishing record score of 24 under par to become the fourth foreign winner, after Sandy Lyle (1987), Steve Elkington (1991) and Nick Price (1993) – was not the highest on the circuit. That belonged to the season-ending Tour Championship, without a title sponsor since the withdrawal of Nabisco in 1991, which boasted a staggering purse of $3 million.

Beman presided over the birth and rise of the Senior tour, which was formed in 1980 with two tournaments. Initially built upon the endeavours of the likes of Don January, Miller Barber and Chi Chi Rodriguez, it has been reinvigorated with the 50th birthdays of men like Palmer, Nicklaus and Trevino.

For the record, Palmer hasn't won on the Senior tour since 1988 (it's since 1973 on the regular tour); Nicklaus seldom plays on it, partly because he finds it hard to accept that he struggles to compete with the younger guys any more; Trevino, as one might expect, has taken to it with his customary gusto, being the leading money-winner in 1990 and 1992, the $1,190,518 he accumulated in the former year being more than Greg Norman made in heading the PGA Tour Money List.

In September 1992, Raymond Floyd won the GTE North Classic on the seniors, having won the Doral-Ryder Open six months earlier. He therefore became the first golfer to win on both tours in the same season. In 1993, the Senior tour named the US Senior Open, the PGA Seniors, the Seniors Players Championship and The Tradition as its four major championships. Apart from being possibly an even more questionable concept than the LPGA Tour's majors, this does not accord with Gary Player's idea that the British Seniors is really the fourth of the four (see page 56).

However, there is no disputing that Beman made the US tour a very lucrative place to make a living, and none of the figures mentioned at the start of this chapter take into consideration the vast fees some players can command for endorsing a host of products, not necessarily golf-related. In March 1994, Beman announced his retirement as commissioner, officially with effect from the end of 1995 but in practice as soon as a suitable replacement could be appointed. His

NOT QUITE RIGHT SAID FRED *The smooth-swinging Fred Couples was the dominant American player of 1992, but things didn't go so smoothly for him off the course. Although he won the Masters and headed the Money List, he also got involved in an expensive divorce suit with his ex-wife.*

successor will have a sound base from which to work and an exceedingly tough act to follow.

Several of Beman's decisions have been controversial, notably his determination to get involved in the protracted lawsuit with Karsten (see page 30).

Also, many leading players abhor Beman's introduction of the all-exempt tour, which means the top-125 players on the Money List each year are exempt from pre-qualifying for tournaments. Critics complain that this has led to too many players being content to make a cushy living off tenth-place cheques. But the all-exempt tour, as with so many practices established in the United States, has been copied in Europe, which is where we turn to next.

THE PGA EUROPEAN TOUR

EUROPE'S EXTENDER *Ken Schofield has supervised an astonishing growth in the European tour, not least because of his policy of taking the tour out of Europe.*

SEVEN UP *In 1947 Norman von Nida won a record seven tournaments in England. Dick Burton, who won the Open at St Andrews in 1939 is under the umbrella.*

Madeira. Morocco. Dubai. Thailand. Tenerife. Sounds an exotic itinerary, but those destinations don't sound like what they actually were.

Those places – one in the Middle East, one in the Far East, one in Africa and the other two Atlantic islands that are nearer Africa than Europe – were the first five stops on the 1994 PGA European Tour. There is talk of South Africa and Qatar for the future.

These days, the tour might more appropriately be named the International Tour, with a motto of 'Have clubs, will travel – anywhere'. The pioneers of aviation didn't manage to shrink the globe as much as Ken Schofield has since he took over as the European tour supremo in 1975 and inherited a schedule of 17 tournaments and official prize-money of around £500,000. By 1994, he had converted the equivalent statistics to over 40 official and tour-approved tournaments with prize-money of some £24 million.

The multi-ethnic circuit the modern European tour has become could hardly have been envisaged in the 1930s as British professionals – Henry Cotton excepted, of course – were reluctantly coming to terms with the unpalatable truth that they were a poor second best to the Americans.

The British and Continental tours used to be separate entities. The latter was basically a string of national Opens throughout mainland Europe; the former was operated by the British PGA which, as in the United States, existed primarily for the benefit of club professionals. The tour, such as it was, originally consisted of something like a tournament a month. The Vardon Trophy, named after Harry Vardon and awarded to the season's leading money-winner for topping the Order of Merit (the slightly quaint European term for Money List), was not instituted until 1937, when it was claimed by Charlie Whitcombe.

In the post-war years British golf was dominated by Commonwealth players like Bobby Locke and Peter Thomson, who almost shared the Open Championship between them. Another Australian, Norman von Nida,

won a record seven tournaments, all in England, in 1947. That mark has never been bettered, but in 1953 a Belgian, Flory van Donck, matched it with seven wins in six countries, including five continental Opens.

In 1958, Peter Alliss won the Italian, Spanish and Portuguese Opens in consecutive weeks on one particularly fruitful excursion. Alliss, who is now famous throughout the world as a television commentator, was one of a group of touring British professionals of high, but not the highest, calibre. He, Eric Brown, Bernard Hunt, Dai Rees, Christy O'Connor, Neil Coles and others all made a good living from their travels, but the gulf between the British players and the cream of American golf was distressingly emphasized every two years when the latter would customarily thrash their opponents in the Ryder Cup. The absence of the Open Championship trophy from a British mantelpiece from 1951 to 1969 was a further manifestation of the truth that the tournament circuit in Britain and Europe was merely a pale shadow of the one across the Atlantic.

Then, much as in America, three things happened. In America, these were television, President Eisenhower and Arnold Palmer. In Europe, they were the big ball, Tony Jacklin and John Jacobs.

In 1968 the British PGA, heeding those who considered the 1.68-inch ball to be a factor behind America's supremacy in professional golf, announced that the big ball would be compulsory in all its tournaments for a three-year experimental period. This controversial decision heralded the beginning of the end of the 1.62-inch ball for professionals (though it was permitted in the Open until 1974) and initiated the process by which all club golfers in Britain today play with the big ball.

The chances of the ruling being revoked were reduced within 18 months when Tony Jacklin won the 1969 Open at Lytham (ironically, with the small ball) and within another 12 months they had vanished altogether in the wake of Jacklin's massacre of the Americans in their own national championship (this time with the big one). British golf had its king, and the time was ripe to capitalize on his success.

In 1971, John Jacobs was appointed Tournament Director-General of the PGA, relieving the then secretary, Major John Bywaters, of a massive chunk of his colossal workload. Jacobs was brought in to make the tour side more business-like, and that he did, proving himself to be as astute an administrator as he was capable professional and is esteemed teacher.

He did not have an easy baptism. Three major sponsors had pulled out after the 1970 season, including Players following the fiasco mentioned in the introduction to this chapter. The continental tournaments suddenly looked extremely attractive, and six of them – the Algarve, Spanish, Italian, French, German and Swiss Opens – counted for the Ryder Cup points table and the Order of Merit in 1971 by guaranteeing a minimum purse of £10,000, more money than any other event then organized under the auspices of the PGA.

It was into this cold climate that Jacobs stepped. He shuffled the schedule so that the richest tournaments were allocated the best dates, and during those weeks he prohibited his star players from competing outside Europe. He co-ordinated the continental Opens as part of his package and stipulated minimum prize funds for Order of Merit events, which lost him some sponsors but gained others (even John Player again, until the company expensively discovered that Turnberry can be about as suitable as the Arctic for the staging of a golf tournament in the autumn).

Jacobs set himself a target of £200,000 in total prize money for 1972. He doubled that, a spectacular vindication of his insistence on not having to answer to a committee and financial evidence of the drawing power of Jacklin and Peter Oosterhuis. The latter, a huge gangling man of 6'5", collected the Vardon Trophy in four successive seasons from 1971. He then left Britain for America.

Oosterhuis had led the Masters by three shots after three rounds in 1973 and was to finish only a shot adrift of Tom Watson in the 1982 Open at Troon, but he was only to win once in 12 years of arduous campaigning on the US tour, proof positive of how relatively easy it was then to excel in Europe compared

RETURN OF THE NATIVE
Along with Tony Jacklin, Peter Oosterhuis was Europe's other top-class golfer in the early 1970s. He topped the Order of Merit for four straight years before leaving to pursue his competitive career in America. An attempted comeback on the European tour in 1993 proved abortive.

to the United States. Oosterhuis resumed a competitive career in Europe on the eve of his 45th birthday at a tournament in Italy in April 1993. He missed the cut. His total money-winnings of £32,127 in 1974 were less than the cheque New Zealand's Greg Turner pocketed for being runner-up, 19 years on, that week in Rome. Times indeed change, just as they wait for no man. Oosterhuis has since taken the job of Director of Golf at Stockley Park in London. His 'comeback' saw him miss 13 cuts from 13 starts.

The year Oosterhuis departed from British shores also saw the creation of a separate Tournament Players' Division within the PGA (an idea copied from the United States) and the departure of Jacobs from the hot seat. Ken Schofield replaced him and the subsequent increase in the prosperity of the tour has been inexorable.

Schofield would readily admit that he was assisted enormously in his initial endeavours by the exploits of Severiano Ballesteros. These two men were the second wave of the revolution.

Ballesteros was a virtual unknown when he

PART OF A TEAM *Manuel Pinero was one of several fine Spanish professionals to make an impact in Europe around the same time as Ballesteros. Spain won the World Cup with Seve in 1976 and 1977 and without him in 1982 and 1984.*

A FLAVOUR OF EUROPE *Germany's Bernhard Langer in action at Gleneagles during the 1992 Bell's Scottish Open.*

audaciously led the field by two strokes with a round to play in the 1976 Open Championship at Royal Birkdale. His own recklessness and the brilliance of Johnny Miller cost him the title but he finished tied for second with Jack Nicklaus, thanks to a characteristically daring and ingenious chip shot to the final green. Three weeks later Ballesteros won the Dutch Open and from that day on his career flourished almost in tandem with the fortunes of the tour. Exactly 10 years on, he became the first man to earn in excess of £1 million prize-money in Europe when he won the Dutch Open again. On both occasions his victory margin was eight shots.

Ballesteros was not the only successful continental golfer in the mid-1970s. His fellow Spaniards Manuel Pinero, Francisco Abreu and Salvador Balbuena were also tournament victors in 1976, as was Italy's Baldovino Dassu, but the potential of the prodigy from Pedrena excited everybody. He headed the Order of Merit in 1976 and that winter he and Pinero had the nerve to beat the crack American duo of Jerry Pate and Dave Stockton (respectively the reigning US Open and PGA champions) at the World Cup in California.

It is no exaggeration to equate Ballesteros with Arnold Palmer. They both gave the impression of trying to beat the golf course into submission (I use the past tense now that Palmer is beyond his prime and Ballesteros is generally more clinical and less cavalier in his methods of attack). Both men could putt like demons – indeed Ballesteros still can, employing his putter with the deadly precision of a finely-crafted sword. They pulled in the crowds with their exciting brand of golf, which in turn attracted sponsors and television. Finally, both breathed life into their respective circuits at critical moments.

In Europe the timing could not have been more propitious. At the conclusion of the 1976 season, Schofield announced the formal merger of the British and Continental tours under the united banner of the European Tournament Players' Division, outside the PGA. This has subsequently evolved into the modern PGA European Tour.

Ballesteros was the principal reason for players from the continent being drafted in as reinforcements to help the ailing British cause in the Ryder Cup from 1979 onwards. That year he won the Open Championship; the next April he bearded the Americans in their own den by winning the Masters. Such stirring deeds encouraged other Europeans to really believe '*If he can do it, so can I.*'

And they have. The major championship performances of Ballesteros, Bernhard Langer, Sandy Lyle, Nick Faldo, Ian Woosnam and Jose Maria Olazabal – Europe's 'Big Six' – have been outlined in the foregoing chapters, but a few additional details are in order in this section.

After topping the Order of Merit in 1976, Ballesteros retained it the next two years and reclaimed it again in 1986, 1988 and 1991. In both 1986 and 1988 – perhaps his best-ever year, when he won the Open Championship, four other times in Europe and once apiece in the United States and Japan – his stroke average was below 70, a feat that emulated Byron Nelson's sensational and previously unique performance on the US tour in 1945.

Ballesteros had won four of his five majors before any other members of the famous five had won one. Langer was the first to follow him, at the Masters in 1985, a victory he repeated in 1993. He won the Order of Merit in 1981 and 1984, and by May 1994 he had won 29 European tour events plus three in the States, including those two Masters.

Ballesteros and Langer have been inspirations to the development of the game in their respective countries; the three Britons proof that an unreliable and unhelpful climate need not be an insurmountable impediment to exceptional athletic achievement provided the individual has talent and the necessary work ethic. There are few men fortunate enough to be born with the innate skills that Lyle and Woosnam possess; few who have Faldo's absolute self-belief and dedication. And Faldo, of course, having given Ballesteros a 4-0 and 5-1 start in the majors, matched the Spaniard's tally with victory at the 1992 Open.

For the record, by May 1994 Lyle had amassed 18 wins in Europe and six in the United States; Woosnam was on 24 European tour wins and three in America;

THE PAYMASTER

Appearance money was not invented by Seve Ballesteros, but it was his skills in particular that led to its flourishing in Europe.

while Faldo had accumulated 29 European tour titles and three in the States. As with Langer, two of those latter three were Masters titles.

These five are manifestly players of a particular generation. Ranging from Ballesteros through to Woosnam, their birthdays are separated by less than 11 months. Olazabal is almost a decade younger, having turned 28 two months before his Masters victory in 1994. That was his third win in America – one of them being his 12-shot demolition of the field in the World Series in 1990 – to add to the 14 he had in Europe.

But despite the exploits of these stars, it would be a mistake to assume that all has been sweetness and light since the dawn of the 1980s, when the tour moved into its new offices at the Wentworth Club near London.

Back then, there were ructions between the tour and Ballesteros over his demands to be paid appearance money, which, although he by no means invented the concept nor was the sole beneficiary of it, was a crusade indelibly associated with him.

His reasoning was simple. If tournament promoters were prepared to pay money to entice American golfers over to play in their tournament – very possibly players who had not won two major championships, as Ballesteros had at that stage, and who would not be such a draw for spectators – why should he, Ballesteros, be denied the opportunity of receiving similar treatment just because he was a European? Surely, he argued, this was reverse discrimination.

MATCHLESS *The World Matchplay Championship at Wentworth could be described as European golf's rite of autumn. Although the field is small – these days 12 players – it is an excellent international event. Nick Faldo, driving here, was the winner in 1989 and 1992.*

The row reached an unhappy peak in 1981 when Ballesteros shunned the European tour for much of the year. That was why, to his intense chagrin and to the total detriment of any chance Europe had of winning, Ballesteros was left out of the Ryder Cup team at Walton Heath that year.

The subject of appearance money has never been resolved satisfactorily. It has long been prohibited for a player to approach a sponsor or promoter and demand money for playing in his tournament, but so what? There is no need for a player to do that. That's a manager's job, and the rules have never barred managers or agents from doing it. Besides, the best players don't so much have to solicit offers as choose which ones to accept from the plethora of proposals they are deluged with.

With effect from the start of the 1992 season, the European tour announced that sanctions would be imposed against tournaments that paid appearance money, but the chief effect of the revised regulations was simply to redefine 'appearance money'. No longer could a player, legally, be paid merely for turning up to play in a tournament. But if he did something extra – like making a speech, or opening a clubhouse extension – then that could be used to justify whatever fee had been negotiated, which was the same means of getting around the same problem that had long pertained in America.

This exercise in grammatical semantics did something to help Schofield, who had been under pressure from his journeyman pros to outlaw appearance money, but it hasn't remotely hampered the path to riches of the most sought-after stars. Their managers have just had to get a little more creative, more inspired, with the wording of their commitment contracts, while the players may be compelled to attend a few more dinners than they did before. Cynical? Maybe. Accurate? Definitely.

Historically, although Ballesteros lost the battle with the tour over a decade ago, his argument has won the war. Appearance money helped to build the European tour. First, it was the vehicle that tournament promoters used to lure over the best American players

– why else would they have left the superior courses and comforts of their own tour? – and later it was the guarantee of appearance money that persuaded the likes of Ballesteros and Faldo to spend more time on the European circuit rather than amid the bigger cheques and better facilities of the United States. That in turn made the European tour a more attractive proposition for would-be sponsors, and a more well-remunerated place to earn a living for less gifted golfers. You could call it a delicious circle.

The issue of appearance money will never go away so long as sponsors want to attract the best players to their tournament, which means them not playing in someone else's. And that will always be the case. The irony is that if the John Player Classic was to be launched today, the organisers would probably not even try to sign up any Americans. They would be delighted to make do with Messrs Ballesteros, Faldo, Langer, Lyle and Woosnam – for a fee, of course.

Apart from Ballesteros, those players are all managed by Mark McCormack's IMG, which was referred to in the preceding section. Although IMG was founded in the United States, its influence is far more pervasive in Europe. Some would say sinister.

In addition to handling the business affairs of many of the tour's best golfers, IMG promotes and administers several European tournaments, which means it is regularly in what might gently be described as the potentially invidious position of having to make financial arrangements for one of its player-clients to play in one of its tournament-client's events.

McCormack himself has given a lot to golf in Europe, perhaps notably in creating the World Matchplay Championship, held annually at Wentworth, in 1964. The tournament is unquestionably the best individual matchplay event on the calendar and is invariably one of the highlights of the European season. McCormack also founded the Alfred Dunhill Cup nations team event, which is staged each autumn at St Andrews.

McCormack is a member of the R & A and his business acumen played a pertinent part in persuading that august body to become switched on to the commercial possibilities of the Open in the 1970s. But into the 1990s, many people involved in European golf

CLIMACTIC *Since 1988, when Volvo assumed overall sponsorship of the tour, the European season has ended with the Volvo Masters at Valderrama in southern Spain.*

are uneasy about the way in which IMG, through its television arm, TWI, has been allowed to join forces with the PGA European Tour in the establishment of Tour Productions, a joint venture between the two companies that films European tour events and then controls the distribution of the footage outside the country of origin. And disquiet at the way the tour has acquiesced in IMG's expansion into the very hierarchy of the sport was refuelled in October 1992 when the two organizations celebrated the launch of European Golf Design, a merger of their existing golf course architecture operations.

Certainly, all this goes a substantial way towards indicating just how much modern professional tournament golf has inextricably become entangled with high finance and corporate marketing. This was never clearer than in May 1987 when Schofield announced that Volvo, the Swedish car giant, was to be the overall sponsor of the tour for five years from January 1988, an agreement that has since been extended to the end of 1995. The fee remains a secret, but it runs into tens of millions of pounds. In addition

to this munificence, the company also sponsors the PGA Championship, the tour's flagship event, and the Volvo Masters, the season-ending climax held at Valderrama on the Costa del Sol.

And the big money is not confined to the regular tour. The PGA European Seniors Tour had £1.1 million on offer in 13 tournaments in 1994, only its third full season, although the promise of growth in the immediate future surely has to be limited. Unlike in the United States, the best European players of all-time are still in their prime. For Faldo, the seniors is 13 years away. And the PGA European Challenge Tour, the satellite circuit equivalent of the Nike Tour across the Atlantic, which was constituted in 1990, boasted 47 tournaments in 16 different countries in 1994, worth nearly £2 million.

During the course of its development and flourishing, the European tour has adopted several other American innovations, such as the qualifying school (in 1976); the establishment of a separate body, PGA European Tour Enterprises Ltd, to exploit the earnings potential of the tour's activities (1984); and the introduction of the all-exempt tour (1985).

But in some areas at least, things have not changed so dramatically over the years. As the composition of the Ryder Cup teams since 1979 has illustrated, it is still Britain which breeds the majority of Europe's leading players. The highest continental representation in the Ryder Cup was five in 1985, while in the subsequent four matches the figure was respectively four, four, three and five, with Ballesteros and Langer being constants.

Over recent seasons, several British golfers – Faldo, Lyle and Woosnam apart – have made their mark at the top of the sport in Europe while not exactly threatening to win major championships. Howard Clark, Mark James and Sam Torrance have been stalwarts of past Ryder Cup sides, while Ireland's Ronan Rafferty headed the Order of Merit in 1989. As we move deeper into the 1990s, so other British golfers suggest they have the ability to graduate into the serious big-time. Scotland's Colin Montgomerie, who was third in the 1992 US Open, topped the Order of Merit in 1993, thereby maintaining a remarkable progression that saw him improve his Order of Merit placing every year since he turned pro in 1987. A major may be the next step for him. Barry Lane, David Gilford, Paul Broadhurst, Jim Payne and Steven Richardson of England, and David Feherty – who is now based in the United States – and Darren Clarke of Ireland, all have the talent and the potential to develop further.

But the major growth area for golf in Europe undoubtedly lies on the continent. Blinkered British professionals used to complain about their cross-Channel colleagues gaining a larger slice of the tournament cake, which meant extra hassle and cost for them to compete abroad. These days, everyone accepts that's just the way things have to be if the players want all

TRUE BRIT *Throughout the 1980s, Yorkshireman Howard Clark was one of Europe's most reliable performers in the Ryder Cup.*

IN SEVE'S STEPS *Jose Maria Olazabal was a Ryder Cup star in tandem with Ballesteros before he won the Masters in 1994.*

REACHING FOR TOP GEAR *Anders Forsbrand has been at the forefront of the Swedish drive to produce a genuinely world-class male golfer.*

that prize-money. It is not feasible to operate a tour from mid-January to early November without spending a considerable amount of time in the warmer weather of southern Europe – or indeed, spending some of it outside Europe altogether. In fact, of the 38 official events on the 1994 tour schedule, only eight were in mainland Britain or Ireland, although that did not include the Alfred Dunhill Cup or the World Matchplay Championship.

Distinctly, the tour is no longer the preserve of the British. Spain in particular has regularly produced quality players, in numbers out of all proportion to the popularity of the game among Spaniards. Ballesteros is the outstanding example and Olazabal the most recent.

As a first-year 'rookie' professional in 1986,

Olazabal, who had enjoyed a glittering amateur career, was second to Ballesteros on the Order of Merit. In 1987, he was winless on tour but terrific in the Ryder Cup at Muirfield Village, and in the five subsequent seasons he was never worse than seventh on the Order of Merit while never actually winning it. His victory at Augusta in April 1994 was no more than most people expected. His first major had generally been regarded as a case of 'when' rather than 'if'.

The Swedes, too, have quite an impressive array of talent, with players like Joakin Haeggman (who made the Ryder Cup team in 1993 and won his singles match), Anders Forsbrand and Robert Karlsson to the fore. Appropriately, like Volvo, the Swedish golf machine seems able to produce competent performers with admirable rapidity. Sweden won the World Cup and the Dunhill Cup in 1991.

The signs of a continental emergence from the shadow of British numerical superiority were reinforced with Latin and Gallic flavour in spring 1993. Costantino Rocca of Italy won a tournament in Lyon, France, two weeks before Jean Van de Velde of France won a tournament in Rome, Italy – the very one in which Peter Oosterhuis made that belated and unsuccessful return to European action.

Rocca's win was the first by an Italian on the European tour since Massimo Mannelli captured the Italian Open in 1980; Van de Velde's the first by a Frenchman since Jean Garaialde won the German Open in 1970. Whether Van de Velde will ultimately prove to be another Arnaud Massy or merely another 'oh no' remains to be seen, but, as has been the case since Ballesteros first demonstrated that continental golfers could actually play a bit, the European tour promises to be an arena well worth watching over the coming years.

BIG MONTY JOINS THE BIG LEAGUE *By winning the season-ending Volvo Masters in 1993, Colin Montgomerie ended the year as Europe's leading money-winner and now has his sights set on a major championship.*

OTHER INTERNATIONAL CIRCUITS

Tournament golf in Japan has been one of the more remarkable growth stories in sport during the latter half of this century. In a major upset, Japan won the 1957 World Cup (then called the Canada Cup) at Kasumigaseki, just outside Tokyo. Ever since, the country has taken to the game with almost absurd enthusiasm, especially given that the scarcity of suitable land for golf and the consequently exorbitant expense of joining a club – £2 million is the highest point ever reached at the Koganei club in Tokyo – mean it is out of reach for the majority of people who like to call themselves golfers. For them, it's a life of making do with hitting balls on a driving range.

As far as the Japanese PGA Tour goes, by 1994 this state of affairs had led to a calendar of 38 tournaments, running from March to December and worth over £20 million. Close to a further £9 million was available in senior, satellite and other miscellaneous events. However, this represented a total drop of some £1.6 million on 1993, the first such indications of the recession biting into what was previously thought to be a ridiculously resilient marketplace, so the future growth of the tour cannot presently be considered the cert it once seemed.

The stars of that shock World Cup victory – Torakichi (Pete) Nakamura and Koichi Ono – have been superseded by Isao Aoki, Masashi (Jumbo) Ozaki and Tsuneyuki (Tommy) Nakajima as the heroes of Japanese golf. Aoki, as outlined on page 36, has enjoyed success outside his homeland, which is what sets him apart from the rest. On the whole, oriental golfers tend to travel hopelessly.

Of course, being forced to deal with a strange language, indeed a different alphabet, an alien culture and unfamiliar cuisine mean that it is proportionately tougher for Japanese golfers to excel in the west, whether that be in the United States or Europe, but that is what they need to do in order to establish their credentials at the highest level. Aoki alone has managed to do it.

The truth is that the very wealth of Japanese golf is

its malady. It means that the best players are reluctant to forego the huge purses and commercial endorsements available at home, and so they lock themselves into their own circuit. This in turn means that they suffer from a lack of international competition, and sometimes it shows. They are terribly vulnerable to the predators from America and Europe, the marauding 'gaijin' invaders, who swoop down on their three most lucrative tournaments each November.

The three premier events of genuinely international status in Japan – they do not include the Japan Open – are the Taiheiyo Masters, the Dunlop Phoenix and the Casio World Open. The former was inaugurated in 1972 and has only been won by a Japanese golfer seven times; the Dunlop Phoenix, the biggest prize of all, was launched in 1974 and Nakajima (in 1985) has been the only native champion to date; and the Casio tournament began in 1981 and the only Japanese winners have been Aoki, twice, and Ozaki. In 1993, those tournaments were claimed, respectively, by Australia's Greg Norman, South Africa's Ernie Els and America's Tom Lehman, and all told 12 of the 39 titles on the JPGA Tour in 1993 were marked for export.

Jumbo Ozaki has been Japan's most outstanding performer on the domestic stage for so long that his longevity is remarkable however sceptically one views his achievements in a world-wide context. His first full year on the tour was 1971, when he won five times. In 1972, he won ten times. Although the middle years of his career were beset by mediocrity, he was back on track by 1989, when he won seven times. In 1992, aged 45, he won six tournaments to head the Money List again. In 1993, he was second to Hajime Meshiai, although that still netted him close to £900,000.

But Jumbo's image as a golfing giant at home has been dwarfed by his comparative failure overseas, even though in May 1994 he was 11th on the Sony Rankings, a system that rates the best men professional golfers in the world based on their performances on a graded three-year computation. (The system was devised by Mark McCormack and launched by the

IMPORT THREAT *Tommy Nakajima was the only native winner in the first 20 years of the Dunlop Phoenix, Japan's richest tournament.*

SUMMIT MEETING *The imposing snow-capped peak of Mount Fuji, the symbol of Japan, provides a magnificent backdrop for the golfers at the Taiheiyo Masters, held at Gotemba each November.*

Japanese-owned Sony Corporation in April 1986. It has enjoyed a gradually increasing degree of acceptance, helped enormously by having the sanction of the R & A, which guarantees a place in the Open Championship to anyone in the top-50 on the rankings after the preceding US Open.)

Ozaki has finished as high as eighth in the Masters and sixth in the US Open, in 1973 and 1989 respectively, which gives a further indication of how long he has maintained his position at the forefront of Japanese golf, but he has never threatened to win a major. Jumbo has two brothers, Tateo (Jet) and Naomichi (Joe), who can both play a bit, too, especially when they're playing in Japan. Joe topped the JPGA Money List in 1991.

Neither has Nakajima been able to translate his estimable prowess in Japan into titles abroad. His ability deserves a better tribute in history than he is likely to be given on the basis of his foreign forays. He is still remembered for the 13 he took on the 13th hole in the 1978 Masters and for the four swipes he took before emerging from the Road Hole bunker on the 17th at St Andrews while in the course of running up a

nine during the Open Championship three months later. In the 1986 Open at Turnberry, Nakajima trailed the leader, Greg Norman, by one shot entering the final round. He three-putted the first green from 10 feet for a double-bogey six and his challenge was finished before he had hardly started.

Nakajima recently passed his 40th birthday. So has Meshiai. With Jumbo Ozaki, winner of the JPGA Money List in four of the past six seasons, hardly in the first flush of youth either, and with Aoki having already turned 50 and doing very well, thank you, on the US Senior tour – in 1992, he won on his fourth senior outing in between collecting two titles on the regular Japanese circuit – the future success of Japan's golfing dynasty looks decidedly less assured than the perpetuation of its imperial crown. Two or three years ago, there were great hopes for Ryoken (Ricky) Kawagishi, but so far this exciting young prospect has not developed to the extent that one can say anything kinder than he has potential. By and large, Japanese golfers have been held back not so much by their celebrated inscrutability as by their equally notorious insularity. The Japanese may sponsor the Sony

JUMBO HAS NOT FORGOTTEN HOW TO PLAY *Masashi Ozaki, known to golf fans the world over as Jumbo, has been at the top of the game in his home country for over 20 years. He is also one of the most powerful drivers in the game, seeming to launch the ball rather than merely hit it.*

Rankings, but they are a long way from dominating it.

The Japanese tour is not the only source of revenue for tournament golf professionals on the look-out for eastern promise. The 1994 Asian Tour, which was sponsored by Newsweek magazine, comprised ten tournaments worth some £2.3 million. The circuit is an amalgam of the national Opens of exotic eastern countries, like Hong Kong, Malaysia, India and Thailand, and it runs from February to April, concluding with a tournament in Japan before the Japanese tour itself gets underway in earnest. In 1994, Jumbo Ozaki won that tournament, the Dunlop Open,

FAIRWAY TO GO *The Hong Kong Open, one of the stops on the Asian Tour, pays to pull a few stars over to the colony each February. This picture shows Bernhard Langer, while Tom Watson and Seve Ballesteros are among other to have made the trip.*

for a fourth time, but the honour of heading the final Asian Order of Merit went to Carlos Franco, one of the three Paraguayans who had shockingly played a part in his country's victories over Scotland and Wales in the Alfred Dunhill Cup at St Andrews the previous autumn.

The Asian Tour has traditionally been an arena of good pickings for novice players from elsewhere around the world – for example, Payne Stewart plied his trade there in the formative years of his career, winning two tournaments in 1981. Recently, the odd superstar has been lured over. Tom Watson's win in the Hong Kong Open in 1992 was his first anywhere in over four years.

The Asian Tour has spawned some decent players, including Tze-Chung Chen, who should have won the US Open in 1985 and surely would have done had he not taken an eight on the 5th hole in the final round. With that disastrous blemish, Chen's four-shot lead had disappeared. The chief reason he managed to perpetrate that score was by hitting the ball twice with one misplayed chip shot, which earned T. C. the cruel but inevitable nickname of 'Two-Chip'.

Before him there had been another Taiwanese, Lu Liang Huan, known to one and all as Mr Lu, who chased Lee Trevino down to the final putt at the 1971 Open at Royal Birkdale, pausing only, it seemed, to doff his pork pie hat to the crowd at every conceivable excuse.

The heartland of the Asian Tour has also proved to be something of a salvation for the PGA Tour of Australasia, which takes a winter break from the beginning of March to the end of September. Indeed, since the entire future of the Australasian tour was thrown into jeopardy by the cancellation of three of its richest tournaments in 1992, as the local economies buckled and Japanese investment in Australian resorts was cut back, some formal sort of alliance with the Asian Tour had to be the next logical step. Details still have to be finalised, but a meeting between representatives of the two bodies in September 1993 was in favour of a formal merger, thereby creating a 25-tournament schedule, over the next couple of years.

The 1993 Australasian circuit had 18 tournaments, visiting not only Australia and New Zealand but also Singapore, Malaysia and Hong Kong. (Europe's Ken Schofield is evidently not the only tour boss with a

shaky grasp of geography.) The tour's purses amounted to almost £3 million that season, with its major events being the Australian Masters in February and the Australian Open in November.

Down the years, there have been many fine Antipodean golfers, some of whom have won major championships – Peter Thomson, Kel Nagle, David Graham, Greg Norman, Wayne Grady and Ian Baker-Finch from Australia and Bob Charles from New Zealand. As well as winning the British Open in 1986 and 1993, and being Australia's foremost international golfer for most of the time since the late 1970s, Norman has topped the US Money List twice and the European Order of Merit once.

Lately, we have seen the rise of the new breed of golfers from Down Under. Steve Elkington has won two prestigious titles on the US tour – the 1991 Players Championship and the 1992 Tournament of Champions, as well as the 1992 Australian Open – with one of the most widely admired swings in the game. Craig Parry joined the US tour in 1992 after winning

four times in Europe and several times in Australia, including three times in 1992. Parry also held a three-stroke lead with 16 holes to play in the 1992 Masters before a recalcitrant putter and the rooting of the Augusta crowd in favour of his playing partner, Fred Couples, stretched his nerves beyond breaking point. And Brett Ogle, who had only won once in a reasonably prosperous European tour career, had won twice on the US tour by spring 1994, just over 12 months after heading the 1992 qualifying school and while still short of his 30th birthday.

Europe has long been a happy hunting ground for Australian pros, with Peter Senior (who headed the 1993 Australasian Order of Merit), Rodger Davis and Mike Harwood between them collecting some high-calibre events like the PGA Championship, Volvo Masters and European Open to go with their haul of the cream of Australian titles.

But the most potent Australian golfer of the late 1990s and the next century could well be Robert Allenby. Aged 21, the same age as Norman when he

FACE FOR THE FUTURE (1)
Australia's Robert Allenby should be one of golf's bona fide stars into the next century. Aged 21, he was the leading money-winner in his country in 1992.

won on his fourth outing as a professional in 1976, Allenby had two wins and topped Australasian Money List in 1992; this after coming within a stroke of tying for the 1991 Australian Open while still an amateur.

Across the Tasman Sea, two young Maoris who helped New Zealand win the World Amateur Team Championship for the first time in Canada in 1992 could have sensational careers ahead of them. Michael Campbell won the Australian Amateur in 1992 before, aged 24 and in only his fifth professional tournament, winning on the Australasian tour in February 1993. And 19-year-old Philip Tataurangi won the New Zealand Amateur Championship in April 1993 by beating Rob Elkington (brother of Steve) in the final. The previous November, Tataurangi had been third, one shot and one place ahead of Campbell, also then an amateur, in a tournament in New Zealand won by Nick Price. Tataurangi has now joined the professional ranks, so New Zealand looks well placed to maintain its momentum as an emerging force in world golf. Not that it had been doing too badly anyway. In one week in May 1993, three Kiwis – Grant Waite, Greg Turner, and Bob Charles – won on the US tour, the European tour and the US Senior tour, respectively.

Across the Indian Ocean lies South Africa. The sporting prospects for this formerly politically beleaguered and economically ravaged country look brighter these days. The republic has two tours. The

main one, the First National Bank (FNB) Tour, runs from November to March. In the 1993-4 season, it carried 10 tournaments with a total prize fund of around £1 million. The 1994 winter tour, from April to October, was scheduled to have 15 tournaments worth about £200,000. FNB is also pledged to support development programmes for youngsters, especially blacks and coloureds, to encourage growth and opportunites among the disadvantaged members of the community. At present, only some 60 of the 650 members of the PGA of South Africa are non-whites.

The region also boasts the Million Dollar Challenge, a select international, invitational event held at the luxurious Sun City resort in what used to be the controversial 'tribal homeland' of Bophuthatswana, some two hours from Johannesburg, until the South African government peremptorily abolished the 'country' in March 1994, ahead of South Africa's mould-breaking elections the following month. In December 1993, Zimbabwe's Nick Price crowned his glorious season by demolishing the field at Sun City by 12 shots to claim the eponymous first prize.

South African golf owes a massive debt to Bobby Locke, its first international ambassador, and Gary Player, who was a world-class golfer at a time when South Africa was ostracized by most of the civilized world. At least those that attempt to follow in these greats' footsteps should only have on-course

FROST IN AFRICA *The splendour of Sun City, the lavish gambling and entertainment complex in South Africa which hosts the Million Dollar Challenge each December. South Africa's David Frost won it three times in four years from 1989 – worth $1 million each time!*

traumas to contend with.

No one seems more surely destined to beat a hasty path to the top than Ernie Els, a strapping blond young man of 6' 3" who either side of his 23rd birthday won six of his home tour events in 1992, including the South African Open, PGA and Masters. Since he joined the European tour, he has continued to mature. He was fifth in the 1992 Open and sixth in 1993, seventh at the 1993 US Open, and eighth at the 1994 Masters. In addition to his aforementioned win at the Dunlop Phoenix in Japan in November 1993, in January 1994 Els opened with an 11-under-par 61 to set up his win in the Dubai Desert Classic, his first on the European tour.

The 1994 FNB Order of Merit was headed by Tony Johnstone, another regular European tour campaigner, as is his fellow-Zimbabwean, Mark McNulty. Johnstone won three times in the season, taking his career haul to 20. He also won his country's national Open in Harare in what was a landmark year for the championship. The Zimbabwe Open used to be a stop on the Safari Tour, which until a few years ago served European golfers as an alternative winter tune-up destination to Australia or South Africa. These days, the Safari Tour lumbers on in truncated form as part of the PGA European Challenge Tour but the 1993 'Zim Open', as the natives call it, was the first to be run by the PGA of South Africa, and it is likely that one day soon the administration of all Africa's major golf tournaments will be organized from Johannesburg.

The Australasian and South African tours offer alternative tournament golf on generally excellent courses not only for journeymen pros but also for the game's top players while the US and European tours are taking their brief winter breaks in the northern hemisphere. As it has in the development of the tour in Europe, appearance money plays a substantial role in determining which tournaments command the support of the elite; indeed, in South Africa, both FNB and the PGA openly embrace the payment of appearance money, acknowledging it to be the only way for them to get strong international fields.

This section began with a reference to golf's World Cup, which these days is one of many team competitions that occupy the autumn schedule. The World Cup, which is contested by two-man teams, the winners being the team with the lowest aggregate score over four rounds, was founded as the Canada Cup in Montreal in 1953, the realization of the cherished dream of an American philanthropist, John Jay Hopkins. Thirty years later, the organizers had learned that its principles, while worthy (the event sought to foster goodwill through golf), were no longer sufficient to grab the attention of the players. Its prize-money was meagre at a time when purses were soaring. That situation was eventually rectified and the World Cup has recouped some of its former status. Fred Couples and Davis Love won the trophy for the United States in both 1992 and 1993.

Other team events now clutter up the calendar. The rise in prize-money in the World Cup coincided with the launch of the Dunhill Cup, now Alfred Dunhill Cup, in 1985. This is a three-man team knockout tournament played annually at St Andrews. As if the fixture list were not congested enough already, another team event commenced in 1985, the Nissan Cup, for six-man teams from the tours of the United States, Europe, Australasia and Japan. That went through two more sponsors before 1991, when it died through lack of interest. You can have too much of a good thing. Time will tell whether the President's Cup, launched in September 1994 and contested between the United States and the Rest of the World except Europe (a sort of 'Not the Ryder Cup') will stay the distance.

Although there has been sporadic talk of some potentate, perhaps Mark McCormack, disturbing the current order of things by starting a maverick 'World Tour', golf is truly a world-wide sport already, the men's professional game practically inundated with companies apparently eager to pour ever more cash into its brimming coffers. McCormack himself was the prime mover behind the creation of the $2.7 million Johnnie Walker World Championship in 1991. Held at Tryall in Jamaica just before Christmas, Fred Couples, Nick Faldo and Larry Mize were its first three champions. But if you want to identify a genuine 'world champion', you could do worse than try Fiji's Vijay Singh. In 1993, he had top-three finishes on six different tours – in the United States, Europe, Japan, Asia, Australasia and South Africa. World Tour or not, it is safe to say that Vijay is Fiji's best golfer.

FACE FOR THE FUTURE (2)
Ernie Els has quickly matured from being the best young golfer in South Africa to one of the best under-30 golfers in the world.

CHAPTER SIX
WOMEN'S GOLF

The first woman golfer of note was Mary Queen of Scots, although she was not entirely an enviable example. She failed to survive the cut after being espied playing golf within 24 hours of the sudden death of her husband in 1567.

As if her would-be imitators were afraid of courting a similar conclusion to their careers, during the subsequent 300 years there were only desultory references to women playing golf. For example, a Fish Wives' Society was formed at Musselburgh, near Edinburgh, in the late 1700s, and in the first part of the 19th century women played golf at St Andrews, although they risked being branded as near-harlots. One Miss A. M. Stewart wrote: *"A damsel with even one modest putter in her hand was labelled a fast and almost disreputable person, definitely one to be avoided."* Try telling that to the Lady Captain.

Three centuries after Mary Queen of Scots lifted her head for the last time, the first ladies' golf clubs were founded – at St Andrews in 1867 and at Westward Ho! in Devon in 1868.

It has to be said that the cause of women's golf has not progressed a great deal at the cradle of the game. There are still no women members of the R & A and it was as recently as the 1965 Ladies' British Open Amateur Championship (hereinafter referred to as the British Amateur) at St Andrews that there occurred one of the more celebratedly misogynistic anecdotes in the long line of humiliations suffered by women golfers in Britain, where many have become resigned to being treated not so much as second-class citizens as a sub-species. A group of competitors were huddled in front of the R & A clubhouse (even the premises were then out-of-bounds to women), sheltering under their umbrellas from a dreadful storm, when a club official approached. Their immediate hopes that he was about to do the decent thing and invite them in were cruelly dashed when instead he asked them to lower their umbrellas because they were spoiling the view of the Old Course enjoyed by the members, comfortably ensconced in the warmth of the lounge.

Things were not so different when the Westward Ho! and North Devon Ladies' Club had 47 full members (ladies) and 23 associates (men), but at least that was in the last century. The women had their own nine-hole course separate from the men and play was restricted to *"every other Saturday between 1st May and 31st October"*, a regulation which is often retained in spirit today at many British clubs that have not woken up to the fact that some women actually work during the week. But those pioneering women of Westward Ho! did make a contribution to the game that millions of men have since been grateful for. Tired of trying to tuck their clubs under their arms, they invented the golf bag.

While it is probable that women golfers in Scotland played a similar course to the men, their English counterparts at Westward Ho! pursued a shorter form of the game; so short that it was considered reasonable to invoke a rule whereby a wooden putter was the only club allowed on the links. This tied in with the contemporary mores governing the way women played golf, as exemplified by Horace Hutchinson.

"We venture to suggest 70 or 80 yards as the average limit of a drive advisedly; not because we doubt a lady's power to make a longer drive but because that cannot well be done without raising the club above the shoulder. Now we do not presume to dictate, but we must observe that the

VIEW FROM THE TOP *Catrin Nilsmark of Sweden sinks the winning putt (left) in the 1992 Solheim Cup, and her team-mates are not a little jubilant about it.*

EXCUSE ME, MADAM, IS THIS YOURS?
One of the first female golf clubs was the Westward Ho! and North Devon Ladies' Club, founded in 1868.

THE LADIES' WORLD

SEPTEMBER 1900

FIVE CENTS

S. H. MOORE & CO., NEW YORK

EVERY PICTURE MAY NOT TELL THE STORY

Despite the name of the magazine, and the elegant appearance of its cover girl, golf was not always a ladies' world in the new world of America at the turn of the century.

WOMEN'S RULE *Cecil Leitch looks on as the great amateur, Harold Hilton, endeavours to sink a putt during their famous 'Battle of the Sexes' Challenge Match at Walton Heath in 1910 which Miss Leitch won.*

posture and gestures requisite for a full swing are not particularly graceful when the player is clad in female dress." So there you have it.

Despite this sort of over-zealous anxiety for the ladies' welfare, which caused several clubs to limit their activities to the putting green, by 1900 there were about 130 women's golf clubs. One might guess from the comments of Hutchinson and Miss Stewart that women golfers of the day wandered around like floozies. In fact, it was customary for them to be not so much dressed as bedecked. Restricted by 19th-century corsets and girdles, and clad in a long dress which ensured that no man would glimpse anything of her flesh other than her face and hands, it was a wonder that she could play a half pitch, let alone execute a full swing.

We shall return to the subject of changing fashions later, but it is

pertinent here to remark on the privileged background which nurtured women's golf in England around the turn of this century. It was in such genteel surroundings that the movement for the enfranchisement of women was born and flourished, and golf did not escape the consequences of the bid for emancipation. Nobody sought martyrdom from the impact of Harry Vardon's follow-through in the way Emily Davison did when she threw herself under the King's horse at the Derby, but just down the road from Epsom racecourse a band of suffragettes did attempt to debag the Prime Minister, David Lloyd George, while he was playing at Walton Heath.

It was at Walton Heath in 1910 that a more conventional blow was struck for women golfers. Cecilia (Cecil) Leitch, the young heroine of pre-war British women's golf, faced Harold Hilton in a 72-hole challenge match at Walton Heath and Sunningdale. Both players drove from the men's tees, but the fact that Miss Leitch was compensated for her relative lack of length by receiving a stroke every other hole from the great man did not detract from the delight of her vast throng of noisy supporters when she recovered from 4 down after 54 holes to edge home by 2 & 1.

Miss Leitch won the first of her four British Amateurs in 1914. The tournament, like its male equivalent, was contested at matchplay. It had begun in 1893, the year the Ladies' Golf Union (LGU) was created with the aims of holding a championship, promoting women's golf and establishing a handicapping system suitable for women.

That first Ladies' Amateur was appropriately won

by a lady: Lady Margaret Scott, who won the first three championships before retiring. The next dominant figure was May Hezlet, one of three talented Irish sisters, who became champion in 1899 at the age of 17. She won twice more, including 1907 when she defeated her sister Florence in the final, and was beaten at the last hurdle in 1904 by the irrepressible Lottie Dod, who had got bored by winning the Wimbledon Tennis Championships six times and so turned to golf in search of another sport to conquer.

Dorothy Campbell from North Berwick went over to the United States in 1909 following her triumph at Birkdale and became the first woman to win the British and US Amateurs in the same year. The American version had been inaugurated in 1895, the same year as its male counterpart.

One of the earliest female golfing stars in the United States was Alexa Stirling (a childhood friend of Bobby Jones), who won the American crown in 1916, 1919 and 1920, a sequence interrupted only by the First World War. In Britain Cecil Leitch did likewise, winning in 1914, 1920 and 1921, and she also collected the English Ladies' Amateur Championship in 1914 and 1919. She was an inspiration and something of an idol to her fans, who had never before seen a woman give the ball such a mighty thwack. The war cost her several opportunities to add to her considerable achievements, and when that was over Joyce Wethered cost her several more.

Miss Wethered brought an altogether more elegant action to the game, but the grace and fluidity of her swing belied the tremendous power generated by her easy rhythm and wide arc. As well as Bobby Jones (see page 65), Henry Cotton and Walter Hagen both paid effusive tributes to the quality of her play.

Joyce Wethered, more than any other golfer of either sex, is worthy of being compared to Jones. She, too, was a true amateur. Like him she displayed unfailing sportsmanship and warmth both on and off the course and, had she been less modest, she could have pointed to her fantastic record of winning more often than she lost. Apart from Miss Leitch, Miss Wethered is the only person to win the British Amateur four times. Their clashes in the 1920s popularized women's golf in Britain, and not just among women.

They met in five major finals. Miss Wethered won three – at the 1920 English Amateur at Sheringham,

A GREAT MOMENT IN GOLF *The end of the morning round in the final of the 1929 British Ladies' Championship. This was the middle point of Joyce Wethered's tremendous recovery against the American champion, Glenna Collett, in what is commonly regarded as the finest women's golf match ever played.*

TRIPLE-WIN TWINS *Two of the finest women amateurs ever produced by the US – Alexa Stirling (left), a childhood friend of Bobby Jones and winner of three consecutive US Amateurs, and Glenna Collett (later Vare), who emulated Miss Sirling's hat-trick and went on to win her national title a record six times.*

42nd **WOMEN'S AMATEUR CHAMPIONSHIP**
OF THE UNITED STATES GOLF ASSOCIATION

WESTMORELAND COUNTRY CLUB, WILMETTE, ILLINOIS ● PRICE 25 CENTS

With a record of eight wins and two seconds from
11 championship appearances, Miss Wethered retired.
She returned for the 1929 British Amateur, largely
because it was held at St Andrews, and made her way
to the final. There she met Glenna Collett, the reigning
American champion who had already won her national
title in 1922 and 1925 and was by then embarked on a
hat-trick of wins from 1928 to 1930. Miss Wethered was
5 down after nine holes but covered the next 18 in 73
strokes in an era when 80 was an excellent score. She
won by 3 & 1.

Two anecdotes concerning Miss Wethered are
legendary. She is the source of the famous phrase
"*What train?*", a remark she made after journalists at
the 1920 English final enquired if her concentration
had been disturbed by a passing locomotive as she was
putting on Sheringham's 17th green.

And then there is the tale of the postman patrolling
the streets of St Andrews in 1929, gloomily relaying the
news "*She's five doon*" as Miss Wethered reached her
nadir in the match against Glenna Collett. Of course,
there weren't many folk listening. Most of the town
was out on the Old Course, watching.

Joyce Wethered's defeat of Miss Collett emphasized
her pre-eminence in the game. In the words of Charles
Price: "*She did not have to play in America to convince
the Americans that she was perhaps the best female
golfer who ever lived.*" Miss Collett was the queen of the
American scene and, following her marriage, she went
on to collect a record sixth US Amateur as Glenna

despite having stood 6 down at one stage of the
afternoon round, and in the British Amateurs of 1922
and 1925. Miss Leitch countered with both the British
and French titles in 1921.

The 1920 English Amateur was the first remotely
important competition Joyce Wethered entered. In
learning the game she had been driven by the
exhortations of her brother, Roger, a fine
amateur golfer who lost a playoff for the
Open in 1921. Following her success in
1920, Miss Wethered participated in each
of the next four English Amateurs and
won the lot. From 1921 to 1925 she
played in the British Amateur five times
and was victorious on three occasions,
twice when her last opponent was Miss
Leitch. In 1922 they went into lunch all-
square but Miss Wethered was rampant in
the afternoon and by the 11th it was all
over. Three years later, an epic encounter
remained in the balance until Miss Leitch
bowed the knee at the 37th.

Collett Vare. She lost twice in the final as well, once to Virginia van Wie, who emulated the hat-tricks of Mrs Vare, Alexa Stirling and Beatrix Hoyt by completing one of her own between 1932 and 1934.

There was no second comeback for Miss Wethered, assuming one discounts her regular subsequent appearances in the friendly ambience of the Worplesdon Mixed Foursomes, which she won a record eight times between 1922 and 1936.

Her career was conducted at the same time as Bobby Jones was establishing his place among golf's immortals, and even in retirement the parallel between the two was maintained. Both quit at the age of 28. Both forfeited their amateur status in the 1930s to allow themselves, independently, to reap material gain from their reputations, though neither had any intention of competing as a professional.

Miss Wethered, who took the title Lady Heathcoat-Amory on her marriage in 1937, was reinstated as an amateur after the Second World War. It was only fitting that she was. There will never be another amateur to match her or Jones.

But women's amateur golf in Britain did not wither without Wethered. Enid Wilson annexed the British Amateur from 1931 to 1933. Helen Holm managed to fit in a couple of wins before the war, as did Pam Barton. In 1936, aged 19, the latter repeated the performance of Dorothy Campbell (who, as Mrs Hurd, had won a third American title in 1924) by winning the British and US Amateurs in the same season. Jessie Anderson (later Valentine) succeeded Miss Barton in 1937 and won the British title for a third time in 1958.

It was during the 1930s that the Curtis Cup matches between the two nations were started. The countries had met sporadically in friendly matches since 1905. Two of the Americans who took part in the first informal meeting at Cromer in England were the sisters Harriot and Margaret Curtis, later to be US Amateur champions once and three times, respectively. They offered a cup to the USGA "*To stimulate friendly rivalry between the women golfers of many lands*", but the competition started as Great Britain & Ireland versus the United States, and that is the way the Curtis Cup has stayed.

Of the 23 contests between 1932 and 1984, the

Americans won 19. They lost twice and tied twice. But in a remarkable reversal of fortunes, the British won three of the next four meetings.

The British lost the first match at Wentworth in 1932 by 5 1/2 points to 3 1/2, despite having Joyce Wethered, Enid Wilson, Wanda Morgan and Diana Fishwick in their line-up. In 1936, the home team did better, grabbing a share of the spoils at Gleneagles, thanks to Jessie Anderson sinking a putt of 20 feet on the last green of the match, but it wasn't until the seventh fixture, at Muirfield in 1952, that the British won; Elizabeth Price securing the crucial point. The 5-4 margin was repeated at Prince's four years later when Frances (Bunty) Smith made a five at the final hole to Polly Riley's six. To complete a decade of unparalleled joy for a British team against the Americans, the visitors retained the trophy with a tie in Massachusetts in 1958. Again the principals in the concluding drama were Mrs Smith and Miss Riley, and again the former was triumphant. Needing to halve the last hole to secure the tie, she won it.

If British successes have been emphasized here, that is because American victories were the norm, and hence hardly noteworthy. They won every encounter from 1960 to 1984, sometimes narrowly but usually with a great deal in hand.

Then in 1986, in perhaps the biggest shock in amateur golf since Jones lost in the first round of the 1929 US Amateur, the British and Irish won in the

HALL OVER *When Caroline Hall beat Vicki Goetze on the last green in 1992, Great Britain & Ireland had won the Curtis Cup for the third time in four goes. Here the Duke of York presents the trophy to the victorious captain, Liz Boatman.*

fatiguing heat and humidity of a Kansas August with a team of reputed has-beens and no-hopers. They annihilated the Americans 13-5 at Prairie Dunes, an achievement put into its proper historical context when one considers that it was the first time the United States had ever lost a Ryder, Walker or Curtis Cup match on home soil. (Mind you, they have since lost the other two at home as well.)

Great Britain & Ireland retained the cup by 11-7 at Royal St George's in 1988, lost it by by a 10-point margin in New Jersey two years later, but regained it at Royal Liverpool in 1992. Ultimately, Caroline Hall needed to halve the final singles to win the match, but she was 1 down with three to play against Vicki Goetze, probably the most talented player on either team. Miss Hall then won the 16th with a birdie and got a solid par to win the last as Miss Goetze faltered.

While the British were relishing their dominance of the Curtis Cup in the 1950s, the leading women amateurs were no longer the best women golfers. In America, women – no doubt to the posthumous chagrin and astonishment of Horace Hutchinson – were playing professional golf.

The stage was set by Babe Zaharias, whose brief biography appears on page 67. She was the nearest thing the women's game has had to a natural, to a Sam Snead. She drove the ball immense distances, and when asked how a woman of 5' 7" and weighing 10 stone could find such power, she would reply, in an answer guaranteed to have Hutchinson wincing as he rotated in his grave: "*I just hitch up my girdle and let it rip.*" She made money by touring the country with top men professionals, being paid up to $600 an appearance for demonstrating her booming tee shots, which was about $100 more than Hogan and Snead could command. This

THE VICTORY VICTOR

Kathy Whitworth's mark of 88 wins on the LPGA Tour is a record for men as well as women, despite what Sam Snead might say about his obscure tournament victories in the deep, dark past.

made her a professional in the eyes of the USGA, but in 1943, having learned that there is more to golf than hitting the ball over 250 yards, Babe Zaharias was reinstated as an amateur.

The Babe wasted no time in making her mark. She won the US and British Amateurs and when she turned pro once more she won 31 tournaments, including the US Women's Open in 1948, 1950 and 1954. The latter was effectively her epitaph. She never defended the title and died of cancer in 1956.

The US Women's Open is now the most prestigious championship in ladies' golf. It was first held in 1946 under the auspices of the fledgling Women's PGA of America. Although the Open ran continuously, the WPGA had a chequered five-year existence from 1944 to 1948. The moribund body was revived in 1950 under the banner of the Ladies' PGA, but the tour was close to bankruptcy before Ray Volpe was appointed its first commissioner in 1975.

Volpe resurrected the tour's fortunes with his astute marketing policies before handing over to John Laupheimer in 1982. Laupheimer doubled prize-money but resigned in 1988 after player dissatisfaction. He was succeeded by Bill Blue, who quit after two unhappy years and was replaced by Charles Mechem. The 37-tournament, $22-million 1993 LPGA Tour compared nicely with the $45,000 the father of the circuit, Fred Corcoran, rustled up in 1950, although it will be noted that the men's senior tour in the States has rather left the women in its wake.

The leading lights of the LPGA Tour in its formative years, and the women who virtually played pass the parcel with the US Open trophy, were Zaharias, Patty Berg, Betty Jameson and Louise Suggs – all previous winners of the US Amateur. Betsy Rawls won the Open in 1951 and then twice more in 1953 and 1957. Her second and third victories were especially painful for the Hawaiian golfer Jacqui Pung.

Pung was decisively beaten by Rawls in a playoff for the Open in 1953, the first season it was administered by the USGA. But Pung appeared to have gained her revenge four years later when she handed in a card for 298 to pip Rawls by a stroke at Winged Foot. Soon after Pung returned her score, it was discovered she had mistakenly signed for a five on a hole where she had actually taken six.

She had attested to the correct total but had not checked the arithmetic. Whereas 11 years later Roberto de Vicenzo would deny himself the chance of a Masters playoff by signing for a higher score than he had taken, Pung was disqualified. She had won – and then she hadn't. She had finished first – and suddenly she had finished nowhere. The members of the host club organized a whip-round and raised $3,000 for her; $1,200 more than the first prize. It was a marvellous gesture but scant consolation.

Rawls added a fourth Open medal to her collection in 1960, a tally since equalled by Mickey Wright. Just as Joyce Wethered was the greatest amateur to grace women's golf, and Zaharias the perfect link between the two codes, so Wright is arguably the finest professional the female game has ever produced.

Her first US Open was, coincidentally, Zaharias's last, and the two were paired for the last day's double round in 1954. Wright turned pro the next season and from 1956, when she won her first LPGA event, until 1969 she won 81 tournaments. She notched up her 82nd triumph in 1973. Kathy Whitworth has since taken her total of victories to 88, but she never matched the stranglehold that Wright had on her contemporaries. One might, mindful of an even more powerful grip exerted on the men's tour in 1945, say that Wright held her rivals in a half-Nelson.

The precis of Wright's career covered on page 66 amply illustrates the point. Above all, she won four US Opens, four LPGA Championships, three Western Opens and two Titleholders' Championships. They then constituted the four legs of the women's Grand Slam, giving her a record 13 major championships, one more than Berg. Incidentally, Wright won three of the four majors in 1961, although Zaharias had gone one better by winning the only three on offer in 1950, and Sandra Haynie was to win the Open and LPGA Championships in 1974 during a period when the two other majors had fallen by the wayside.

As this lack of continuity suggests, the concept of the female Grand Slam carries less kudos than it does for the men. This is borne out by the fact that the Western and Titleholders' events have now been replaced by the Dinah Shore tournament and the du Maurier Classic. These were accorded their exalted rating with retrospective effect and it has to be said that commercially sponsored majors do not have quite the same ring of authenticity. Even the LPGA Championship is not immune to such fluctuations. From 1994, McDonald's replaced Mazda as its sponsor.

Whitworth and Nancy Lopez are the two members of the LPGA's exclusive Hall of Fame who have never captured the crown the players covet most – the US Open. Since Wright's heyday, the tradition of multiple winners in the championship has been maintained: Susie Berning and Hollis Stacy three times each, and Donna Caponi, Joanne Carner and Betsy King twice. Conversely, and perversely, the US Open has also provided debut professional wins in America for a startling number of players – Murle Lindstrom, Mary Mills, Sandra Spuzich, Donna Caponi, Jerilyn Britz, Janet Anderson (nee Alex), Kathy Baker, Jane Geddes, Laura Davies and Liselotte Neumann. In 1993, Lauri Merten took the title for her first win in nine years. Both she and the runner-up, Donna Andrews, became the first players to break par in all four rounds of the championship.

Of the characters in the previous paragraph, Carner and Lopez and are dealt with in Chapter 3, but a few details about some of their peers are apposite here. In 1986, Pat Bradley won three legs of the Grand Slam, thereby matching Wright's feat of 1961 and giving herself a complete set of four. In 1991, she became the 12th inductee into the Hall of Fame (for which entry requirements are strictly stipulated), following, in order, Berg, Jameson, Suggs, Zaharias, Rawls, Wright, Whitworth, Haynie, Carol Mann, Carner and Lopez. All have won at least 30 official tournaments.

Among the best of the rest of contemporary players are Amy Alcott and Betsy King, both winners of five major championships. King has won all hers since 1987, including the US Open in 1989 and 1990 and the LPGA Championship by 11 strokes in 1992 *en route* to becoming the first player to break 70 in all four rounds of a women's major.

The popular winner of the 1992 US Open was Patty Sheehan, who in 1990 had squandered an 11-shot lead by playing the last 27 holes in eight over par, thus leaving the door open for King. Two years on, she

which she won. Two months later, she took the Women's British Open, the first player to achieve that double in the same season, although King, Geddes and Davies have also won both. In March 1993, Sheehan won her 30th LPGA tournament to become the 13th entrant inducted into the Hall of Fame.

The LPGA Tour is no longer an all-American affair. Jan Stephenson of Australia, Sally Little of South Africa and Ayako Okamoto of Japan were among the best players on the circuit in the 1980s, but these days the foreign invasion is spearheaded by the Europeans, in similar fashion to the way things were on the men's US tour a decade ago.

In the vanguard of the invasion was Laura Davies, the best British woman professional ever and an inordinately and innately talented golfer. After winning the British Open in 1986, she won the US Open the next summer, beating Carner and Okamoto in a playoff. Like Zaharias, Davies is a prodigiously strong hitter with an engaging personality. Having turned 30 in October 1993, she is the elder statesman of a bunch of outstanding young European women golfers.

Twelve months after Davies had won the US Open, Sweden's Liselotte Neumann did likewise. In August 1992, Florence Descampe from Belgium won on the LPGA Tour, although by the end of the season Helen Alfredsson, another Swede, had pipped her for the honour of being Rookie of the Year. Alfredsson confirmed that accolade by taking the Dinah Shore tournament, the first major of the year, in 1993, while Davies blew her chance of winning it in 1994 when she bogeyed the last hole to let Donna Andrews pass her with a birdie. Alfredsson, too, is a past winner of the British Open, that being in 1990.

In October 1992, Europe won the second Solheim Cup match, the women's version of the Ryder Cup, by 11½ points to 6½ at Dalmahoy, Edinburgh, primarily because they won seven of the ten singles. The United States had won the first match in 1990 and will stage the third in 1994, but this defeat defied all logic since, apart from Davies, whose combative example inspired her team-mates, on paper the Americans had 10 of the best 11 players on view. But then golf is played on grass, not on paper, and the European captain, Mickey Walker – winner of the

VERY SELECT COMPANY
Pat Bradley is the only player to have won all four modern major champion-ships on the LPGA Tour.

SIX YEARS OF SUCCESS
Between 1987 and 1992, Betsy King won five major championships on the LPGA Tour, including back-to-back US Women's Opens.

won in courageous and theatrical circumstances. After hitting their drives on the 71st hole, Sheehan and Juli Inkster, who led by two shots, had to wait for two hours as a torrential storm hit Oakmont. On the resumption, Sheehan hit her approach shot to 10 feet for one birdie and at the last she rolled in an 18-footer for another to force a playoff,

British Amateur in both 1971 and 1972 – deployed her troops splendidly.

Apart from the European successes of Davies and Alfreddson, England's Trish Johnson and Helen Dobson both won on the LPGA Tour in 1993, and Davies began her 1994 campaign by winning in Arizona and Tennessee, and then claiming the LPGA Championship, her second American major, in Delaware. All this, of course, begs the question about what was happening in Europe.

The Women's Professional Golfers' European Tour (WPGET) began life as the Women's PGA (WPGA) in 1978 under the directorship of Barry Edwards. By the early 1980s it was beset by internal squabbling and Colin Snape, the Executive Director of the British PGA, took control in 1982. He used the influence and connections of his organization to strengthen the circuit by taking it on to the continent. This move enabled the £1 million prize-money barrier to be broken in 1987, an announcement made a few weeks after Snape had 'resigned' – in fact, been dismissed over what was considered his dictatorial attitude.

The WPGET was formed on its break from the PGA in April 1988. Its first boss was an avuncular Irishman and tournament promoter, Joe Flanagan, who left prematurely in 1991 because the players felt he had not done well enough and because he was fed up with their sly criticisms of his performance. Andrea Doyle, a former travel company executive, took over the job but

was sacked in March 1993 (the very week that Alfredsson was winning the Dinah Shore) because the players felt she had not done well enough, etc., etc. Sounds familiar?

The circuit, which had 27 tournaments in 1988, had just 11 in 1993 and was worth less than £1.5 million, some £400,000 below the high of 1990. Terry Coates, a man with a high-powered business background and a keen golfer, succeeded Doyle with an optimistic demeanour but aware that – as Laupheimer, Blue, Snape, Flanagan and Doyle have discovered – running a women's golf tour can be a turbulent post. But his first moves indicated reason for optimism, and assuming he remains able to rely on the continued support of Europe's top players – particularly Davies – the signs may be encouraging. The 1994 schedule carried a minumum of £1.8 in prize-money, maybe going up to £2 million, spread over 16 tournaments, of which 11 were on the continent.

The emphasis of the WPGET may increasingly lie

GREAT WOMAN DRIVER
Laura Davies is the most powerful golfer in the contemporary women's game, capable of blasting her drives close to 300 yards in competition. She was also the inspiration who proved to other Europeans that the Americans were not invincible.

AT LAST *After years of trying, and after an inordinate share of hard-luck stories, Patty Sheehan (left) won the US Women's Open in 1992, beating Juli Inkster in dramatic style at Oakmont.*

ALFIE KNOWS WHAT IT'S ALL ABOUT *Helen Alfredsson, Rookie of the Year on the LPGA Tour in 1992 and winner of a major championship there in 1993. She is one of several fine Swedish golfers.*

WELCOME CONTAGION *Sweden is not the only continental country producing top-class women golfers. Belgium's Florence Descampe got her first win in the United States before Alfredsson did.*

on mainland Europe, where the women's game is more readily embraced and free of sexual prejudice. Also, in most continental countries there are fewer men's professional tournaments vying for attention.

Continental golf is not short of female role models. Neumann, Alfredsson and Descampe – plus Sweden's Catrin Nilsmark, who won the opening event of the 1994 season, the Ford Classic – were among the 10 members of the Solheim Cup class of 1992. Sandrine Mendiburu of France looks ready to supplant the elegant Marie-Laure de Lorenzi as her country's most accomplished woman golfer. Annika Sorenstam, yet another Swede, had a sparkling amateur record at university in the United States and an encouraging start to her pro career. And Valerie Michaud of France and Pernille Pederson of Denmark won the British Amateur in 1991 and 1992, respectively.

Elsewhere around the world, there are tours to tempt the amateurs to turn pro in Australia, Asia and Japan. An Australian, Karen Lunn, won the Women's British Open and topped the European Order of Merit in 1993. In Japan, where the LPGA holds its season-ending event and plays an annual match against the natives, the 1993 JLPGA Tour had 49 tournaments and was worth over £12 million.

The growth of the LPGA Tour meant that after the Second World War few prominent American amateurs were encouraged to retain their status. Most, like Juli Inkster, who won the US Women's Amateur in three consecutive years from 1980, and Beth Daniel and Vicki Goetze, who both won it twice, chose to convert their class into cash. Anne Sander (nee Quast) was one who didn't. She won three US Amateurs and a British Amateur, the latter coming 22 years and three marriages after her first national title in 1958.

The outstanding woman amateur since the war has probably been Catherine Lacoste of France. She won the British and US Amateurs in 1969 to become only the third person (after Dorothy Campbell and Pam Barton) to do the double. In the former she ended the reign of her compatriot, Brigitte Varangot, who had ruled for three of the preceding six years. But it was what Miss Lacoste did in 1967 that set the world alight and left several American professionals with red faces and hot tempers. As a 22-year-old, she won the US

Open, the only amateur to do so. In 1964, Miss Lacoste had helped France to win the first biennial Women's World Amateur Team Championship for the Espirito Santo Trophy. Since then the United States has emphasized its superiority, being denied only by Australia in 1978 and by Spain in 1986 and 1992.

Women's golf has not only altered with the introduction of professionalism in the last 50 years. In the 100 years that have elapsed since Lady Margaret Scott adorned the fairways dressed in a sailor's hat, a blouse with billowing sleeves and starched collar, and a skirt that brushed the ground, modes of attire have changed, too.

When Gladys Ravenscroft, who would later win the British and American titles, rolled up her sleeves on the course in the 1909 British Amateur at Birkdale, it nearly caused a scandal. And one might have thought the apocalypse was nigh when the exotically-named Gloria Minoprio arrived on the first tee for the opening round of the 1933 English Amateur clad in tight-fitting navy blue trousers, with a matching sweater which did nothing to hide the contours of her body. She played with just one club, which she employed a caddie to carry along with a spare, and was beaten 5 & 4. Henry Longhurst filed his piece for the Evening Standard that night under the headline 'Sic transit Gloria Monday!', a line he was able to repeat in every year except one for the next five. He was almost foiled once when Miss Minoprio somehow got through the first round. Then Longhurst's line, delayed by a day, read 'Sic transit Gloria Tuesday'.

A flustered LGU retaliated immediately in 1933 by announcing it "deplored any departure from the traditional costume of the game". Those committee members would be appalled by subsequent developments. Thirty years later Marley Spearman, a former professional dancer, not only burst into the limelight with her golf but also popularized brightly coloured clothing on the course in Britain, but she could not have envisaged the skimpy skirts, tight shorts and T-shirts that would become the norm. Even the most prescient early statesmen of the LPGA Tour would not have imagined the day that some of their players could make more money by modelling for posters than by playing in tournaments.

Laura Baugh, who won the US Amateur as a precocious 16-year-old in 1971, has made a fortune from her calendars but never won a tournament as a professional. Jan Stephenson, who has won the US Open and two other majors, has capitalized on her good looks and film-star figure.

One wonders what Horace Hutchinson would have made of it all.

ROLE MODEL *Jan Stephenson has more than doubled her substantial on-course income from lucrative modelling work.*

CHAPTER SEVEN

THE AMATEURS

Professionals constitute the vast majority of the golfers discussed in this book. They represent, of course, the tiniest tip of the iceberg, numerically an insignificant minority compared to the millions of amateurs who play the game.

It would be wrong to say that a massive proportion of amateurs play golf for fun. Most of them do at least some of the time, but on other occasions there is nothing the humblest exponent of the game takes more seriously than a three-foot putt. This chapter is not concerned with him, the archetypal club golfer, but with the top echelon of amateur golfers: men whose abilities justified some on-course solemnity; many of whom could have made handsome livings as professionals had they wished to, and some who later did; and a few who were as good as anyone produced from the paid ranks of their contemporaries. And, despite the past tense employed in that last sentence, there are still some amateurs around today who fulfil the first two of those three categories.

Just as Prestwick founded the Open in 1860, it also hosted the tournament which was the precursor of the Amateur Championship (or British Amateur as it is often known to avoid confusion). The club inaugurated a foursomes competition in 1857, but in the two subsequent years, prior to the birth of the Open, the event was held as an individual knockout. The Amateur itself did not begin until 1885, when it was staged at Royal Liverpool, Hoylake, and won by a local member, Allan MacFie. For a long time it was not regarded as the first official British Amateur – that distinction belonged to the 1886 event at St Andrews – but it was belatedly accorded the honour in 1922 after the R & A had assumed sole responsibility for the organization of the championship.

The early years were dominated by John Ball and Harold Hilton (see pages 37 and 43), though Horace Hutchinson, Johnny Laidlay, Freddie Tait and Robert Maxwell were each

AT THE PINNACLE OF THE GAME *Michael Bonallack – now secretary of the R & A but in his competitive days perhaps the finest post-war amateur golfer in the world never to turn professional.*

victorious twice before the First World War. Ball's record of eight titles is as safe as Byron Nelson's mark of 11 consecutive professional tournament wins. When Michael Bonallack retired in the 1970s with his name engraved five times on the trophy (which, incidentally, dwarfs the claret jug presented to the Open champion), the already remote possibility of Ball being overhauled vanished completely. It is surely inconceivable that today anyone good enough to threaten Ball's mark would remain an amateur sufficiently long to rewrite the history books.

Perhaps the strangest statistic about Ball's remarkable tally is that he never won the Amateur in consecutive years. It seemed he might retain the title at St Andrews in 1895 but in the final Leslie Balfour-Melville beat him at the first extra hole after Ball's approach had found the Swilcan Burn. This maintained a remarkable sequence. Balfour-Melville had won his quarter-final and semi-final matches in exactly the same fashion.

Across the Atlantic at this time, the United States Amateur Championship had survived a false start before eventually getting the winner that the winner thought it deserved. As described on page 22, the egotistical Charles Blair Macdonald became the first official US Amateur champion in 1895. In strictly tournament terms though, a more significant occurrence was Walter Travis's triumph in 1900.

Travis was born in Australia but emigrated to the United States in his early teens and became an American citizen. He didn't take up golf until he was 35, yet at the age of 39 he won the Amateur Championship of his adopted country. By 1903 he had won it three times, and the following year he astounded and appalled his ill-tempered hosts at Sandwich by becoming the first overseas winner of the British Amateur. Travis was startled and upset by the lukewarm, not to say intermittently hostile, reception that

YOU'RE NEVER TOO OLD

Chick Evans (right) won the US Open and the US Amateur in 1916 and was still playing in the latter tournament in the 1960s.

greeted him at Royal St George's, which was in stark contrast to the friendly treatment he had sampled when in Britain previously. The difference then was that he had not been a competitor.

In Travis's own words: "*I have always enjoyed the reputation of being a short driver.*" He also had another reputation as a deadly putter, but just before the championship he had lost his customarily uncanny feel and touch. In desperation he borrowed a centre-shafted 'Schenectady' putter from an American spectator. He then proceeded to putt players of the calibre of Hilton and Hutchinson into defeat before wearing down the long-hitting Ted Blackwell by 4 & 3 in the 36-hole final.

Deafening silence acknowledged the denouement.

IT'S NEVER TOO LATE *Walter Travis was born in Australia, and became a citizen of the United States. He was the first foreign winner of the Amateur Championship in Britain and he was one of golf's great late developers.*

Lord Northbourne was less than gracious in commenting at the prize-giving ceremony: "*Never since the days of Caesar has the British nation been subjected to such humiliation.*" Not surprisingly, Travis didn't play in the British Amateur again. Ironically, nor could he ever recapture that magic with the Schenectady. But just in case, the R & A quickly moved to ban the centre-shafted putter.

Travis was in the very vanguard of the American challenge to the British dominance of the game; a challenge which was to prove utterly successful after the First World War. The 'Old Man', as he was nicknamed back home, was an inspiration to his countrymen, an outstanding example of how doggedness and diligence could reap substantial rewards. It was amateur golf that appealed to the American public at the turn of the century, partly because they realised their home-bred professionals were no match for the Great Triumvirate and a few other leading Britons and because Travis had demonstrated that American amateurs could lick the British in their own backyard.

Travis's mantle was taken up by Jerome Travers, the son of a wealthy New York family, who combined a remorselessly competitive tenacity with a socialite existence. Travers won four US Amateurs and a US Open between 1907 and 1915, although he indulged his sybaritic tendencies to such an extent that twice he didn't even bother to enter the US Amateur during that period.

Francis Ouimet, who preceded Travers as US Open champion by two years, immediately succeeded him as US Amateur champion in 1914. Bob Gardner then emulated H. J. Whigham, Macdonald's son-in-law, and Chandler Egan by winning for a second time, while in 1916 Chick Evans did what only John Ball (1890) had done and Bobby Jones (1930) was to do by winning a country's Open and Amateur Championships in the same year. Evans won the US Open at Minikahda and the Amateur at Merion in Philadelphia.

Evans was to win the US Amateur once more, in 1920, and was a solid enough golfer to play in it until 1962. Ouimet was also to win the title once more, in the far off future of 1931, before he – like Bobby Jones and Joyce Wethered – turned professional for a while.

The time between Ouimet's two wins in the US Amateur belonged to Bobby Jones. After 1923 – when he won his first major championship, the US Open – Jones won the US Amateur in five of the next seven seasons. On the two occasions he missed out (1926 and 1929) he compensated in style by taking his second and third US Opens.

Jones didn't just win in his finals: he slaughtered his adversaries. Remembering that all matches were then played over 36 holes (though none went anywhere near the distance), consider these facts. In 1924, Jones thrashed George von Elm by 9 & 8 having disposed of Ouimet by 11 & 10 in the semi-finals. The following September he beat Watts Gunn, his colleague and protege from the East Lake club in his hometown of Atlanta, by 8 & 7.

Chick Evans succumbed by the same margin in 1927, this after poor Ouimet had again gone down by 11 & 10 in the semi-finals. No wonder Ouimet would later claim: *"I played some pretty darn creditable golf in the Amateur in the twenties. Then I'd run into Bobby, and he would absolutely annihilate me. You have no idea how good Bobby was!"*

In 1928 Jones provided further incontrovertible evidence of his superiority. He faced Phil Perkins, the British Amateur champion, in the final of the US Amateur and crushed him 10 & 9. It was probably no consolation to Perkins that Jones had prevailed in the two previous rounds by 14 & 13 and 13 & 12, because the Englishman's humiliation occurred a mere fortnight after Jones had inflicted a 13 & 12 defeat on him in the top singles in the fifth Walker Cup match, of which more in a moment.

By the end of 1929 Jones had done more than enough to be regarded by posterity as a giant among golfers. Within another 12 months he had established himself as one of the most accomplished sportsmen in history. His Impregnable Quadrilateral in 1930 is the epitome of athletic perfection. It is also truly impregnable. Jones won the British Amateur at St Andrews on May 31 by beating Roger Wethered 7 & 6 in the final; lifted the British Open at Hoylake on June 20, having two shots to spare over his professional compatriots, Leo Diegel and Macdonald Smith; retained his US Open title on July 12 at Interlachen, Minneapolis, with Smith again two strokes in arrears;

MOMENTOUS MOMENT
The completion of the Impregnable Quadrilateral. The spectators rush on to the 11th green (bottom, left) at Merion where Bobby Jones had just beaten Gene Homans to win the 1930 US Amateur and with it golf's original Grand Slam.

PRIZE COLLECTION *'Grand Slammer' Bobby Jones (below, on the right) with his biographer O.B. Keeler and, from left to right, the trophies of the British Amateur, the Open Championship, the Walker Cup (Jones had captained the United States to victory at Royal St George's in 1930), the US Open and the US Amateur.*

and finally won his fifth US Amateur on September 27 at Merion, where he had also won his first, by overwhelming Gene Homans 8 & 7 in his last seriously competitive round.

The *New York Times* declared on the morning after Merion that "*Bobby Jones not only became the national Amateur champion for 1930 but the holder of a record that probably will survive through the ages.*" That's as safe a wager as betting on the religion of the next Pope. The feat will never be matched; nor, surely, will Jones's performance of beating the field for eight years, and at the highest level, more regularly than it beat him. Byron Nelson did it memorably for one long year in 1945. Ben Hogan did it for one brief glorious season in 1953. Nobody else, not even Jack Nicklaus, has come close.

Maintaining this peak drained Jones. On telling his biographer, O. B. Keeler, of his intention to retire, he added: "*I'll never give up golf. I love it too well, and it has meant too much in my life. But it will be an easier and more gracious trail from now on.*"

In November 1930, Jones signed a contract with Warner Brothers to make a series of instructional films. This meant he had to renounce his amateur status. He publicly declared his retirement from competition (although he remains the epitome of amateur ideals). The *New York Times* announced the news and summed up their view of Jones with the following rhyming tribute:

"*With dignity he quit the memorable scene on which he nothing common did, or mean.*"

How true that is. Jones was so brutal with his brilliance that his hapless rivals may have been excused for loathing him. But he was deified, not despised. Gene Sarazen once said of partnering Jones in a tournament: "*He made you feel that you were playing with a friend, and you were.*" Raymond Oppenheimer, a golfing philanthropist and a fine amateur who played with Jones during the 1930 Open Championship, said: "*Jones was the most genuinely modest person I have ever met. When one had talked with him for a short time he gave you the feeling that the only difference between your golf and his was that he had been much more lucky.*"

Jones's win in the British Amateur in 1930 made him the only man to have a complete collection of all four legs of the Impregnable Quadrilateral. A select few – Harold Hilton, Lawson Little, Arnold Palmer and Jack Nicklaus – have won three. Anyone who suggests that Jones's victories in the two Amateurs cannot be considered to have the status of those in the Opens need only reflect that in 1926 he won both Opens but went down in both the major Amateurs. Amateur golf was extraordinarily strong in the 1920s.

In the two Amateurs Jones lost in America, his conquerors were an avenging George von Elm in the final of 1926 (you may recall him from the marathon US Open of 1931) and Johnny Goodman in the first round in 1929. Goodman was a rising star who fulfilled his immense potential by winning the US Open in 1933, making him the last amateur to win a major championship open to professionals, and the US Amateur in 1937.

It is obvious that, quite apart from Jones, the Americans were then producing amateurs of the highest quality: men who could beat their professional counterparts in the US Open. They could also beat the British, as they have proved repeatedly since the inception of the Walker Cup between the United States and Great Britain & Ireland in 1922, which is where we left the British scene in those pre-Jones days.

The Walker Cup takes its name from George Herbert Walker, the President of the USGA in 1920. (In 1988, Walker's grandson, a notoriously keen golfer

TWO-TALENTED AT GOLF
Bernard Darwin (below, right) with Paul Hunter of the United States, whom he beat by 2 & 1 at Hoylake in the unofficial amateur international of 1921. Darwin is revered as one of the greatest of all golf writers but he was a fine golfer, too. He proved the point again when he won a singles in the first Walker Cup match in 1922.

called George Bush, was elected President of the USA.) Walker offered to donate an International Challenge Trophy for a competition involving all countries who wished to send amateur teams to the United States in 1921. Nobody pitched up.

Disconcerted but not discouraged, the Americans quickly dispatched an elite eight-man party (it included Jones, Ouimet and Evans) to tackle the British in an international at Hoylake. The visitors won 9-3. Tommy Armour represented the hosts, which is a historical curiosity because, having changed nationalities, he played for the United States at Wentworth in the professionals' match of 1926 which led Sam Ryder to inaugurate his cup. Armour, on the losing side in both unofficial matches, never actually took part in either the Walker or Ryder Cups.

In the spring of 1922, the R & A announced it would send a team to the United States to contest the Walker Cup. The rest of the world had blown its chance – the Walker Cup was to be exclusively between the old power and the new.

It has to be said that the old has not done very well. The Americans have won 30 of the 34 meetings. The British and Irish won in 1938 and 1971 (both times at St Andrews), tied a memorable match at Baltimore in 1965 and, shockingly, won a breathtaking one in Atlanta in 1989, but that's as far as it goes.

As befits an amateur gathering, the Walker Cup is proud of its Olympian spirit. The taking part is what matters. Winning is important, too, but the making or missing of a three-foot putt is not relevant to the meaning of life or the whereabouts of the next gin and tonic. Try telling that to the players, of course – they're the ones who sweat over those short putts. But the Walker Cup has admirably maintained its ideals, and at times that has been all that has kept it going. Unlike the Ryder Cup, there was no semblance of equality in the results in the early days, and in the modern era there is no obvious association with mainland Europe or anywhere else that could justify a strengthening of the British challenge without fundamentally altering the special nature of the event.

In a burst of enthusiasm, the Walker Cup was initially an annual reunion. It began in 1922 at Charlie Macdonald's National Golf Links, when it featured an unscheduled performance by Bernard Darwin, who had been sent to cover the occasion for *The Times* and found himself playing in place of the indisposed British captain, Robert Harris. Darwin recovered from 3 down after three holes to beat William Fownes in the singles, thus furthering his reputation as the best of all golf writers to one as the best golfer of all golf writers.

The 1923 match at St Andrews provided a reliable indicator of how the British could snatch defeat from the jaws of victory. Willis Mackenzie lost having been 6 up after 14 (all matches were over 36 holes) while Roger Wethered and Ernest Holderness halved with Francis Ouimet and lost to Frederick Wright, respectively, despite both having been 2 up with three to play. The upshot of these disasters was that the home team lost 6½–5½, a margin that swelled to 9-3 the following September at Garden City, New York.

The match became a biennial fixture after that, which spared a few Britons from the torture of playing Bobby Jones. Either side of pulverising Phil Perkins, he

A FAMILIAR ROUTINE
The American captain, in this case Bob Gardner (below, right) in 1923, takes possession of the Walker Cup.

and was one over threes for the five holes in the afternoon. His record winning margin of 14 & 13 was also of Jonesian dimensions and is likely to remain unsurpassed.

To the surprise of most people, the debacle at Pine Valley was followed by a British victory at the tenth attempt in 1938. They won by three points and had the added satisfaction of holding on to the trophy for nine years until the Walker Cup was resumed in 1947. The British hosted it again then because post-war circumstances made it more difficult for them to travel.

The Second World War coincidentally brought down the curtain on the halcyon days of amateur golf, though after it there were several outstanding amateurs – particularly Americans like Bill Campbell, Frank Stranahan, Charlie Coe, Dick Chapman, Willie Turnesa, Harvie Ward and Deane Beman, who is more well known as the US tour commissioner who announced his retirement in March 1994. The latter four won both major Amateurs, and Chapman also took the national titles of Canada, France, Italy and Portugal. Ward, Stranahan and Beman all turned professional eventually, the latter two having limited success on the US tour after they made the transition.

Those seven were not quite in the same class of the professional stars of the day, but several of the young US Amateur champions of the 1950s chose to seek the fast lane to fame and fortune. Some of them found it, notably Gene Littler, Arnold Palmer and Jack Nicklaus (who, as in so many respects, was the exception that proved the rule because he was a threat to the professionals even before he joined them). The route they took has been frequently followed, and if one mentions only Lanny Wadkins, Craig Stadler, Jerry Pate and Hal Sutton, that is because they are the ones who have gone on to lift major professional championships as well.

These days, the standard career path for the promising American golfer means that if he wins his

HIGH-PERFORMANCE CARR *Ireland's Joe Carr won the Amateur Championship three times. He is pictured here getting a drive away against Harvie Ward, then widely considered to be the best amateur golfer in the world, in the 1953 final at Hoylake, which Carr won by 2 holes.*

beat Cyril Tolley 12 & 11 in 1926 and Wethered 9 & 8 in 1930. Those three, together with Holderness, were the best amateurs in Britain in the 1920s, and yet putting them in with Jones was like sending lambs to the slaughter.

The lambs were well and truly slaughtered at Pine Valley in 1936. They halved three matches and lost the other nine. Without a point to show for his country's endeavours, Henry Longhurst observed: "*The British side of the scoreboard looked like a daisy chain, with twelve noughts one beneath the other.*"

Things could have been still more embarrassing had Lawson Little not turned pro earlier that year. Little had accomplished the unique feat of winning the British and US Amateurs in both 1934 and 1935; a back-to-back double that not even Jones had achieved. Little's golf at Prestwick in the first of those years was particularly awesome. Aged 23, he destroyed Jack Wallace with a 66 in the morning round of the final,

national Amateur he is already likely to be benefiting from a university sports scholarship, during which he will mature with a regular diet of competitive golf. The aspiring golfer will then probably play in one Walker Cup before turning pro.

Phil Mickelson is an outstanding example; indeed, he is an outstanding golfer. He actually played in two Walker Cups, in 1989 and 1991. He won the US Amateur in 1990, won the Tucson Open the following January while still an amateur, and won in San Diego in February 1993 in his first full season as a pro. Mickelson may well emulate Bob Charles by becoming a left-handed winner of a major championship. He and Jack Nicklaus are the only golfers to have won four events on the US tour prior to their 24th birthdays. But he will be aware of the case of Scott Verplank, who had been the last amateur winner of a US tour event, in 1985 at the age of 21. Verplank's subsequent professional career has been a disaster. In the game of golf there are few dead certs for stardom.

Some leading American amateurs do not look on their successes as a stepping stone to professionalism and are not tempted by the uncertain riches of life on tour, but they are in the minority. Affairs in Britain, as might be expected, have been less ordered. Instead of the support of a university sports scholarship (unless, like Colin Montgomerie for one, they get it in the United States) many of the best prospects since the Second World War have been dependent on assistance from various voluntary organizations or charitable institutions, such as the Golf Foundation, and encouragement from wealthy individual benefactors like Gerald Micklem. Twice an English Amateur champion and four times a Walker Cup player, Micklem occupied just about every important post at the R & A except honorary professional. In 1985 he was elected president of Sunningdale, and in 1987, the year before he died, the beautiful old Berkshire course became the first inland club in Britain to host the Walker Cup.

Micklem rendered sterling service to the R & A for many years, and the R & A's present secretary did as much for British golf in the 1960s and 1970s. Michael Bonallack succeeded Ireland's Joe Carr, who won the Amateur Championship three times, as the foremost amateur in the British Isles. He established a record which would justify a less unassuming personality to claim himself to be the world's best post-war amateur, certainly of those who never became professionals.

He won the British Amateur on his five appearances in the final: in 1961, 1965 and 1968-70. That last flourish made him the only man to achieve a hat-trick of victories in either of the two main Amateurs. Like Little in the 1930s, he could boast of something Jones would have been proud of but had not accomplished. Bonallack also collected nine English Amateur titles at either matchplay or strokeplay. These included the demolition of David Kelley by 12 & 11 in the final at Ganton in 1968, when Bonallack shot 61, with just two tiny putts conceded, in the morning round.

Bonallack was naturally in both Walker Cup teams that avoided defeat in the period he was at the top. In 1965 the British had seemed certain to clinch a momentous victory at Five Farms, but needing just two points from eight in the second series of singles (18-hole matches had been introduced in 1963), they could manage only 1½. It was left to Clive Clark, now a BBC commentator, to square the contest by holing from 35 feet on the last green.

Six years later Bonallack was the captain when Britain won six singles on the second afternoon to turn the tide in improbably dramatic fashion at St Andrews. Victory was secured when David Marsh found the heart of the treacherous 17th green with a 3-iron to go to dormie-1 up on Bill Hyndman. In a sequence which was wholly out of keeping with precedent, the British won all four singles that went to the 18th hole.

Normality was restored for 18 years, although at both Hoylake in 1983 and Pine Valley

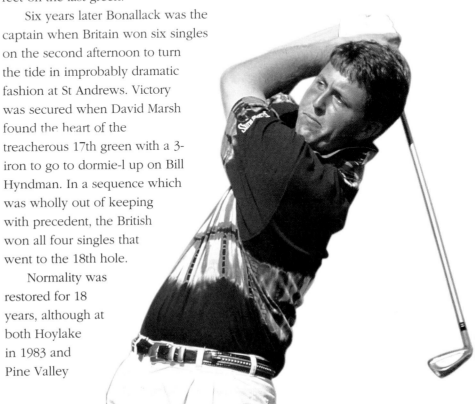

LEFT BUT NOT LEAST
America's Phil Mickelson is the best left-handed golfer in the world. Formerly the world's best amateur, period, he is now one of the best professionals on the US tour.

in 1985, an enthralling contest was not resolved until late in the day. Then at Peachtree in 1989, even better placed than in 1965, GB&I needed only 1½ points from the final session of eight singles to win for the first time in the United States. But they could only manage two halves from the first seven and it came down to the final game, which Jim Milligan needed to halve in order to claim the Walker Cup for his team but in which he was 2 down with three to play against the American veteran Jay Sigel, winner of the British Amateur in 1979 and of the US Amateur in 1982-3, and, in 1994, a victorious professional rookie on the US Senior tour.

Suddenly, Sigel's short game collapsed. He mishit chip shots on each of the last three holes. Meanwhile, Milligan birdied the 16th and chipped in for a par at the 17th to level matters. He could afford to take two putts from 10 feet to halve the last in bogey fives, so he did.

However, at Portmarnock, near Dublin, two years later, the British and Irish never recovered after losing all four opening foursomes, and four points was their margin of defeat. They would have been eternally grateful for that at Interlachen in 1993. The United States won by 19-5, the most emphatic demolition job since 24 points began to be contested in 1963.

Back to individual matters. The Americans had continued to plunder the British Amateur even in the days when

A HARD ACT TO FOLLOW *Twice winner of the Amateur Championship, Peter McEvoy has long been Britain's best amateur golfer since Michael Bonallack.*

Bonallack was installed as guardian in residence. Among them, in 1967, was Bob Dickson. A few months later he earned himself a place in the exalted company of Hilton, Jones and Little by adding the US Amateur, which in an ill-fated experiment was conducted at strokeplay from 1965 until 1973. Steve Melnyk lifted the British Amateur in 1971, two years after taking the American title. Another American, Dick Siderowf, won the British Amateur twice in the 1970s, as did two Englishmen, Trevor Homer and Peter McEvoy. The latter, who these days runs his own sports promotions company, was at the top long enough to be in the victorious Walker Cup team of 1989.

Whether continental golfers will ever be recruited to help the British in the Walker Cup, as they have in the Ryder Cup, remains to be seen, but their emergence as a serious force cannot be disputed. Jose Maria Olazabal, the 1994 Masters champion, won the 1984 Amateur at Formby, beating his now Ryder Cup colleague, Colin Montgomerie, in the final. That was the meat in a sandwich that was built upon victory in the British Boys' Championship in 1983 and topped off with the British Youths' in 1985. That hat-trick, in a chapter littered with outstanding achievements, is something else that may remain unique. Olazabal was denied by three years the privilege of being the first continental winner of the Amateur. Philippe Ploujoux of France secured that honour at St Andrews in 1981 – and he wasn't the last either. Sweden's Christian Hardin was champion in 1988 and Holland's Rolf Muntz was victorious in 1990.

This cosmopolitan spreading of the rewards is indicative of the healthy state of the sport around the world. This has been demonstrated in the World Amateur Team Championship, contested in the even-numbered years for the Eisenhower Trophy, which was offered by the late American president "*To foster friendship and sportsmanship among the Peoples of the World*". It was put up at the instigation of the USGA in 1958 and is operated jointly with the R & A. The United States won nine of the first 13 stagings, but since 1984 the winners have been Japan, Canada, Great Britain & Ireland, Sweden and New Zealand.

Not that American golf is bereft of fresh talent, as the likes of David Duval and Justin Leonard have

HAPPY TOGETHER *Jim Milligan's team-mates and friends (above) congratulate him after his chip-in on the 17th hole of the final singles match set up a historic British Walker Cup victory in Atlanta in 1989.*

demonstrated even since Mickelson turned pro. And in Eldrick 'Tiger' Woods, the black teenage sensation who in 1993 became the first player to win the US Junior Amateur Championship three times (no one else had ever done it twice before), they may have the golfing prodigy of the late 1990s (*pace* Robert Allenby and others).

However, just as there is a huge difference between that calibre of player and the average club golfer, so there is a great gulf between the top level of the amateur game and the professional ranks. Some of the men discussed here have bridged the gap, some have not. Other amateurs might have had they tried, but many others make the move without realistically assessing their chances.

By forfeiting their amateur status to turn pro, the unsuccessful ones are consigning themselves to an uncertain future, dependent on the mercy of the R & A or USGA for reinstatement as an amateur or else existing in the awful limbo of being neither professional nor amateur: simply a non-amateur.

Many golfers have learned what a tough transition that is to attempt. But then as an amateur it's not easy keeping up with the Joneses.

NOT SO SIMPLE NOW *Iain Pyman not only won the Amateur Championship in 1993 but also put on an impressive display in the Open. The 1994 Masters was his last event as an amateur, though – like so many of his talented predecessors, he then took the professional plunge.*

CHAPTER EIGHT
THE ARCHITECTS

Golf in Scotland began on those stretches of sandy ground along the British coastline that were bequeathed by the receding seas following the last Ice Age. The wind blasted the sand deposits into the shapes we now know as dunes and generally ensured the land was undulating rather than perfectly flat. This was then fertilized by the guano of indigenous or migrating birds and eventually many strains of grass took root. These came to provide the fine, firm turf on which links golf established itself; they were the origins of the sward upon which the first recognizable golf courses were created and upon which millions of disciples proclaim the game is best enjoyed. Eventually heather and gorse found a home there, too, inhabiting those areas of a links familiar only to the errant golfer and his lost ball.

I t has taken one inadequate italicized paragraph to describe centuries of evolution, and it would have taken several centuries more for Mother Nature to learn to prepare greens and plant flagsticks all over the Scottish countryside. That was where man stepped in, if sometimes reluctantly.

The earliest architects tended to treat as sacrosanct the ground they were given to work with, which was fine for Old Tom Morris when he laid out Lahinch in Ireland but was a totally useless attitude when the planner was confronted with the heavy, clay-based soils often encountered inland.

Old Tom took to golf course design in a simplistic fashion at first, but subsequently he refined his craft and imaginatively avoided the traditional concept of nine holes out, nine holes back when he designed Muirfield in Scotland and Royal County Down at Newcastle in Northern Ireland. This sophisticated routing called for the holes to tack at different directions for two separate loops of nine, not only eliminating the tedium of playing in the same direction as well as having to confront the same wind conditions for nine consecutive holes, but also offering organizers and players the advantage of two possible starting points.

Despite this touch of ingenuity, Morris and the early pioneers were frequently guilty of including such integral St Andrean features as stone walls and hidden bunkers on courses where they appeared as anachronisms and excrescences, not the natural hazards their proponents had envisaged. Although they did their work cheaply and thereby enabled course construction to flourish and more people to take up golf, the late years of the 19th century were dubbed the "*dark ages of golf architecture*" by Tom Simpson, who was one of the men to do something substantial about altering that state of affairs.

Salvation was at hand with the realization that the best turf for golf courses was that which was least suitable for farming. The characteristics of the arable land which the purists deplored – thick grass on impervious loam – were rejected where possible in favour of fine close-cropped turf and fast-draining soil, such as was to be found on the heathlands to the south and west of London. The sandy subsoil of the region was a heaven-sent gift for golfers, once the heather and bracken had been cleared, and it spawned a new breed of golf course architects. They were called

NATIONAL EXAMPLE *The National Golf Links, on Long Island east of New York City, was designed by Charles Blair Macdonald. It was the first great golf course in the United States and its magnificence owed much to the inspiration Macdonald had derived from British courses.*

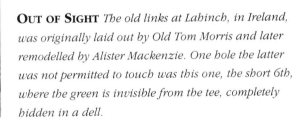

OUT OF SIGHT *The old links at Lahinch, in Ireland, was originally laid out by Old Tom Morris and later remodelled by Alister Mackenzie. One hole the latter was not permitted to touch was this one, the short 6th, where the green is invisible from the tee, completely hidden in a dell.*

THE HAND OF MAN *In the early days, golf course construction was a labour-intensive affair, as seen here with workmen reconstructing the 10th green at the Royal Mid-Surrey course, near London.*

amateurs, because they had not earned a living from playing the game as their forerunners had, but they were really the first professionals in their field.

To the fore were men like Willie Park Jr., John Abercromby, Harry Colt and Herbert Fowler. Park, son of the first Open champion and twice winner himself, was a genuine innovator who has since been acclaimed as the first proper, capable golf architect. Park laid out Sunningdale and Huntercombe and began work on Worplesdon. That task was completed by the aforementioned Abercromby, who also built Coombe Hill and The Addington.

Colt's first job was to design Rye, a superb links on the Sussex coast. He quit his vocation, the law, to realize his ambition to become a golf course architect. He accepted the position of secretary at the newly-opened Sunningdale club in 1901 and was responsible for planting the hundreds of pines which today adorn that beautiful course.

Colt was a master. He later designed Swinley Forest (which he called "*the least bad course*" he ever built), Stoke Poges, St George's Hill, the West and East courses at Wentworth and the New Course at Sunningdale. He did other admirable work, too, including the extensive revision of both courses at Royal Portrush in Ireland and the building of Le

Touquet in France, Kennemer in Holland, Falkenstein at Hamburg and Puerta de Hierro at Madrid.

Herbert Fowler's most renowned creations were at two 36-hole golf clubs near London, Walton Heath and the Berkshire. Nobody had a surer sense than he of making the best use of the land available. James Braid was appointed the club's professional when it opened in 1904, and he and his fellow-members of the Great Triumvirate followed in the footsteps of the professionals-cum-architects of the 19th century. Braid remained true to his Scottish roots with his commitments at Gleneagles, Carnoustie, Blairgowrie and Dalmahoy; J. H. Taylor collaborated with Fred Hawtree in a huge number of remodelling projects, notably Royal Birkdale; while Harry Vardon, though less prolific, was involved at Ganton in Yorkshire and Little Aston near Birmingham.

Tom Simpson became a prominent figure in the field after the First World War. He joined forces with Fowler and left his mark by altering existing heathland courses like Sunningdale New and New Zealand (which is in Surrey, not the southern hemisphere); improving the glorious links of Cruden Bay in Scotland; and designing magnificent courses in France at Morfontaine, Chantilly, Deauville and Hossegor.

These men had an eye for aesthetic values and as a

result they created features which were in empathy with the surroundings: greens and hazards of subtle patterns and contours rather than hideous geometric shapes which only looked right on a drawing board. In short, they elevated what had generally been a crude pastime into an art. Another great name from the annals of course architecture, Dr Alister Mackenzie, left the imprint of his genius in several places but, though he was a Scotsman, it was in the United States that he was to make his most seminal impression.

American golf course architecture was originally a primitive task, too. One Tom Bendelow resigned from his job on the *New York Herald* in 1895 and set himself up under the grandiose and flattering title of 'design consultant'. His sole qualification was his Scottish accent. His courses were known euphemistically as 'Sunday Specials' because a weekend afternoon was all they took to stake out – one stake for the tee, another for a simple rectangular cross-bunker, a third for a pile of dirt-covered stones, known in the vernacular as 'chocolate drop mounds', and finally one for the green, which would invariably be flat. The only element of intrigue and curiosity on Bendelow courses was whether the greens would be round or square.

Bendelow perpetrated 600 of these abominations across America. His limited vision, not to say blindness, was allowed to go unrebuked simply because few of his clients had ever seen a proper course. But he was also limited by a budget of $25 for nine holes, and like the novices in Britain he did provide plenty of playgrounds – if hardly great courses – on which the public were able to become acquainted with golf. He and his ilk at least deserve credit for that.

Of more permanent impact than Bendelow's rough and ready endeavours were the Chicago Golf Club, the Myopia Hunt Club near Boston and the Garden City course on Long Island, the former being the first 18-hole course in America. It was built by Charles Blair Macdonald and staged numerous national championships in its early years. But the most influential pre-war course in America was a different creation of Macdonald's: the National Golf Links of America, along the shore of Long Island.

The typically immodest nomenclature not only indicates the identity of its arrogant author, it also belies its actual status as one of the country's most exclusive and under-played clubs. But the suggestion of some sort of model which is also inherent in the title is not misleading. The National showed up the standard Bendelow course for what it was, a field with holes in it.

Macdonald conceived the idea in 1901 after reading an issue of the British magazine *Golf Illustrated*, which conducted a survey of leading golfers to ascertain their opinions on the best holes in the British Isles. Seldom can such a pleasant exercise have had such profound consequences. Macdonald travelled extensively in Britain to see and learn from those holes the panellists had selected. He took some features from them all but copied none absolutely. He spared no expense in acquiring the best expert advice and in altering the natural terrain to enable him to sculpt 18 exemplary holes. There were to be no weak links on the National. When it was opened it was greeted with gasps of envy and incredulity by his American rivals and unreserved admiration from knowledgeable British observers. Soon the United States was revelling in a golden age of golf course architecture.

Two sons of Philadelphia, George Thomas and Albert Tillinghast, were responsible for several marvellous Californian courses. Thomas bequeathed Riviera and the North and South Courses at the Los Angeles Country Club to the film star city. Tillinghast built the San Francisco Golf Club, a worthy companion to his superb north-eastern layouts which included both courses at Winged Foot and Baltusrol.

Yet two more Philadelphians left their individual marks upon golf course design. The first was Hugh Wilson, an insurance broker who built a great course, Merion, in just 126 acres in the Philadelphia suburb of Ardmore. And then there was George Crump. This millionaire Philadelphia hotelier disappeared into the pine-clad sandhills of neighbouring New Jersey in 1913 and, bar four holes which were completed by Wilson and Harry Colt along the lines he had ordered, by the time of his death in 1918 he had produced the most daunting golf course in the world. He called it Pine Valley. This beautiful course is still the supreme test, relentlessly demanding of every shot. The reward for excellence is all the greater for realizing the consequences of failure. It is often heralded as the greatest inland golf course in the world, a fitting epitaph to George Crump's perseverance and his belief in the scheme into which he also poured so much of his own money.

Pine Valley reinforced the continuing vogue for penal course architecture. Two men in particular, both Scottish expatriates, changed the trend.

The first was Donald Ross. In the 1920s, Ross's name on the blueprint of a golf course was as coveted as any designer label today. He had learned his craft at Dornoch. In his formative years in the United States he benefited from his heritage in the same way as Bendelow had. Not averse to doing a few 'quickies' himself, Ross was involved with hundreds of American courses, though only peripherally with most. Those to which he earnestly devoted his time were landmark courses and are of the highest calibre. In an eight-year spell from 1919, six Ross courses were selected for the US Open (Brae Burn, Inverness, Skokie, Oakland Hills, Worcester and Scioto), though it is for two others – the No 2 Course at Pinehurst, North Carolina, and Seminole in Florida – that he is chiefly renowned.

THE GOOD DOCTOR *Dr Alister Mackenzie, who represented the architectural amalgamation of the old world and the new. A Scotsman by birth, it was in the United States that he made his most lasting impressions.*

And then there was Alister Mackenzie. Like Harry Colt, he renounced his original profession, in his case medicine, to turn to course architecture. Two English courses, Alwoodley and Moortown at Leeds, established his reputation. He enhanced it with his modifications to Lahinch and followed that up with the West Course at Royal Melbourne in Australia and Cypress Point in California – two of the indisputably great courses of the world. When Bobby Jones was surprisingly knocked out in the first round of the 1929 US Amateur at Pebble Beach, he took his clubs down to Cypress for a game and was so impressed by what he saw

(who wouldn't be?) that Mackenzie became the man Jones sought for the job at Augusta shortly after his retirement from competitive golf. Ironically, Mackenzie only received the commission at Cypress Point when the club's first choice, Seth Raynor, died.

Mackenzie certainly made the optimum use of his chance at Cypress and again at Augusta. Augusta National had a profound influence on golf course architecture. With its wide fairways, dearth of bunkers and huge greens, it was the ultimate exposition of strategic design, although in subsequent years too many architects imitated its greens on the misconceived premise that big was beautiful. The strategy seldom works elsewhere – but at Augusta it is exactly right. There was a sad footnote. Alister Mackenzie, like George Crump, did not live to see his course in play.

The appearance of Augusta National coincided with the Great Depression. More clubs closed than opened in the States during the 1930s and 1940s. By the 1950s, though, the country had emerged from its economic trough. Its golf course architects had two paramount advantages over their British rivals – finance and property – and they did not squander their superiority. They dominated their field as their professionals did the tournament scene, no one more so than Robert Trent Jones – not a bad name for a man to have if he is going to be involved in golf.

Perhaps the simplest way to salute Jones's significance is to quote from *The Golf Course*, the authoritative book on the subject, written by Geoffrey Cornish and Ron Whitten. They called Jones "*the man who had the greatest impact on the profession of golf course architecture, and upon the game of golf itself*".

That's a pretty effusive and unequivocal tribute, but Jones has certainly been the influential post-war figure in a profession which for him was never anything other than his intended vocation. He even devised his own syllabus for his studies at Cornell University. When he graduated he walked into a world of affluence, with scores of people eager to supply the land on which they wanted a first-rate golf course and the money with which to build it. Trent Jones was happy to oblige.

He is as esteemed for the courses he has revised as for those he has built. The former group includes

Oakland Hills, which Ben Hogan called the "*monster*" at the 1951 US Open, Augusta National and Baltusrol. Trent Jones teamed up with Bobby Jones not only at Augusta but also at Peachtree in the latter's home-town of Atlanta, where the length of the tees (around 40 yards) and the size of the greens (averaging 8,000 square feet) are extraordinary.

Long tees became almost a patented Trent Jones trademark. They allow the high-handicap golfer to enjoy his game off the front markers while keeping the professionals in check off the back, and the hazards come into play for both. Jones also expounded the notion that every hole should be a tough par but an easy bogey. His big greens can play easily or severely, depending on their pace and the location of the flag.

Among Jones's original American courses are those at superb resort destinations like Dorado Beach on the island of Puerto Rico and Mauna Kea in Hawaii. They catered for the boom in demand for luxury golf holidays and they are not out of place beside Jones's mainland accomplishments such as Peachtree, Spyglass Hill in California and Firestone in Ohio.

Jones has not been without his critics, and often vehement ones. When Tony Jacklin won the 1970 US Open at Jones's Hazeltine, the runner-up, Dave Hill, was fined for saying that all it lacked was 80 acres of corn and a few cows. "*They ruined a good farm when they built this course,*" he said. Other critics have alleged that his courses are too expensive to maintain; look too much alike because he has accepted too many assignments; and rely too heavily on water as a hazard in an exaggerated attempt to counteract the golfer's increasing proficiency with the sand wedge.

Some of Jones's best work has been achieved outside America. His New Course at Ballybunion is a stunning companion to the magnificence of the Old, though a few holes may be a little on the quirky side. Jones has also had several successes on the continent, including Valderrama, Sotogrande and Las Brisas, the jewels of Spain's Costa del Sol; I Roveri, a parkland gem in Turin; Troia, a controversial quasi-links near Lisbon; and Pevero, dramatically blasted out of volcanic rock on the Mediterranean island of Sardinia. Altogether Jones has designed over 400 courses in 25 countries, and even recently new projects bearing his

EXPORTED EXPERTISE
Like Mackenzie, Donald Ross took his talent from Scotland and applied it to great effect in America. He produced such gems as Seminole in Florida.

imprimatur have sprung up all over the continent, like Moliets in France and Castelconturbia in Italy.

Jones's sons, Bobby and Rees, have followed in his footsteps. Bobby was responsible for perhaps the nearest thing the Americans have to a links – Spanish Bay, next door to Cypress Point on the Monterey Peninsula, and he built one of England's most exclusive clubs, The Wisley in Surrey, which opened in 1991. Rees's work includes the widely acclaimed Haig Point in South Carolina, and he has also spread his wings into Britain, building The Oxfordshire, a lavish development that opened in summer 1993.

It may be that the most famous – or infamous – golf course architect of the modern generation has been another American, Paul (Pete) Dye. He has now joined his compatriots in exploiting the vast potential of Europe, but it is in and around the United States that he established a reputation which has carried around the world. His breathtakingly beautiful holes at Casa de Campo, beside the Caribbean surf of the Dominican Republic, epitomize his inventiveness and ability to

TREND SETTER *Robert Trent Jones Snr (below) has probably been the most influential American golf course architect in history, and he has also had a substantial impact outside his native country. His son, Robert Trent Jones Jnr, is also a golf course architect. The Wisley Golf Club in Surrey (below, right) which Jones Jnr designed, is one of several top-quality new courses built by Americans to open in the British Isles in recent years. It's a reversal of the pattern established by the likes of Mackenzie and Ross decades before.*

harness the machinery and implement the research which now makes it possible to drain marshes, irrigate deserts and replace a wilderness with paradise. The golf course architect today has to be an expert in agronomy, botany, chemistry, geology and civil engineering, or have access to someone who is, and combine these practical qualifications with the eye of an aesthete. Karl Litten's sculpting of the Emirates course from the desert of Dubai is an emblematic example of the genre.

Admiration and controversy have followed Dye's career in approximately equal measure. His signature mark is the use of railroad ties, or sleepers, an idea he stole from Scotland and took to America for inclusion at places like the Tournament Players' Club (at the PGA Tour's headquarters) in Florida and at Harbour Town in South Carolina. Across the US mainland in California, Lee Trevino said of Dye's PGA West: *"I know some courses which are easier than the practice ground here."*

Dye, like Trent Jones, has two sons – Perry and P. B. – in the architecture business, and with the latter he has collaborated on European projects like Domaine Imperial in Switzerland and Barbaroux in France. He and Jones are not alone among American designers in having designs on the continent. Bob von Hagge, to name just one other, has done notable work at Seignosse and Les Bordes in France.

Just as the original golf course architects were professional golfers, so many contemporary golfers – too many, some would complain – have done the opposite. Jack Nicklaus is the probably foremost professional golfer turned course architect. Several others (Arnold Palmer, Seve Ballesteros, Nick Faldo, Greg Norman – you name them, the chances are they're at it) have also taken the plunge, but most have not produced anything of the quality of Nicklaus's best. He has additionally undertaken work in Australia, Japan, continental Europe and Britain, where his debut effort was St Mellion in Cornwall. Mount Juliet, host to the Irish Open in 1993 and 1994, is another of Nicklaus's high-standard designs.

The British have not been moribund in the meantime. Fred Hawtree, whose father had been associated with J. H. Taylor, designed Royal Waterloo in Belgium, Hubbelrath in Germany and St Nom-la-Breteche near Paris. Ken Cotton produced Olgiata in Italy, while Frank Pennink numbered Halmstad in Sweden, Noordwijk in Holland and Vilamoura in

Portugal among his most impressive performances. These two formed a company with Charles Lawrie, and both courses at Woburn in Buckinghamshire are part of their British collection. Though those three are now dead, the firm continues to prosper at home and overseas with Donald Steel, formerly a distinguished golf correspondent, at the helm.

A lack of land and financial constraints led to precious few post-war courses of the quality of Southerness and Woburn adding to the enjoyment of golfers in the British Isles until the late 1980s and 1990s when, in addition to those already mentioned, further high-profile and high-quality new courses such as the Buckinghamshire and East Sussex, which has two excellent 18-hole layouts, were unveiled.

Of course, while everyone would like to be able to afford to build their dream course, and others would love to play it, the obvious need is for more rudimentary courses so that more people can take up the game and later experience the thrill of playing on some of the classics discussed in this chapter.

This is an era in which the demand is for courses that possess the 'natural look' – although cynics would say that in America this involves digging up the site at huge expense and then putting things back much as they were. Almost everywhere in the world these days, conservationist lobbies are, rightly, urging that the development of new golf courses be kept in check so as not to impair the natural scheme of things, and as we move inexorably towards the next century, the course architects will have to be sensitive of their obligations to the world as a whole and not merely to their clients. But properly conceived, the existence of a golf course can enhance the environment, indeed may protect it, rather than detract from it.

For *aficionados*, the course provides the reason for our affection and addiction to the sport. Undoubtedly, the greatest glory of golf lies in being out there, playing the game.

COMPUTER COURSE *These days, as in so many fields of professional life, golf courses can be designed (above) on computers and with the assistance of other high-tech office machinery.*

THE MASTER BUILDERS *Gary Player is just one of several eminent professional golfers today who are trying their hand at golf course architecture, just as Old Tom Morris was doing 100 years ago. This is his Lost City course (left) at Bophuthatswana, South Africa, during construction.*

CHAPTER NINE

CLASSIC COURSES

This selection of 30 golf courses takes in 13 from the British Isles – including the Republic of Ireland – nine from the United States, five from continental Europe and one each from South Africa, Canada and Australia. The list has, admittedly, been arrived at after a more arbitrary process than was used to choose the 40 'Household Names' profiled in Chapter 3 – a straw poll of one person; myself.

When embarking on the perilous task of comparing great golfers of one era with those of another, at least there are a few facts in the record books to substantiate one's opinions. The same is not true of courses.

Comparing golf courses is not only invidious but pretty pointless. Since one of the manifold attractions of playing the game is that no two courses are the same, one is invariably trying to draw a comparison between contrasts. For example, take Augusta National and the Old Course at St Andrews, the two courses afforded extended study in this chapter. Leaving aside their immense reputations and their position in the lore of the game as places where great sporting deeds and tragedies have been enacted (in Augusta's case, even though it is only 60 years old), and also the fact that they both have 18 holes, and you find they have little in common.

Augusta is lined with trees, has no rough to speak of, is built on hugely undulating terrain, has gleaming white fairway bunkers from which almost anyone could blithely escape with a 5-wood, has five holes on which water provides the major means of defence, has greens that are intimidatingly quick and fairways that are smoother than the greens at most other clubs. All this can be achieved because Augusta National is one of the most private clubs in the world and it shuts down for five months of the year.

The Old Course has no trees, is lined with gorse bushes, is – the odd bump apart – as flat as a pancake, has bunkers which even the best golfers in the world sometimes struggle to extricate themselves from at the first attempt, has greens of even speed and it used to be maintained to a standard which memorably caused Sam Snead to say in the week before he won the 1946 Open there that it looked "*an old abandoned*

sort of place ... so raggedy and beat up I was surprised to see what looked like fairway among the weeds." All this is because the Old Course is a public facility that caters for over 40,000 rounds a year and the only respite it gets from the visitors who flock to make their pilgrimage is on Sundays, when it's closed.

The Old Course is kept in rather better condition these days than it was just after the war, and granted it does have water in play on one hole, the notorious Swilcan Burn at the first, so it is not entirely a different specimen to Augusta. On the other hand, although both courses have large greens, St Andrews only has 11 of them!

The following certainly does not pretend to be a ranking of the best 30 courses in the world. But what these courses, specifically selected to give some geographical sweep, do illustrate is golf at its best; sometimes at its most exotic. They offer a glimpse of its infinite temptations and myriad charms – the splendid solitude of Morfontaine and Pine Valley; the tranquil beauty of Killarney and Sunningdale; the breathtaking views of Cypress Point and Turnberry; the ancient appeal of Carnoustie and Royal Dornoch; the rugged grandeur of Ballybunion and Royal St George's. All these and more, including Augusta and St Andrews, are here.

No doubt every reader and golfer would be able to suggest

courses they feel to be more deserving of inclusion but, as the saying goes, I have the typewriter. And whatever the rights and wrongs of my choices, all these courses could be adduced in evidence as part of the case for claiming that golf is the greatest game there is.

Early morning light and shadows throw Turnberry's humps and bumps into relief (opposite); while the huts (left) by the first tee greet golfers teeing off at Royal St George's.

AUGUSTA NATIONAL GEORGIA, USA

The genesis and subsequent elevation of Augusta National into an indisputably prominent position in the pantheon of the world's great golf courses is umbilically connected to its role as the permanent home of the Masters Tournament, which began in 1934.

The story of the Masters is related in Chapter 4 of this book. It is almost impossible to talk about the course without referring to the tournament, and vice versa. Bobby Jones founded the tournament with Clifford Roberts and he worked on the design of the course with Alister Mackenzie. It is hard to say whether the course or the tournament is more talked about by golfers the world over, even though only a precious few of them will ever get closer than their television sets to either.

When Augusta opened, it was revolutionary. There were only 22 bunkers on the whole course when it

Augusta's 10th hole may be the most beautiful par-4 in golf. Although it is not apparent from this photograph, the hole plays massively downhill, the sprawling bunker in the centre of the fairway is some 100 yards from the front of the green, and the green itself is raised about 25 feet above the fairway.

staged the first Masters and there remain fewer than 50 today (it doesn't pay to be too precise or dogmatic about such things because one never knows when a couple may be added or subtracted). The rough is negligible, the fairways are massively wide, the greens vast. The philosophy was to make the course easy for club members to play to their handicaps while posing severe problems for tournament golfers in search of birdies. Jones and Mackenzie achieved this by the judicious siting of the tees and by cultivating extremely fast, contoured greens which set as tough an examination of putting as is to be found anywhere.

At Augusta, getting to the green is only half the battle. There are places from which three-putting is almost mandatory, a consequence of the emphasis and value the course puts on iron play. The location of the pin is everything. When the course is set up for the Masters, nothing less than an exemplary approach shot will give the golfer a realistic chance of making a birdie. An indifferent one means a likely bogey.

Augusta demands decisions with almost every shot it takes, as on the dogleg-left 13th – at 485 yards, only just of par-5 length, but nevertheless one of the finest of the species in captivity.

The questions it poses include: does one play safe off the tee, to the right side of the fairway, bearing in mind that too far right lands you in the trees? Or does one try to cut the corner with the drive and risk tangling with those awesome pines on the left? And after an adequate drive, is it worth attempting the carry over the creek in front of the green with the second shot, thereby setting up a four or even a three, but at the same time risking a six or a seven as a result of going in the water?

The stories of golfers simultaneously losing their way and the Masters on the 13th are legion. Many have been recounted elsewhere in these pages. But

while water, golf's least compassionate hazard, guards the greens at Amen Corner (the 11th, 12th and 13th) and on the 15th and 16th, the intensity of the drama that annually unfolds in those places each April should not obscure the quality of the other holes at Augusta, perhaps notably the 10th. It's a magnificent, sweeping downhill hole of 485 yards (technically too long for a par-4, but Mackenzie and Jones refused to be hidebound by convention), where the green sits on a plateau in the shadow of a magnificent cathedral of pines.

The 10th, maybe more than any other hole, symbolizes the majesty of the course. But as many Masters contestants have painfully discovered down the years, Augusta can be both a beauty and a beast.

With bunkers to the left, a swale over the back and water in front and on the right, no one could ever say the 13th green (above) was defenceless. Meanwhile, the pond on the 16th hole (left) has decided the destiny of many Masters Tournaments.

BALLYBUNION
CO. KERRY, REPUBLIC OF IRELAND

There isn't a bunker on the 11th hole of the Old Course at Ballybunion. That's because it doesn't need one. Both in the way it hugs the sandhills and blends in with the coastal aspect, the hole is in total harmony with nature.

Herbert Warren Wind called the Old Course at Ballybunion "*the finest seaside course I have ever seen*". Robert Trent Jones described the property at his disposal for the building of the New as "*the finest piece of linksland that I had ever seen*".

There is no disagreement as such. Wind was writing in 1967, nearly 20 years before Trent Jones, with the considerable assistance of nature and not a little controversy, sculpted the New Course from this stretch of dramatic, tumbling duneland that, with its imposing peaks and sheltered valleys, is nothing short of perfect terrain for golf.

Tom Simpson recognized the Old for what it was when he was called in to revise it substantially for the 1937 Irish Amateur Championship, won by the 17-year-old native prodigy, Jimmy Bruen. Simpson moved just three greens and inserted one bunker, albeit a

prominent one on what was the 14th but, since the construction of a new clubhouse in 1971, is now the first. Part of Simpson's genius lay in his ability to acknowledge that even he could not improve on what the Almighty had done, and Ballybunion has an enviable selection of God-given holes, like the 7th and 11th, two stirring par-4s that run along the lofty cliff-tops, and the 6th, 10th and 15th, where in each case the approach to the green is framed by the panorama of the Atlantic beyond.

The New Course, too, has several tremendous holes, but one or two others that tend to the unfair or even bizarre, with small greens that would defy even Hogan to hit them with a breeze blowing, as there usually is. Nevertheless, Wind and Trent Jones would agree on one thing. Ballybunion is the possessor of the best 36 holes of links golf in the world.

CARNOUSTIE ANGUS, SCOTLAND

A plethora of golf courses have been described as the toughest in the world. At least when anybody says it about Carnoustie, nobody mocks the statement. With a wind blowing off the Tay Estuary, it can be 7,000 yards of torture.

The course is mercilessly exposed to the elements and unremittingly long. Never do more than two consecutive holes run in the same direction. As a test of golf, its devotees would argue that it is without peer. Its detractors are few and far between, but nobody would brag about its aesthetic appeal. Carnoustie is prosaic rather than poetic; bleak rather than beautiful; harsh rather than handsome. But despite being devoid of shelter and almost devoid of undulation, this otherwise unremarkable piece of property commands massive veneration throughout the golfing world. Although the sea is never in sight, water is. The sinuous Barry Burn

has swallowed up many shots at the 17th and 18th holes over the years.

Allan Robertson and Old Tom Morris both laid out some of the original holes at Carnoustie, and James Braid made alterations before it hosted its first Open, in 1931. Appropriately, for a town which exported so many of its sons to spread the golfing gospel in the United States, that championship was won by Tommy Armour, a Scottish expatriate. Henry Cotton (1937), Ben Hogan (1953), Gary Player (1968) and Tom Watson (1975) have been his successors – a mightily impressive roll-call. But a short one. After Watson's triumph, Carnoustie lost its place on the rota because the town could not cope with the extraneous matters, like access and accommodation, that are essential for the successful staging of the modern Open. But maybe in the 21st century, Carnoustie's time will come again.

This fearsome pot bunker isn't the only problem on the 16th at Carnoustie. The hole measures 250 yards off the back, which is on the limit for a par-3 and too much for most golfers if it is played into the wind. Tom Watson played the hole five times in winning the 1975 Open (once in the playoff) and took four here every day.

CYPRESS POINT
PEBBLE BEACH, CALIFORNIA, USA

This picture conveys the splendour of Cypress Point more powerfully than words ever could. The short 15th is in the foreground; the awesome 16th, a 233-yarder over the ocean, is at the far right.

The substantial and glowing reputation of Cypress Point is almost confined to three of its holes – the 15th, 16th and 17th, all of which are played to the accompanying sound of the Pacific breakers on the rocks below. That is unfortunate, if understandable. They are three of the finest holes on earth and are a major part of the reason why the course has been hailed as *"the Sistine Chapel of Golf"* by Sandy Tatum, a former president of the USGA. That is just one of thousands of compliments that have been bestowed on it. O.B. Keeler, Bobby Jones's biographer, extravagantly called it *"the crystallization of the dream of an artist who had been drinking gin and sobering up on absinthe"*.

Alister Mackenzie was certainly high on inspiration when he built Cypress Point in 1928. It is a magnificent amalgam of the best elements of links, woodland and heathland, and the early holes among the cypress trees and the dunes are worthy companions to their sensational successors beside the ocean. The 5th and 6th are tight, meandering consecutive par-5s; the 15th and 16th, respectively, short and long par-3s. But such transgressions from the orthodox cannot be construed as blemishes when they conspire to produce something as glorious as Cypress Point.

The club is ultra-exclusive, although it was one of the hosts to the AT&T Pro-Am until 1991 when it withdrew from the US tour in the wake of the Shoal Creek controversy (see page 111), but those who know it understand why so many people have said that if they were restricted to playing only one course from here to eternity, Cypress Point would be it.

DURBAN COUNTRY CLUB NATAL, SOUTH AFRICA

Despite the opening of some fine new layouts in recent years, Durban Country Club may well still be the best golf course in Africa. It presents an intriguing mixture of parkland golf in a seaside environment, with the wind off the nearby Indian Ocean a constant factor. And it's not only the presence of the wind that evokes comparisons with golf in Britain. Several holes are reminiscent of a traditional links, such as the par-4 17th, where the humps and hollows would do justice to somewhere like Prestwick.

At just over 6,500 yards, Durban Country Club does not rely on length to bemuse the golfer. It baffles him with its subtleties. The course closes with three par-4s – not, as one might ordinarily anticipate, all arduous monsters but instead all under 400 yards. After the bumpy ride of the 17th, where an uneven lie is almost guaranteed, the 18th is a 276-yard par-4. Not long enough to be a mundane hole, it is short enough to tempt a superior driver to go for broke. Make it, as Jock Brews did in 1928 when he drove the green and sank the eagle putt to win the South African Open by a stroke from his brother, Sid, and the thrill is immense. Carve the drive down the bank to the right and elation may well be substituted by misery.

While there are reminders of Britain in the atmosphere, Durban Country Club resembles many top American courses with its verdant appearance and true, quick greens. But it is also distinctly African. The inclination of the mischievous monkeys to pelt the golfer with nuts from the safety of their tree-tops leaves little doubt as to which continent this course is on.

The 3rd, a par-5 of 506 yards, may be the best hole at the Durban Country Club. With dense bush either side and large bunkers abundant, the narrow ribbon of fairway seems an elusive alley through which to attempt to thread a golf ball.

FALKENSTEIN HAMBURG, GERMANY

Several distinguished golf clubs are more commonly known by a name other than their official title – Royal Liverpool as Hoylake, Royal West Norfolk as Brancaster, for example – and so it is with Falkenstein. In this case, informality may be the best policy. The correct title is Hamburger Golf Club.

The course has a notable pedigree. It was designed by Harry Colt and completed in collaboration with Charles Alison and John Morrison, with later modifications by Bernhard von Limburger, Germany's finest golf course architect. In 1981 it was the setting for the first native victory in the 70-year history of the country's national Open. Bernhard Langer, the finest golfer Germany has ever produced, had to live up to the expectations of his compatriots who – having seen him finish runner-up in the Open Championship at Royal St George's the previous month – felt victory for

him in their Open was nothing more than a formality. Golf isn't that simple, of course, but Langer delivered the goods, much as the other Bernhard had done.

As befits the men who originally created it, Falkenstein is in the traditional English mould. Pine and birch trees dominate the setting, giving the course, which is close to the River Elbe, the ambience of golf in Berkshire or Surrey. The trees assume a threatening rather than a pleasing presence on the 10 dogleg holes in particular, but they always enhance the quality of the course. At under 6,700 yards, and with only one hole – the 2nd – at over 500 yards, Falkenstein is not long but, especially when the heather is out in summer, it plays long enough. Just as Langer has become an example for other German golfers to seek to emulate, so Falkenstein has become a role model for the next generation of German golf course designers.

Threatening bunkers contrast with the imposing gentleness of the birch and pine trees in establishing the mood for a round of golf at Falkenstein.

FALSTERBO
NEAR MALMO, SWEDEN

The par-3 11th hole is one of several to be located on the edge of the marshy sea-water lagoons that shelter bird life and savage golfers at Falsterbo.

The seemingly never-ending supply of good tournament golfers – male and female – coming out of Sweden these days has been one of the most notable developments in European golf, but back in their homeland the most acclaimed golf course is one of the oldest in Scandinavia, and also that relatively rare phenomenon, a classic links outside the British Isles. The holes have even been given names, in a strange mixture of English and Swedish, in the old Scottish fashion.

Falsterbo lies hard by the Baltic Sea and is a heartwarming prospect for an eager golfer in what can be an inhospitable climate. A lighthouse located near the middle of the course is incongruously placed to protect local shipping, but it does symbolically warn of the likelihood of flooding, which happens frequently in winter when the sea-water lagoons encroach on to the

course. Ordinarily, they only threaten errant golfers, as on the 4th hole, where the second shot has to find a green nestled by the edge of the marsh.

The reed-ridden marshes are a haven for a variety of species of bird life, which not only add to the environmental splendour of the place but make this a beguiling rather than dismally remote spot. While water is not a common hazard on a links, at Falsterbo it is entirely empathetic.

Elsewhere, the course reveals its more traditional links-style attributes, with punitive bunkers ready to devour any false or ill-judged stroke. All these facets come together at the closing hole, an imperious par-5 played from a high tee in the dunes overlooking the cold waves of the Baltic to a fairway that at first heads inland before tacking back to a green situated within yards of the beach. A strong finale to a strong course.

GLEN ABBEY
OAKVILLE, ONTARIO, CANADA

Having to hit an approach shot over the waters of Sixteen Mile Creek is the most daunting task facing a golfer on the 452-yard 11th hole at Glen Abbey.

In many respects, Glen Abbey was a pioneering golf course. It was built by Jack Nicklaus for the specific purpose of staging the Canadian Open each year, and consequently his brief included the provision of spectator mounds to make it easier for the public to watch the tournament.

But in between catering for this ancillary requirement, Nicklaus did not neglect his main duty. Glen Abbey is widely considered to be the best course in a country that boasts such excellent tests as Royal Montreal, the National and Banff Springs.

To be strictly accurate, Nicklaus did not so much build Glen Abbey as rebuild it. However, his course bears no resemblance to the original other than it occupies the same appealing site. Although he inserted his own water hazards, Nicklaus also made exemplary use of the natural amphitheatre created by Sixteen Mile

Creek, which is capable of making its presence felt on five holes on the back nine, the 11th to the 15th, which are set in a ravine.

Not for the last time, it has to be said, Nicklaus did not get things exactly right at the first time of asking. There were criticisms that the course overly favoured the golfer who faded the ball (like guess who?) and that some greens were too small.

Appropriate modifications have subsequently been undertaken. Mind you, Lee Trevino wasn't complaining when he won the 1977 Canadian Open, the first at Glen Abbey. The runner-up on that occasion was Peter Oosterhuis, who would win the title there in 1981 – his only ever triumph on the US tour therefore coming, ironically, outside the United States. Nicklaus, incidentally, was second to Oosterhuis, and he has never won over the course he created.

GLENEAGLES
AUCHTERARDER, PERTHSHIRE, SCOTLAND

When a visitor returns from his first visit to Gleneagles he will inevitably wax lyrical for hours on end about the breathtaking beauty and tranquillity of the surrounding hills and the opulent splendour of the famous adjoining hotel. The quality of the golf may well be an after-thought if the spell has enraptured him completely. That is not to cast aspersions on the quality of the courses; it is simply that the enchanting rural location of Gleneagles has a great deal in common with the settings normally associated with another great Scottish pursuit, salmon fishing. The course provides magnificent views of the Ochil Hills, the Trossachs and the Grampians.

The main course at Gleneagles is the King's, host to the Scottish Open on the European tour each July. It was laid out by James Braid as a superior holiday course, a vital ingredient that would lure the right sort of clientele to the hotel when it opened in 1924. Braid did a terrific job – the course is enjoyable and testing for golfers of every level of ability. The golden gorse in spring and the purple heather in late summer add to the serenity of the experience, and the sound of club striking ball off the seductively crisp turf is sometimes accompanied by the bucolic sound of pheasant, partridge or grouse.

Braid also designed the original nine holes of the Queen's Course, which is generally considered to be aesthetically superior to the King's, if a bit less demanding, while May 1993 saw the opening of Jack Nicklaus's Monarch Course. For a country that, Dutch sensibilities notwithstanding, is regarded as the home of golf, Scotland has few inland courses to match the best that England can offer. Gleneagles is the most glorious exception.

From behind the 17th green on the King's Course at Gleneagles, it is hard to say whether the surrounding countryside or the grand hotel is the more impressive sight.

KENNEMER
NEAR AMSTERDAM, HOLLAND

The rugged landscape on view from the 4th tee of the Championship Course at Kennemer gives a fitting impression of the testing nature of arguably the best course in Holland.

G iven that the Dutch have at least a tenable case for claiming that they played a part in the invention of golf, it is fitting to include a Dutch course here – apposite, too, that the choice is a genuine links that in part also resembles the great inland courses of Britain, with pine trees and bushes topping out many of the sandhills. This agreeable hybrid is Kennemer, the setting for Seve Ballesteros's first victory on the European tour, when he won the Dutch Open back in August 1976.

Kennemer consists of three loops of nine holes. These were originally called A, B and C, which demonstrated less ingenuity than Harry Colt brought to the task when he laid out the course in the 1920s. His work was then blighted by wartime fortifications, but the gun turrets and blockhouses were removed in 1947 and the only shooting going on at Kennemer these

days are scores in the 60s from the pros and doubtless some in three figures from the members.

These days, also, the three nines have more imaginative and attractive names. 'A' is called Van Hengel, appropriately enough, in view of the work Steven van Hengel did in establishing Dutch connections with the origins of the game.

The championship course comprises the Van Hengel nine and an amalgam of the other two, and at 6,650 yards and with a stingy par of 70, it represents an enervating challenge. At the 1989 Dutch Open, three under par was the winning score, after which it took Jose Maria Olazabal and Ronan Rafferty nine extra holes to determine the winner. That was the longest playoff in the tour's history – although somewhat shorter than the length of the debate about exactly where golf started.

KILLARNEY
CO. KERRY, REPUBLIC OF IRELAND

Its reputation as the Irish Gleneagles makes for an obvious analogy, but Killarney is capable of happily standing on its own merits. After all, Nick Faldo, no less, won the Irish Open there in both 1991 and 1992. These days, Killarney boasts two 18-hole layouts, Mahony's Point and Killeen, although there are those who preferred it when there was only one course.

That was the one designed by Sir Guy Campbell in 1939 and changed over the next four years by Viscount Castlerosse, the ebullient owner of this idyllic piece of countryside, in collaboration with his friend and fellow-journalist, Henry Longhurst. Castlerosse made significant alterations to 13 holes, sometimes redesigning them completely. The three closing holes on the original course, today the three closing holes on Mahony's Point, remain intact, and remain splendid.

The 16th, a par-5 without a bunker, rushes down towards the lake; the 17th, a par-4 without a bunker, hugs the shoreline of Lough Leane; and the 18th, a par-3 with sand, demands a long iron over the edge of the water to a green tucked into the trees. Longhurst, somewhat immodestly perhaps, called it "*the best short hole in the world*".

When Fred Hawtree laid out the Killeen Course in 1971, the existing course was split, although the clearing of the site did have the great advantage of opening up more land by the lake and therefore improving the golfers' views of Macgillicuddy's Reeks, Ireland's highest mountain range, which overlooks the scene. If now we have to play 36 holes to sample the best of Killarney, it has to be said that there are worse ways to pass the time.

When surveying the demands of the tee shot on the last hole at Mahony's Point, perhaps the biggest obstacle to overcome is to avoid being distracted by the breathtaking scenery.

MERION
PHILADELPHIA, PENNSYLVANIA, USA

The 13th hole at Merion only measures 127 yards, little more than a full wedge shot for most professionals, yet the small green and punitive bunkering, complete with the course's distinctive Scotch broom in the sand, can make the target an elusive one to find for even the best players.

From the 7th to the 13th on the East Course at Merion, there isn't a hole over 375 yards, and only two of those are par-3s. A triumph of routing and subtlety, it reflects the inspiration that its designer Hugh Wilson, an expatriate Scot, derived from Britain, notably in his use of severe bunkers – "*the white faces of Merion*" – dotted with wild broom to make them even more punitive. He also copied the idea of using wicker baskets instead of flags atop the sticks on the greens, something he had first seen at Sunningdale.

The first six holes include two gargantuan par-5s before players reach that stretch from the 7th that looks so simple on the card but in fact can destroy it. Over those seven holes, almost every shot has to be unerringly struck.

And then Merion has its big finish, the last three holes comprising a long par-3 sandwiched between two long par-4s, all built around an old quarry.

The flair Wilson demonstrated in conjuring up this perplexing blend of extremely demanding long holes and equally difficult short ones was immense. And his sagacity has seen Merion rewarded with some of the most memorable occasions in golf. Ben Hogan won the 1950 US Open, just over a year on from his horrendous car crash, after drilling a 1-iron into the heart of the final green to get into a playoff.

Lee Trevino beat Jack Nicklaus in another playoff at the '71 US Open, while in 1930 Bobby Jones completed the Grand Slam by closing out Gene Homans with a par-4 on the 11th hole of the afternoon round in the final of the US Amateur.

Another Gene, Sarazen, came to grief at that hole in the 1934 US Open, hitting into the Baffling Brook and running up a seven. He lost by a stroke to Olin Dutra. Merion has had its major moments all right.

MORFONTAINE
NEAR PARIS, FRANCE

No man did more to provide the French with golf courses of the highest order than Tom Simpson. Morfontaine was reputedly his first project across the Channel and it may well be the best. At 6,750 yards it is considered too short for men tour professionals, but that is their misfortune, not our problem. For the rest of us it is paradise, and no pushover. Pines, heather and sandy scrub represent the chief problems; its flawless condition and ethereal quiet are among the many pleasures.

The club is situated just outside the tiny village of Mortefontaine (no, that's not a misprint), about 30 miles north of central Paris. In many respects, it's the golfing equivalent of the Louvre. Despite being close to both Charles de Gaulle airport and the relentless traffic of the autoroute out of the city, the course is veritably a sylvan treasure, where rabbits and deer often outnumber the golfers. Apart from being exquisite, Morfontaine is also exclusive.

For Britons, the course might recall Woodhall Spa; for Americans, Pine Valley. Morfontaine is of that sort of calibre. Henry Longhurst called it "*the most attractive course in France*", and he could safely have cast the net wider than that. And although it is not daunting in terms of length, there are plenty of challenging holes. The course opens with a 470-yard par-4 and a 220-yard par-3, while the 15th and 16th are two fours that total over 940 yards. In addition to its superlative 18-hole course, Morfontaine has a marvellous par-35 nine-holer, another quality effort from Simpson where several greens have contours that make those at Augusta National seem gentle.

As well as showing that the hole obviously demands an accurate drive, something of the peacefulness that is an inherent part of the experience of playing golf at Morfontaine is captured in this view from the 9th tee.

MUIRFIELD
GULLANE, EAST LOTHIAN, SCOTLAND

It was from just off the back of this green that Lee Trevino crucially chipped in during the last round of the 1972 Open; on this green that John Cook missed a two-foot putt that opened the door again for Nick Faldo in 1992. Muirfield's 17th hole has played a significant part in Open history.

Despite the misgivings and insults which greeted its debut as a host to the Open Championship in 1892, Muirfield is today regarded as the fairest test on the rota. The vituperative comments of Andrew Kirkaldy and other staunch St Andreans (see page 72) have been replaced by an overwhelming accord that Muirfield is a fair yet testing examination of skill.

It represents a blend of two schools of thought about links golf, with the traditionalists being delighted at the sight of this fabulous stretch of genuine golfing ground close to the Firth of Forth and the modernists enraptured by the lack of blind shots, hidden hazards and irregular bounces. Like all links, Muirfield is the better for having a breeze blowing across it, but its touchy greens and the apparently magnetic properties of its deep bunkers provide adequate defence even in calm conditions. Muirfield's impressive roll of Open

champions – Harold Hilton, Harry Vardon, James Braid, Ted Ray, Walter Hagen, Alf Perry, Henry Cotton, Gary Player, Jack Nicklaus, Lee Trevino, Tom Watson and Nick Faldo – does not flatter it one bit. Fittingly, that's pretty exclusive company. The Honourable Company of Edinburgh Golfers, for whom Muirfield is home, is perhaps Britain's most exclusive golf club.

Like Braid, Faldo has won two Open Championships there – the last two, in 1987 and 1992. He won both times by a shot, respectively striking an imperious 5-iron and a towering 3-iron to the final green to set up the par that would bring him victory on each occasion. Nicklaus (in 1966) and Trevino (1972) also made solid fours there to win, Trevino having already produced an unreasonable degree of sorcery to destroy Tony Jacklin, but Player prevailed in 1958 despite a six at the last. There is always more than one way to win a championship.

MUIRFIELD VILLAGE DUBLIN, OHIO, USA

This is the definitive version of the course that Jack built. In recent years Jack Nicklaus has attempted to step out of his own immense shadow as the greatest professional golfer of his and maybe all generations to take on the golf course architects. Muirfield Village was only opened in 1974 yet already there are many experts who unhesitatingly award it a position among the top-10 courses in the United States.

The course is built on the outskirts of his home town of Columbus and is named in honour of the Scottish links where he made his Walker Cup debut in 1959 and won his first Open Championship, in 1966, although it inevitably bears no resemblance to its near-namesake. However, some holes seem to pay more than a merely passing compliment to Augusta National, where Nicklaus has won six Masters titles. The 12th, a par-3 across water, is like a hybrid of the 12th and 16th at Augusta. Elsewhere, the course highlights one of Nicklaus's user-friendly ideas about course architecture, with the first five holes and several others thereafter being played from a tee raised above the level of the green. The course requires every shot in the bag and it is always in immaculate condition. But that is no surprise. Nicklaus has never accepted anything less than excellence in himself, either when playing courses or when building them.

Apart from staging Nicklaus's own creation, the Memorial Tournament, each spring on the US tour, Muirfield Village was the scene of Europe's epic Ryder Cup victory in 1987. The theory beforehand was that the Europeans would not feel comfortable on such a quintessentially American golf course. In fact, they relished the perfection of Muirfield Village's maintenance and revelled in a historic triumph. The United States captain that year? Jack Nicklaus.

The 17th at Muirfield Village requires that the drive be struck to the left half of the fairway in order to open up the green for the second shot. Seve Ballesteros played the hole to perfection in his singles match against Curtis Strange in the 1987 Ryder Cup, and when he beat him by 2 & 1 on this green, that sealed Europe's victory.

PEBBLE BEACH
CALIFORNIA, USA

The 7th hole at Pebble Beach is a mere 107 yards, downhill at that. But the green is severely bunkered and when the wind blows in from off the Pacific, just over the back of the green, a medium iron may be needed from the tee. Tom Kite needed that much in the 1992 US Open, and then missed the green to the left. One pitch shot later he had an improbable birdie two and was on his way to the title.

Given their proximity to each other, comparisons between Pebble Beach and Cypress Point are inevitable. Much the same may be said about Rome and Venice because they both happen to be in Italy. Like those two great cities, the courses have differences and similarities but they are united by brilliance. All considered, the Italian analogy is not too grand.

Robert Louis Stevenson described Carmel Bay, which the best and most spectacular holes at Pebble Beach overlook, as "*the finest meeting of land and sea in the world*". That sets the appropriate tone. It may be that Pebble has more mundane holes than its illustrious neighbour but it probably possesses more holes of genuine championship quality, and its greater length means that it is able to test the best far more rigorously than Cypress can. Pebble Beach's holes beside the Pacific – from the 6th to the 10th, and then 17 and 18 –

command such glorious views that if the course were to be built today rather than in the 1920s, that land would be used for apartments. The 8th to the 10th are wild, glorious, daunting par-4s along the cliff-tops. Jack Nicklaus has called the approach to the 8th "*the finest second shot on any golf course I have ever seen*". It demands a blow across a chasm to a green 190 yards away. The beach is so close at this part of the course that even Nicklaus has played his second shot to the 10th hole from it.

That was in 1972, when he won the first US Open to be held at Pebble Beach. Ten years later Tom Watson thwarted the Golden Bear in a thrilling finale, and ten years after that Tom Kite claimed his first major championship when he survived the wind and the tension created by the many near-misses he had previously endured in the majors. In 2000, Pebble Beach will host the US Open for a fourth time.

PINEHURST
NORTH CAROLINA, USA

There are now seven courses at Pinehurst and, given the way new ones are springing up all over this pine-clad sand belt, there could be one or two more by the end of the century. But even if there are, it is a safe wager that none will eclipse Donald Ross's masterpiece.

The No. 2 course is synonymous with Pinehurst as surely as the Old Course is with St Andrews. It has an almost flamboyantly prosaic name, and granted it would not win a beauty contest against Cypress Point or Pebble Beach, but it constantly puzzles the golfer with the decisions it demands and baffles him with its insidious undulations. It is a particularly searching examination of chipping, and the manner in which the greens tend to repel anything less than a good shot is reminiscent of Royal Dornoch, where Ross learned his

craft. The course will succumb to great golf and 62s have been recorded in professional tournaments. The players that have achieved those scores should cherish them forever, because they enhance their reputations rather than detract from Pinehurst's. Tommy Armour summed up No. 2's appeal when he said: "*The man who doesn't feel emotionally stirred when he golfs at Pinehurst...should be ruled out of golf for life.*"

Ross's *tour de force* was opened in 1925 and it complements to perfection the grand scale, grace and tastefulness of what has long been one of America's most salubrious golf resorts. It has staged the US PGA Championship and the Ryder Cup in the past, and in 1991 and 1992 it hosted the season-ending Tour Championship on the US tour. And in 1999, the ultimate accolade – No. 2 will get the US Open.

With an overhanging pine by the tee and an unbroken line of them running the whole length of a par-5, Pinehurst is an appropriately named golf club. The 16th hole on No. 2 encapsulates its ageless appeal.

PINE VALLEY
CLEMENTON, NEW JERSEY, USA

The 10th hole at Pine Valley only measures 146 yards, and the bunker in the front-right portion of the green isn't that big. But it is deep. Very deep. A player once arrived at the 10th having played the front nine in 38. He went into the bunker and took 38 on this hole alone. One fourball reputedly took an aggregate of 88 shots to complete it. All in all, it's some short hole.

One disheartened American professional called Pine Valley "*a 184-acre bunker*". An awestruck English visitor once stood on the 2nd tee and asked: "*Do you play this hole or do you photograph it?*" Bernard Darwin, having once taken nine shots on the 327-yard 8th hole and still not being in the cup, picked up and remarked: "*It is all very well to punish a bad stroke, but the right of eternal punishment should be reserved for a higher tribunal than a green committee.*"

The above comments sum up Pine Valley, created almost whimsically by George Crump while the First World War was raging in Europe. The emerald fairways and greens are generous enough but the penalty for missing either is so severe that one is intimidated into doing exactly that. Thousands of courses afford plenty of opportunities to lose balls. At Pine Valley, it's easy to lose count. People have even lost their playing partners. The rough isn't rough, it's jungle in a desert. Horror stories are legion – a man taking 44 on a par-3, the club championship being won with a 33-over-par total of 173, and much more. It is the ultimate matchplay course – which made it a wonderful venue for the Walker Cup in 1985.

But in addition to being capable of causing so much terror, Pine Valley is also beautiful, both to behold and in the indescribable pleasure to be experienced from courting all that disaster and still pulling off the intended shot. One day a leading amateur, Woody Platt, played the first four holes in six under par: two birdies, an eagle and an ace. He knew that sort of thing couldn't last so he retired to the bar (conveniently located beside the 5th tee). Pine Valley has driven many golfers to drink, but the place is so bewitching that no one would wish to stay away for long. In golf, there's always the hope of the next time.

PORTMARNOCK
DUBLIN, REPUBLIC OF IRELAND

If it were British, Portmarnock would make an outstanding venue for the Open Championship. Instead, it is just outside Dublin, capital of the Irish Republic, so political considerations alone make the proposition an impossibility these days, even though in 1949 it held the only Amateur Championship to be played outside the British Isles. Nevertheless, it has been a regular and esteemed host to the Irish Open, and it has a significant reputation as an international venue, one that was enhanced by its staging of the World Cup in 1960 (when Arnold Palmer and Sam Snead were victorious for the United States) and the Walker Cup in 1991, and it holds realistic hopes of putting on the Ryder Cup in 2005.

Portmarnock shares several qualities with Muirfield. It presents all its problems with a frankness that immediately repudiates any allegation that the golfer's card has been ruined by clandestine means, and it is arranged in two loops of nine, thus avoiding the monotony often inherent in old-style links of having the wind in your face for nine consecutive holes. With a blue sky and scudding clouds above, its marvellous crisp turf beneath, and views over the estuary to the mainland in the distance, Portmarnock is an idyllic place to play golf, although when the weather turns nasty, so does the course. It measures over 7,100 yards off the back.

The site was initially annexed for its present purpose in 1893 by two locals who rowed across the estuary and found this ideal tract of golfing ground. After many alterations to the original layout, it is today a links of the highest order. Just look at the last five winners of the Irish Open there – Ballesteros, Langer, Woosnam (twice) and Olazabal.

The 15th brings together all the elements that make Portmarnock such a wonderful place to play golf. But as beautiful as the setting is, this is one of the most demanding par-3s to be found on any links.

ROYAL DORNOCH SUTHERLAND, SCOTLAND

Golf has been played at Dornoch since the early years of the 17th century, but its invariably undulating terrain, deep bunkers and upraised greens mean that it still presents a stringent test for contemporary golfers.

A trip to Royal Dornoch has acquired the mystique of being the golfing equivalent of the search for the Holy Grail. The place has acquired an almost mystical reputation, rather like a modern Camelot, an impression largely due to its geographical location, being some 60 miles north of Inverness. The good news about this, of course, is that Dornoch is surely the easiest great golf course in the world on which to get a game. And despite its remoteness, the course did host the Amateur Championship in 1985.

It has been established that golf was played at Dornoch at least as early as 1616, making it the third oldest-known course in the world after St Andrews and Leith. Donald Ross learned his skills as a golf course architect under the tutelage of Old Tom Morris, who laid out the second nine, and John Sutherland, the club's first secretary, while he was professional and greenkeeper at Dornoch late in the last century. In 1963, Pete Dye, one of the most renowned American architects of the modern era, was a neophyte when he visited the course for the first time. He returned home professing a fascination for its unspoilt qualities, its "*ageless aura*". Tom Watson has described it as "*a natural masterpiece*".

It was the replacement of six weak holes after the last war that upgraded the course's quality, a fundamental alteration enforced on the club because the RAF had requisitioned part of its land for an airstrip. The six new holes, the 6th to the 11th, blend in well with the old, maintaining Dornoch's chief characteristic – its upraised plateau greens, which make it unsurpassed as a links in its demands on the accuracy of the approach shot and the touch required with the short game.

ROYAL MELBOURNE VICTORIA, AUSTRALIA

Some of the most respected experts on the subject reckon that the sand belt of Melbourne has spawned as great a concentration of excellent golf courses as any other area of comparable size in the world. The pick of an unquestionably outstanding bunch is Royal Melbourne. There are two layouts – the West (by Alister Mackenzie) and the East (by Alex Russell) – but when authoritative voices proclaim that the club has one of the finest courses in the world, they are referring to a composite 18 which relies on 12 holes from Mackenzie's design and six from Russell's. This layout has hosted many prestigious tournaments, including several Australian Opens and the 1988 World Cup of Golf.

Two eminent professionals have declared this to be the best course in the world, period. One is Greg Norman, who may be biased by his nationality, and the other is Ben Crenshaw, who isn't. The course demands length and finesse, and an ability to plot one's way round and handle the fearsome pace of its greens. When they are set up for a tournament, it is doubtful that any course in the world – Augusta National included – has greens that are as quick.

The course is a glorious sight, a compelling blend of heathland and links to delight every golfer – and bedevil him. Its greens are the American model speeded up; its sand bunkers are evil places to escape from unscathed. Although the Composite Course stretches to almost 7,000 yards, it is discriminating in its use of length. The first eight holes have two par-4s under 350 yards and a par-3 of less than 150. In contrast, the round concludes with an uphill par-3 of 210 yards, a par-5 of 575 and an uphill par-4 of 432. Three pars to win is a tall order here.

The 5th hole at Royal Melbourne epitomizes the grandeur of Australia's best golf course and, along with renowned holes like the 12th at Augusta National and the 15th and 16th at Cypress Point, which are featured in this section, it emphasizes that Alister Mackenzie could design a pretty fine short hole.

ROYAL ST GEORGE'S SANDWICH, KENT, ENGLAND

The 6th hole at Royal St George's is called the 'Maiden'. While no pushover of a par-3 today, it used to be much more fearsome in the days when the green was obscured by the huge mound that gave the hole its name.

After a hiatus of 32 years, Royal St George's, which in 1894 had been the first English course to stage the Open Championship, returned to the Open rota in 1981. So successful was that championship – especially if you happened to be Bill Rogers – that the R & A awarded the club the championship again in 1985. The 1993 Open, one of the greatest of all time, was thus its third in 13 years and its twelfth altogether.

The club was founded in 1887 by a Scotsman, Dr Laidlaw Purves, and the links reflects many of the elements of the courses with which Purves would have been familiar. In the contemporary climate, Sandwich's tendency to uneven stances, occasional blind shots (though these days 'blind' doesn't so much mean blind as an inability to see the bottom of the flag with the approach shot) and unpredictable bounces frustrates professional golfers, even infuriates them, but when the course has a hint of green about it, as opposed to being hard, fast and dry, those awkward kicks are not quite so pronounced and even the most temperamental of modern tournament pros would concede – albeit maybe reluctantly – that St George's is a dragon not devoid of merit.

The sequence of holes from the 4th to the 8th is where the golfer is most at the mercy of the wind off the Channel, while the final four holes stand comparison with any. In the 1922 Open, George Duncan came to the last needing a four for a 68 (an incredible effort in those days) to tie Walter Hagen. His second shot found the depression to the left of the green and he took three more to get down. 'Duncan's Hollow' it became known as, and although Sandy Lyle took three to get down from much the same spot in 1985, the difference was that he won. The hollow caused no depression for him.

SEMINOLE
NORTH PALM BEACH, FLORIDA, USA

This is both a thinking man's course and a rich man's club. Palm Beach is one of the most exclusive winter playgrounds in the United States and Seminole reflects the Florida season by closing during the hot and humid summer months. For the rest of the year it provides arguably the best golf in the Sunshine State, albeit that only members and their guests get the chance to enjoy it. Seminole is not your average Florida resort course.

Seminole is said to be the only one of the hundreds of Donald Ross designs that he actually campaigned for; for the others he was sought out. He was doubtless attracted by the echoes of Scotland in the closeness of the ocean, the sea breezes and the fine, firm turf. It has other attributes that bear no resemblance to Ross's native country – such as warm winter air, omnipresent palm trees and over 200 gleaming white sand bunkers

which Ross created in harmony with the rolling Atlantic surf nearby – but its class transcends frontiers. The course also epitomizes the strategic, as opposed to penal, school of golf course design. Seminole presents a number of options on each tee and fairway, rewarding the bold golfer who executes a difficult shot but allowing the less audacious or less gifted player the opportunity to play the hole an easier way. Those who bite off more than they can chew are penalized in proportion to the gravity of their error, not irretrievably condemned to run up double figures.

Ben Hogan, who used the club as a place to hone his game each spring for the forthcoming season, and a man who is hardly free and easy with compliments, once said: "*If you can play Seminole, you can play any course in the world.*" But first of all, there's the very real problem of actually getting on it!

A Seminole experience. The 13th green is perched just above the Atlantic shoreline, and in the shaping and colouring of the bunkers, Donald Ross made this hole, among others, resemble the breaking waves of the ocean.

ST ANDREWS FIFE, SCOTLAND

While St Andrews may or may not be the place where golf began, it is its spiritual home. Although no hard evidence exists to substantiate the oft-repeated claim that the Old Course is the oldest course in the world (the first recorded reference to golf at St Andrews dates from January 25, 1552), it is reasonably regarded as the original golf course – the prototype on which all others are based.

Today, the graceful 'auld grey toun' has 99 holes of golf on its six courses, and the unique atmosphere and fascination of St Andrews lies in the manner in which golf is so integrally connected with the life of the town. Through times when religious, political and commercial fortunes were subjected to fluctuations, the Old Course remained a constant – not only in being there but in that its character has hardly changed since it was reduced from 22 holes to 18 in 1764.

While it has served as a paradigm of course design down the ages, its shared fairways and massive double greens – only the 1st, 9th, 17th and 18th have single greens – mean it could never supply a satisfactory blueprint for the courses that followed. For one thing, it only has two par-3s (the 8th and 11th) and two par-5s (the 5th and 14th). Robert Trent Jones, the American golf course architect, said: "*The Old Course is only right at St Andrews.*" It was built by nature, shaped by man.

Looping the Loop. The far end of the Old Course, out by the Eden Estuary, is where golfers are most confident of either consolidating a good score or retrieving a bad start.

The bunkers on the Old Course are pernicious. Many of these satanic orifices, often formed by sheltering sheep or foraging foxes and frequently hidden from view until you see your ball in one, contain just enough room "*for an angry man and his niblick*", to borrow Bernard Darwin's

memorable expression. Several have appropriately alarming names: 'Lion's Mouth', 'Hell', and 'Coffins'.

The course opens with the prospect of the joint widest fairway in the world, a distinction the first hole shares with the last since they share the same fairway. After that the direction of the wind will dictate whether it is the outward or the inward half that will play the easier. The stretch of shortish holes from the 7th to the 12th, known as 'The Loop', is where good scores are generally fashioned.

The wind is fundamental to the protection of the Old Course's integrity, but the punitive nature of its less capricious hazards mean that it is by no means outdated when it comes to repelling the best golfers in the world during an Open. The 17th, the Road Hole, with its nefarious bunker in front, "*eating its way into the very vitals*" of the green (to quote Darwin again), and the road beyond awaiting anything long, is the hardest hole in championship golf.

The Old Course is alive with the phantoms of champions past, an intangible thrill that may provide some compensation for one's inability to grasp its finer points as one encounters the hanging lies and hidden bunkers for the first time. The splendid subtleties are not revealed until the golfer returns, as he will surely endeavour to, but eventually he will appreciate that St Andrews is a wonderful test of strategic golf. The course favours the player who draws the ball, but while driving to the left will generally be a safe policy, the approach to the green will be harder from there. The reward for taking the intrepid line from the tee is always the pleasure of

being confronted by a much more straightforward shot to the flag.

Bobby Jones hated the course on his first visit in 1921. By the time he had won the Open and the Amateur there, he loved it. When he was made a Freeman of St Andrews in 1958, he spoke with eloquence about his conversion, saying: *"The more I studied the Old Course the more I loved it, and the more I loved it the more I studied it."* He added: *"There is always a way at St Andrews, although it is not always the obvious way."* As a tribute to its beguiling charms, that is as hard to beat as Jones was.

The R & A clubhouse in the distance (above) and the sinuous Swilcan Burn in the foreground are landmarks of St Andrews. Even from the road side of the green, it is obvious that the 17th (right) is a brute of a hole.

SHINNECOCK HILLS
SOUTHAMPTON, LONG ISLAND, NEW YORK, USA

This aerial shot indicates the perfect siting of Stanford White's clubhouse at Shinnecock Hills, while the natural flow of the holes over the land immediately invigorate the desire to go out and play the course.

This selection of nine American courses includes only three that have held the US Open: Merion, Pebble Beach – and Shinnecock Hills. The country is well endowed with great courses which do not need/want the honour/hassle of staging their country's national golf championship. Shinnecock went without it for 90 years, between the second US Open in 1896 and its second in 1986, because it was considered not to have the extraneous facilities necessary for a modern major championship.

The USGA eventually decided to return to America's first great golf course, and when the players arrived there in June 1986 they found the old course still a great one. Ben Crenshaw, the 1984 Masters champion, remarked: *"At the US Open, the golfers will have the privilege of playing Shinnecock."* What's more,

they will have it again when the US Open returns there in 1995, its centenary year. When the players had the privilege of playing the course in the 1986 US Open, Raymond Floyd had the privilege of winning the title with 279, just one under par.

The course is laid out on Long Island Sound, about two miles from the Atlantic and some 90 miles east of New York city. The original course is unrecognizable from the magnificent one that occupies the same terrain today, the latter having undergone substantial alterations between the wars, but the Stanford White clubhouse remains an elegant monument to a bygone age. In the design of both its course and its clubhouse, the club was ahead of its time at the end of the last century, and Floyd's winning total in 1986 suggests Shinnecock is not out of time at the end of this one.

SUNNINGDALE
BERKSHIRE, ENGLAND

Sunningdale is generally acclaimed to epitomize the most splendid qualities of inland golf in Britain. On a summer's evening, the birch, pine and heather conspire to create an intoxicating environment. The view from the 5th tee, with the 4th green in the foreground and the next two holes stretching out to the horizon between a gracious avenue of trees, has frequently been captured on film and canvas and it adorns clubhouse walls throughout the world. The panorama from the 10th tee is equally exhilarating, giving the impression that not only a sturdy par-4 but also most of the Home Counties are awaiting your drive.

The way it looks now, one could easily imagine that Sunningdale was carved through a forest by its designer, Willie Park, but in fact the trees were added by Harry Colt, the master architect, after he had been appointed secretary in 1901. The course is only just over 6,500 yards but it is crammed with artful holes. Two par-4s, the 3rd and 9th, are under 300 yards but often result in bogeys, while the 11th is a wonderfully delicate gem of just 325 yards. The course can be butchered by modern professionals – Ian Woosnam shot a 20-under-par total of 260 in winning the European Open in 1988 – but mostly it remains a thoroughly valid championship venue. The most famous score over it was Bobby Jones's 66 in a qualifying round for the 1926 Open, an almost unheard-of achievement in those days.

The Old Course, to which the foregoing refers, now has a worthy companion in the New, built by Colt in 1922. It may suffer by comparison in visual beauty but it is marginally tougher. In short, Sunningdale is one of the finest 36-hole golf clubs in the world.

The 7th hole on the Old Course at Sunningdale is unusual for that course in presenting the golfer with a blind tee shot. But the green, nestling seductively among the trees and the heather, is apparent enough for the next shot.

TURNBERRY AYRSHIRE, SCOTLAND

The distant tower of the lighthouse and the distant mass of the rock, Ailsa Craig, are two of the incidental delights of playing at Turnberry on a balmy summer's evening.

In 1994, Turnberry got its third stab at hosting the Open. It seems almost remarkable that this spectacular links on the west coast of Scotland – indeed, on some holes, absolutely on the coast – never held the championship before 1977, the year Tom Watson beat Jack Nicklaus by a stroke after playing the last 36 holes head-to-head, Watson taking 130 to his rival's 131. The so-called 'Duel in the Sun' was perhaps golf's greatest ever shoot-out. Any references to the sun were reserved for the last day in 1986, when Greg Norman strolled home unthreatened after setting up his victory with his excellent golf on the three previous, tempestuous days, notably with his truly astonishing 63 in the second round.

This is a magical spot; comparisons with Cypress Point and Pebble Beach are not entirely fanciful. The formidable mass of Ailsa Craig – the championship

links at Turnberry is called the Ailsa, the other being the Arran – rises from the Firth of Clyde and is one distinctive landmark. Chief among the others are the lighthouse close to the 9th tee, which itself is set on a rocky outcrop that does nothing to help the composure of anyone who suffers even mild vertigo, and the white-faced, terracotta-roofed hotel which was built by the Glasgow and South Western Railway Company to lure holiday-makers to the area in the early 1900s.

The golf courses, spread out below the hotel, have survived two world wars, during which they were seized by the authorities for use as an airstrip. But in the 1950s Philip Mackenzie Ross tore up the tarmac and restored the fairways and greens so effectively that the Ailsa Course is better than it ever was before. Mind you, with names like Mackenzie and Ross, how could he fail in his task?

VALDERRAMA
SOTOGRANDE, COSTA DEL SOL, SPAIN

Originally called Sotogrande New, to distinguish it from the famous old course of that name built by Robert Trent Jones across the main Gibraltar-Malaga road, this course's name was at first changed to Los Aves before Valderrama became the third attempt at getting it right. But then the course's owner, Jaime Ortiz-Patino, an extraordinarily wealthy and determined Bolivian businessman, will go to any lengths to get things right at his beloved golf club. Money is no object; perfection is.

Patino acquired the course in 1985 and brought in Trent Jones to make some improvements. The outcome is the toughest course on the European tour, one which has hosted the Volvo Masters, the annual climax to the season, each autumn since 1988. It is an outstanding examination of technique, ruthlessly exposing any flaws in a golfer's game both through the green and on

it. In the first five Volvo Masters, par was only broken eight times altogether at the end of 72 holes, and Nick Faldo was responsible for three of those efforts. When even he, indisputably the best golfer in the game, said in 1992: "*You have to play like God out there to shoot par*", one gets a sense of how demanding Valderrama can be. Sandy Lyle won with a three-over-par 287 that year. All week, there were only six rounds below 70 but 14 rounds in the 80s.

Valderrama commands gorgeous views out over the Mediterranean, which in turn means it is exposed to the capricious breezes that circulate between sea and mountains. Cork and olive trees line the fairways, at times encroaching almost claustrophobically into them. The bunkering is rigorous, too, and the greens are as slick and tricky as anything to be found in America. It is indeed a sort of European Augusta National.

It never pays to stray too far from the straight and narrow at Valderrama. The cork trees tend to ensnare the wayward drive and the gleaming white bunkers await anything awry with the approach.

WENTWORTH
VIRGINIA WATER, SURREY, ENGLAND

On the West Course at Wentworth, it is the holes on the back nine that are the best known, as a result of being shown on thousands of hours of television coverage. But that doesn't mean holes like the 7th are undeserving of attention.

Just as Augusta is synonymous with the Masters, so Wentworth is invariably associated with the World Matchplay Championship. Launched in 1964, since when it has run through three different sponsors before being presently ensconced with the Japanese car company Toyota, this is the world's premier individual matchplay event. Many of the game's great players – like Jack Nicklaus, Arnold Palmer and Nick Faldo – have won it. Gary Player and Seve Ballesteros share the record of five victories apiece.

The Matchplay is held over Wentworth's West Course, one of three 18-holers the club has. The East was the scene of the first Curtis Cup match in 1932 and, like the West, it was designed by Harry Colt. The Edinburgh is the latest addition, being opened in 1992 by the Duke of Edinburgh, hence the name. The club's professional, Bernard Gallacher, who collaborated in its design, is the present European Ryder Cup captain.

Throw in the fact that Wentworth is also the headquarters of the PGA European Tour, and it is apparent that the club is at the hub of the tournament scene in both Britain and Europe.

The West Course is two miles nearer London and 400 yards longer than Sunningdale Old. Its turf is heavier, too, and at the Matchplay in the autumn the course can play every bit of its 7,000 yards. When it hosts the British PGA Championship each spring, it tends to play shorter. When Colt laid out the West Course, which carries the exotic nickname of the Burma Road, in the 1920s, he made admirable use of the tree-lined estate. Most subsequent changes have been merely cosmetic, and Wentworth remains a searching test of golf. Its two closing holes, both par-5s, where the hope of a three can so quickly become the agonising reality of a seven, bring the round to a rousing finish.

WOODHALL SPA
LINCOLNSHIRE, ENGLAND

A small Lincolnshire town may seem an incongruous place in which to find what many would suggest is the finest inland course in the British Isles, but the suggestion is a far from preposterous one. The sandy-soiled, pine-clad, heather-covered terrain has been turned into a glorious golf course, and although Woodhall Spa has not hosted major professional tournaments, that is a consequence of its rural isolation – well away from the hurly-burly of big cities and major roads – rather than an aspersion on its quality. Besides, the club has its roots solidly founded in amateur golf, having hosted many important events on the international calendar.

A great golfer, Harry Vardon, completed the first nine holes on the current site at Woodhall Spa in 1905 and a great course architect, Harry Colt, added a second nine in 1912. In the 1920s, Colonel Stafford Hotchkin undertook a wholesale revision of their work and installed 17 new greens. That is essentially the course which provides such pleasure for golfers today. Hotchkin later built such esteemed layouts as West Sussex golf course in England, and also Humewood at Port Elizabeth in South Africa.

While no course on earth truly resembles Pine Valley, Woodhall Spa comes closer than most. It is one of those courses that can be tougher to get round in an economical number of strokes the better you know it. On the short 5th, for example, the green looks small enough from the tee, but only when you get there and see the cavernous bunkers surrounding it are you aware of just how demanding that tee shot was. Overall, though, it is in the mix of its par-4s that Woodhall Spa most impresses, with several stout two-shotters intermingling with a handful of fine drive-and-pitch holes. Overall, it's a masterpiece that all golfers should enjoy and all course architects could learn from.

There are few places in golf as serene or agreeable as Woodhall Spa. As on all the finest inland courses in England, heather plays a prominent role in adding both colour to the environment as well as teeth to the course.

CHAPTER TEN

REFERENCE TABLES

On the following pages are the winners of each of the most significant

international competitions in golf since their inception. Appropriate details are carried in the

foregoing chapters of this book.

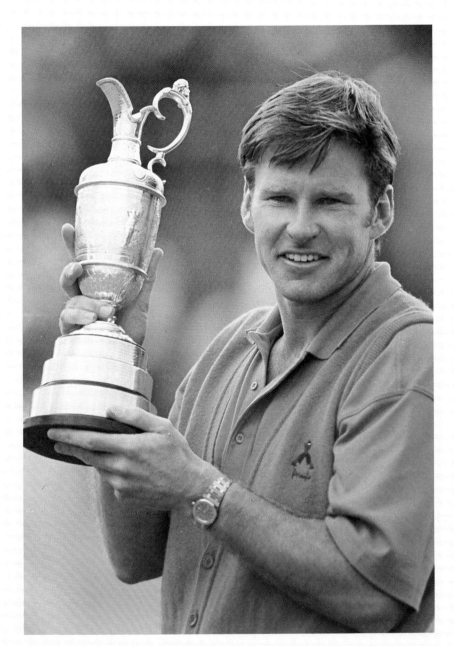

WE ARE THE CHAMPIONS *Walter Hagen graciously accepts the Open trophy for the second time in succession in 1929 (left). It was his fourth win in the event and the sixth in succession for US players. In modern times, British golfers have done rather better, notably Nick Faldo (right), whose win at Muirfield in 1992 was his third in the championship in six years.*

THE OPEN CHAMPIONSHIP

Year	Venue	Winner	Score
1860	Prestwick	Willie Park Snr	174
1861	Prestwick	Tom Morris Snr	163
1862	Prestwick	Tom Morris Snr	163
1863	Prestwick	Willie Park Snr	168
1864	Prestwick	Tom Morris Snr	167
1865	Prestwick	Andrew Strath	162
1866	Prestwick	Willie Park Snr	169
1867	Prestwick	Tom Morris Snr	170
1868	Prestwick	Tom Morris Jnr	157
1869	Prestwick	Tom Morris Jnr	154
1870	Prestwick	Tom Morris Jnr	149
1872	Prestwick	Tom Morris Jnr	166
1873	St Andrews	Tom Kidd	179
1874	Musselburgh	Mungo Park	159
1875	Prestwick	Willie Park Snr	166
1876	St Andrews	Bob Martin	176
1877	Royal Musselburgh	Jamie Anderson	160
1878	Prestwick	Jamie Anderson	157
1879	St Andrews	Jamie Anderson	169
1880	Royal Musselburgh	Bob Ferguson	162
1881	Prestwick	Bob Ferguson	170
1882	St Andrews	Bob Ferguson	171
1883	Royal Musselburgh	Willie Fernie	159*
1884	Prestwick	Jack Simpson	160
1885	St Andrews	Bob Martin	171
1886	Royal Musselburgh	David Brown	157
1887	Prestwick	Willie Park Jnr	161
1888	St Andrews	Jack Burns	171
1889	Royal Musselburgh	Willie Park Jnr	155*
1890	Prestwick	John Ball †	164
1891	St Andrews	Hugh Kirkaldy	166

Competition extended from 36 to 72 holes

Year	Venue	Winner	Score
1892	Muirfield	Harold Hilton †	305
1893	Prestwick	William Auchterlonie	322
1894	St George's	J.H. Taylor	326
1895	St Andrews	J.H. Taylor	322
1896	Muirfield	Harry Vardon	316*
1897	Royal Liverpool	Harold Hilton †	314
1898	Prestwick	Harry Vardon	307
1899	St George's	Harry Vardon	310
1900	St Andrews	J.H. Taylor	309
1901	Muirfield	James Braid	309

Year	Venue	Winner	Score
1902	Royal Liverpool	Sandy Herd	307
1903	Prestwick	Harry Vardon	300
1904	Royal St George's	Jack White	296
1905	St Andrews	James Braid	318
1906	Muirfield	James Braid	300
1907	Royal Liverpool	Arnaud Massy	312
1908	Prestwick	James Braid	291
1909	Cinque Ports (Deal)	J.H. Taylor	295
1910	St Andrews	James Braid	299
1911	Royal St George's	Harry Vardon	303
1912	Muirfield	Ted Ray	295
1913	Royal Liverpool	J.H. Taylor	304
1914	Prestwick	Harry Vardon	306
1920	Cinque Ports (Deal)	George Duncan	303
1921	St Andrews	Jock Hutchison	296*
1922	Royal St George's	Walter Hagen	300
1923	Troon	Arthur Havers	295
1924	Royal Liverpool	Walter Hagen	301
1925	Prestwick	Jim Barnes	300
1926	Royal Lytham & St Annes	Bobby Jones †	291
1927	St Andrews	Bobby Jones †	285
1928	Royal St George's	Walter Hagen	292
1929	Muirfield	Walter Hagen	292
1930	Royal Liverpool	Bobby Jones †	291
1931	Carnoustie	Tommy Armour	296
1932	Prince's	Gene Sarazen	283
1933	St Andrews	Densmore Shute	292*
1934	Royal St George's	Henry Cotton	283
1935	Muirfield	Alf Perry	283
1936	Royal Liverpool	Alf Padgham	287
1937	Carnoustie	Henry Cotton	290
1938	Royal St George's	Reg Whitcombe	295
1939	St Andrews	Dick Burton	290
1946	St Andrews	Sam Snead	290
1947	Royal Liverpool	Fred Daly	293
1948	Muirfield	Henry Cotton	284
1949	Royal St George's	Bobby Locke	283*
1950	Troon	Bobby Locke	279
1951	Royal Portrush	Max Faulkner	285
1952	Royal Lytham & St Annes	Bobby Locke	287
1953	Carnoustie	Ben Hogan	282
1954	Royal Birkdale	Peter Thomson	283
1955	St Andrews	Peter Thomson	281
1956	Royal Liverpool	Peter Thomson	286
1957	St Andrews	Bobby Locke	279
1958	Royal Lytham & St Annes	Peter Thomson	278*

* playoff † amateur

Year	Venue	Winner	Score
1959	Muirfield	Gary Player	284
1960	St Andrews	Kel Nagle	278
1961	Royal Birkdale	Arnold Palmer	284
1962	Troon	Arnold Palmer	276
1963	Royal Lytham & St Annes	Bob Charles	277*
1964	St Andrews	Tony Lema	279
1965	Royal Birkdale	Peter Thomson	285
1966	Muirfield	Jack Nicklaus	282
1967	Royal Liverpool	Roberto de Vicenzo	278
1968	Carnoustie	Gary Player	289
1969	Royal Lytham & St Annes	Tony Jacklin	280
1970	St Andrews	Jack Nicklaus	283*
1971	Royal Birkdale	Lee Trevino	278
1972	Muirfield	Lee Trevino	278
1973	Troon	Tom Weiskopf	276
1974	Royal Lytham & St Annes	Gary Player	282
1975	Carnoustie	Tom Watson	279*
1976	Royal Birkdale	Johnny Miller	279
1977	Turnberry	Tom Watson	268
1978	St Andrews	Jack Nicklaus	281
1979	Royal Lytham & St Annes	Seve Ballesteros	283
1980	Muirfield	Tom Watson	271
1981	Royal St George s	Bill Rogers	276
1982	Royal Troon	Tom Watson	284
1983	Royal Birkdale	Tom Watson	275
1984	St Andrews	Seve Ballesteros	276
1985	Royal St George s	Sandy Lyle	282
1986	Turnberry	Greg Norman	280
1987	Muirfield	Nick Faldo	279
1988	Royal Lytham & St Annes	Seve Ballesteros	273
1989	Royal Troon	Mark Calcavecchia	275*
1990	St Andrews	Nick Faldo	270
1991	Royal Birkdale	Ian Baker–Finch	272
1992	Muirfield	Nick Faldo	272
1993	Royal St George's	Greg Norman	267

* playoff † amateur

THE US OPEN CHAMPIONSHIP

Year	Venue	Winner	Score
1895	Newport	Horace Rawlins	173
1896	Shinnecock Hills	James Foulis	152

YEAR	VENUE	WINNER	SCORE	YEAR	VENUE	WINNER	SCORE
1897	Chicago	Joe Lloyd	162	1949	Medinah	Cary Middlecoff	286
				1950	Merion	Ben Hogan	287*
Competition extended from 36 to 72 holes				1951	Oakland Hills	Ben Hogan	287
				1952	Northwood	Julius Boros	281
1898	Myopia Hunt	Fred Herd	328	1953	Oakmont	Ben Hogan	283
1899	Baltimore	Willie Smith	315	1954	Baltusrol	Ed Furgol	284
1900	Chicago	Harry Vardon	313	1955	Olympic	Jack Fleck	287*
1901	Myopia Hunt	Willie Anderson	331*	1956	Oak Hill	Cary Middlecoff	281
1902	Garden City	Laurie Auchterlonie	307	1957	Inverness	Dick Mayer	282*
1903	Baltusrol	Willie Anderson	307*	1958	Southern Hills	Tommy Bolt	283
1904	Glen View	Willie Anderson	303	1959	Winged Foot	Billy Casper	282
1905	Myopia Hunt	Willie Anderson	314	1960	Cherry Hills	Arnold Palmer	280
1906	Onwentsia	Alex Smith	295	1961	Oakland Hills	Gene Littler	281
1907	Philadelphia	Alex Ross	302	1962	Oakmont	Jack Nicklaus	283*
1908	Myopia Hunt	Fred McLeod	322*	1963	Brookline	Julius Boros	293*
1909	Englewood	George Sargent	290	1964	Congressional	Ken Venturi	278
1910	Philadelphia	Alex Smith	298*	1965	Bellerive	Gary Player	282*
1911	Chicago	John McDermott	307*	1966	Olympic	Billy Casper	278*
1912	Buffalo	John McDermott	294	1967	Baltusrol	Jack Nicklaus	275
1913	Brookline	Francis Ouimet †	304*	1968	Oak Hill	Lee Trevino	275
1914	Midlothian	Walter Hagen	290	1969	Champions	Orville Moody	281
1915	Baltusrol	Jerome Travers †	297	1970	Hazeltine	Tony Jacklin	281
1916	Minikahda	Chick Evans †	286	1971	Merion	Lee Trevino	280*
1919	Brae Burn	Walter Hagen	301*	1972	Pebble Beach	Jack Nicklaus	290
1920	Inverness	Ted Ray	295	1973	Oakmont	Johnny Miller	279
1921	Columbia	Jim Barnes	289	1974	Winged Foot	Hale Irwin	287
1922	Skokie	Gene Sarazen	288	1975	Medinah	Lou Graham	287*
1923	Inwood	Bobby Jones †	296*	1976	Atlanta	Jerry Pate	277
1924	Oakland Hills	Cyril Walker	297	1977	Southern Hills	Hubert Green	278
1925	Worcester	Willie MacFarlane	291*	1978	Cherry Hills	Andy North	285
1926	Scioto	Bobby Jones †	293	1979	Inverness	Hale Irwin	284
1927	Oakmont	Tommy Armour	301*	1980	Baltusrol	Jack Nicklaus	272
1928	Olympia Fields	Johnny Farrell	294*	1981	Merion	David Graham	273
1929	Winged Foot	Bobby Jones †	294*	1982	Pebble Beach	Tom Watson	282
1930	Interlachen	Bobby Jones †	287	1983	Oakmont	Larry Nelson	280
1931	Inverness	Billy Burke	292*	1984	Winged Foot	Fuzzy Zoeller	276*
1932	Fresh Meadow	Gene Sarazen	286	1985	Oakland Hills	Andy North	279
1933	North Shore	Johnny Goodman †	287	1986	Shinnecock Hills	Ray Floyd	279
1934	Merion	Olin Dutra	293	1987	Olympic	Scott Simpson	277
1935	Oakmont	Sam Parks	299	1988	Brookline	Curtis Strange	278*
1936	Baltusrol	Tony Manero	282	1989	Oak Hill	Curtis Strange	278
1937	Oakland Hills	Ralph Guldahl	281	1990	Medinah	Hale Irwin	280*
1938	Cherry Hills	Ralph Guldahl	284	1991	Hazeltine	Payne Stewart	282*
1939	Philadelphia	Byron Nelson	284*	1992	Pebble Beach	Tom Kite	285
1940	Canterbury	Lawson Little	287*	1993	Baltusrol	Lee Janzen	272
1941	Colonial	Craig Wood	284	*playoff† amateur*			
1946	Canterbury	Lloyd Mangrum	284*				
1947	St Louis	Lew Worsham	282*				
1948	Riviera	Ben Hogan	276				

THE MASTERS TOURNAMENT

HELD AT AUGUSTA NATIONAL GOLF CLUB

YEAR	WINNER	SCORE
1934	Horton Smith	284
1935	Gene Sarazen	282*
1936	Horton Smith	285
1937	Byron Nelson	283
1938	Henry Picard	285
1939	Ralph Guldahl	279
1940	Jimmy Demaret	280
1941	Craig Wood	280
1942	Byron Nelson	280*
1946	Herman Keiser	282
1947	Jimmy Demaret	281
1948	Claude Harmon	279
1949	Sam Snead	282
1950	Jimmy Demaret	283
1951	Ben Hogan	280
1952	Sam Snead	286
1953	Ben Hogan	274
1954	Sam Snead	289*
1955	Cary Middlecoff	279
1956	Jack Burke	289
1957	Doug Ford	283
1958	Arnold Palmer	284
1959	Art Wall	284
1960	Arnold Palmer	282
1961	Gary Player	280
1962	Arnold Palmer	280*
1963	Jack Nicklaus	286
1964	Arnold Palmer	276
1965	Jack Nicklaus	271
1966	Jack Nicklaus	288
1967	Gay Brewer	280
1968	Bob Goalby	277
1969	George Archer	281
1970	Billy Casper	279*
1971	Charles Coody	279
1972	Jack Nicklaus	286
1973	Tommy Aaron	283
1974	Gary Player	278
1975	Jack Nicklaus	276
1976	Ray Floyd	271
1977	Tom Watson	276
1978	Gary Player	277
1979	Fuzzy Zoeller	280*
1980	Seve Ballesteros	275

Year	Winner	Score
1981	Tom Watson	280
1982	Craig Stadler	284
1983	Seve Ballesteros	280
1984	Ben Crenshaw	277
1985	Bernhard Langer	282
1986	Jack Nicklaus	279
1987	Larry Mize	285*
1988	Sandy Lyle	281
1989	Nick Faldo	283*
1990	Nick Faldo	278*
1991	Ian Woosnam	277
1992	Fred Couples	275
1993	Bernhard Langer	277
1994	Jose Maria Olazabal	279

playoff

THE US PGA CHAMPIONSHIP

Year	Venue	Winner	Margin
1916	Siwanoy	Jim Barnes	1 up
1919	Engineers	Jim Barnes	6 & 5
1920	Flossmoor	Jock Hutchison	1 up
1921	Inwood	Walter Hagen	3 & 2
1922	Oakmont	Gene Sarazen	4 & 3
1923	Pelham	Gene Sarazen	at 38th
1924	French Lick	Walter Hagen	2 up
1925	Olympia Fields	Walter Hagen	6 & 5
1926	Salisbury	Walter Hagen	5 & 3
1927	Cedar Crest	Walter Hagen	1 up
1928	Five Farms	Leo Diegel	6 & 5
1929	Hillcrest	Leo Diegel	6 & 4
1930	Fresh Meadow	Tommy Armour	1 up
1931	Wannamoisett	Tom Creavy	2 & 1
1932	Keller	Olin Dutra	4 & 3
1933	Blue Mound	Gene Sarazen	5 & 4
1934	Park	Paul Runyan	at 38th
1935	Twin Hills	Johnny Revolta	5 & 4
1936	Pinehurst	Densmore Shute	3 & 2
1937	Pittsburgh	Densmore Shute	at 37th
1938	Shawnee	Paul Runyan	8 & 7
1939	Pomonok	Henry Picard	at 37th
1940	Hershey	Byron Nelson	1 up
1941	Cherry Hills	Vic Ghezzi	at 38th
1942	Seaview	Sam Snead	2 & 1
1944	Manito	Bob Hamilton	1 up
1945	Morraine	Byron Nelson	4 & 3
1946	Portland	Ben Hogan	6 & 4
1947	Plum Hollow	Jim Ferrier	2 & 1
1948	Norwood Hills	Ben Hogan	7 & 6
1949	Hermitage	Sam Snead	3 & 2
1950	Scioto	Chandler Harper	4 & 3
1951	Oakmont	Sam Snead	7 & 6
1952	Big Spring	Jim Turnesa	1 up
1953	Birmingham	Walter Burkemo	2 & 1
1954	Keller	Chick Harbert	4 & 3
1955	Meadowbrook	Doug Ford	4 & 3
1956	Blue Hill	Jack Burke	3 & 2
1957	Miami Valley	Lionel Hebert	2 & 1

Competition changed to strokeplay

Year	Venue	Winner	Score
1958	Llanerch	Dow Finsterwald	276
1959	Minneapolis	Bob Rosburg	277
1960	Firestone	Jay Hebert	281
1961	Olympia Fields	Jerry Barber	277*
1962	Aronimink	Gary Player	278
1963	Dallas	Jack Nicklaus	279
1964	Columbus	Bobby Nichols	271
1965	Laurel Valley	Dave Marr	280
1966	Firestone	Al Geiberger	280
1967	Columbine	Don January	281*
1968	Pecan Valley	Julius Boros	281
1969	NCR (Dayton)	Ray Floyd	276
1970	Southern Hills	Dave Stockton	279
1971	PGA National	Jack Nicklaus	281
1972	Oakland Hills	Gary Player	281
1973	Canterbury	Jack Nicklaus	277
1974	Tanglewood	Lee Trevino	276
1975	Firestone	Jack Nicklaus	276
1976	Congressional	Dave Stockton	281
1977	Pebble Beach	Lanny Wadkins	282*
1978	Oakmont	John Mahaffey	276*
1979	Oakland Hills	David Graham	272*
1980	Oak Hill	Jack Nicklaus	274
1981	Atlanta	Larry Nelson	273
1982	Southern Hills	Ray Floyd	272
1983	Riviera	Hal Sutton	274
1984	Shoal Creek	Lee Trevino	273
1985	Cherry Hills	Hubert Green	278
1986	Inverness	Bob Tway	276
1987	PGA National	Larry Nelson	287*
1988	Oak Tree	Jeff Sluman	272
1989	Kemper Lakes	Payne Stewart	276
1990	Shoal Creek	Wayne Grady	282
1991	Crooked Stick	John Daly	276
1992	St Louis	Nick Price	278
1993	Inverness	Paul Azinger	272*

playoff

THE RYDER CUP

Year	Venue	Winners	Margin
1927	Worcester	USA	9½-2½
1929	Moortown	GB & I	7-5
1931	Scioto	USA	9-3
1933	Southport & Ainsdale	GB & I	6½-5½
1935	Ridgewood	USA	9-3
1937	Southport & Ainsdale	USA	8-4
1947	Portland	USA	11-1
1949	Ganton	USA	7-5
1951	Pinehurst	USA	9½-2½
1953	Wentworth	USA	6½-5½
1955	Thunderbird	USA	8-4
1957	Lindrick	GB & I	7½-4½
1959	Eldorado	USA	8½-3½
1961	Royal Lytham & St Annes	USA	14½-9½
1963	East Lake	USA	23-9
1965	Royal Birkdale	USA	19½-12½
1967	Champions	USA	23½-8½
1969	Royal Birkdale	tie	16-16
1971	Old Warson	USA	18½-13½
1973	Muirfield	USA	19-13
1975	Laurel Valley	USA	21-11
1977	Royal Lytham & St Annes	USA	12½-7½
1979	Greenbrier	USA	17-11
1981	Walton Heath	USA	18½-9½
1983	PGA National	USA	14½-13½
1985	The Belfry	Europe	16½-11½
1987	Muirfield Village	Europe	15-13
1989	The Belfry	tie	14-14
1991	Kiawah Island	USA	14½-13½
1993	The Belfry	USA	15-13

THE US WOMEN'S OPEN CHAMPIONSHIP

Year	Venue	Winner	Margin
1946	Spokane	Patty Berg	5 & 4

Competition changed to strokeplay

| 1947 | Greensboro | Betty Jameson | 295 |

REFERENCE TABLES 215

YEAR	VENUE	WINNERS	SCORE
1948	Atlantic City	Babe Zaharias	300
1949	Landover	Louise Suggs	291
1950	Wichita	Babe Zaharias	291
1951	Atlanta	Betsy Rawls	293
1952	Bala	Louise Suggs	284
1953	Rochester	Betsy Rawls	302*
1954	Salem	Babe Zaharias	291
1955	Wichita	Fay Crocker	299
1956	Duluth	Kathy Cornelius	302*
1957	Winged Foot	Betsy Rawls	299
1958	Bloomfield Hills	Mickey Wright	290
1959	Pittsburgh	Mickey Wright	287
1960	Worcester	Betsy Rawls	292
1961	Baltusrol	Mickey Wright	293
1962	Myrtle Beach	Murle Lindstrom	301
1963	Kenwood	Mary Mills	289
1964	San Diego	Mickey Wright	290
1965	Atlantic City	Carol Mann	290*
1966	Hazeltine National	Sandra Spuzich	297
1967	Hot Springs	Catherine Lacoste †	294
1968	Moselem Springs	Susie Berning	289
1969	Scenic Hills	Donna Caponi	294
1970	Muskogee	Donna Caponi	287
1971	Erie	JoAnne Gunderson Carner	288
1972	Winged Foot	Susie Berning	299
1973	Rochester	Susie Berning	290
1974	La Grange	Sandra Haynie	295
1975	Atlantic City	Sandra Palmer	295
1976	Springfield	JoAnne Gunderson Carner	292*
1977	Hazeltine National	Hollis Stacy	292
1978	Indianapolis	Hollis Stacy	289
1979	Brooklawn	Jerilyn Britz	284
1980	Richland	Amy Alcott	280
1981	La Grange	Pat Bradley	279
1982	Del Paso	Janet Alex	283
1983	Cedar Ridge	Jan Stephenson	290
1984	Salem	Hollis Stacy	290
1985	Baltusrol	Kathy Baker	280
1986	NCR (Dayton)	Jane Geddes	287*
1987	Plainfield	Laura Davies	285*
1988	Baltimore	Liselotte Neumann	277
1989	Indianwood	Betsy King	278
1990	Duluth	Betsy King	284
1991	Colonial	Meg Mallon	283
1992	Oakmont	Patty Sheehan	280
1993	Crooked Stick	Lauri Merten	280

*playoff † amateur

THE WOMEN'S BRITISH OPEN CHAMPIONSHIP

YEAR	VENUE	WINNER	SCORE
1976	Fulford	Jenny Lee Smith †	299
1977	Lindrick	Vivien Saunders	306
1978	Foxhills	Janet Melville †	310
1979	Southport & Ainsdale	Alison Sheard	301
1980	Wentworth	Debbie Massey	294
1981	Northumberland	Debbie Massey	295
1982	Royal Birkdale	Marta Figueras-Dotti †	296
1984	Woburn	Ayako Okamoto	289
1985	Moor Park	Betsy King	300
1986	Royal Birkdale	Laura Davies	283
1987	St Mellion	Alison Nicholas	296
1988	Lindrick	Corinne Dibnah	295*
1989	Ferndown	Jane Geddes	274
1990	Woburn	Helen Alfredsson	288*
1991	Woburn	Penny Grice–Whittaker	284
1992	Woburn	Patty Sheehan (reduced to 54 holes)	207
1993	Woburn	Karen Lunn	275

* playoff † amateur

THE SOLHEIM CUP

YEAR	VENUE	WINNER	MARGIN
1990	Lake Nona	USA	11½-4½
1992	Dalmahoy	Europe	11½-6½

THE AMATEUR CHAMPIONSHIP

YEAR	VENUE	WINNER	MARGIN
1885	Royal Liverpool	Allan MacFie	7 & 6
1886	St Andrews	Horace Hutchinson	7 & 6
1887	Royal Liverpool	Horace Hutchinson	1 hole
1888	Prestwick	John Ball	5 & 4
1889	St Andrews	Johnny Laidlay	2 & 1
1890	Royal Liverpool	John Ball	4 & 3
1891	St Andrews	Johnny Laidlay	at 20th
1892	St George's	John Ball	3 & 1
1893	Prestwick	Peter Anderson	1 hole
1894	Royal Liverpool	John Ball	1 hole
1895	St Andrews Melville	Leslie Balfour	at 19th
1896	St George's	Freddie Tait	8 & 7
1897	Muirfield	Jack Allan	4 & 2
1898	Royal Liverpool	Freddie Tait	7 & 5
1899	Prestwick	John Ball	at 37th
1900	St George's	Harold Hilton	8 & 7
1901	St Andrews	Harold Hilton	1 hole
1902	Royal Liverpool	Charles Hutchings	1 hole
1903	Muirfield	Robert Maxwell	7 & 5
1904	Royal St George's	Walter Travis	4 & 3
1905	Prestwick	Gordon Barry	3 & 2
1906	Royal Liverpool	James Robb	4 & 3
1907	St Andrews	John Ball	6 & 4
1908	Royal St George's	E.A. Lassen	7 & 6
1909	Muirfield	Robert Maxwell	1 hole
1910	Royal Liverpool	John Ball	10 & 9
1911	Prestwick	Harold Hilton	4 & 3
1912	Royal North Devon	John Ball	at 38th
1913	St Andrews	Harold Hilton	6 & 5
1914	Royal St George's	J.L.C. Jenkins	3 & 2
1920	Muirfield	Cyril Tolley	at 37th
1921	Royal Liverpool	Willie Hunter	12 & 11
1922	Prestwick	Ernest Holderness	1 hole
1923	Cinque Ports (Deal)	Roger Wethered	7 & 6
1924	St Andrews	Ernest Holderness	3 & 2
1925	Royal North Devon	Robert Harris	13 & 12
1926	Muirfield	Jess Sweetser	6 & 5
1927	Royal Liverpool	William Tweddell	7 & 6
1928	Prestwick	Philip Perkins	6 & 4
1929	Royal St George's	Cyril Tolley	4 & 3
1930	St Andrews	Bobby Jones	7 & 6
1931	Royal North Devon	Eric Martin Smith	1 hole
1932	Muirfield	John de Forest	3 & 1
1933	Royal Liverpool	Hon. Michael Scott	4 & 3
1934	Prestwick	Lawson Little	14 & 13
1935	Royal Lytham & St Annes	Lawson Little	1 hole
1936	St Andrews	Hector Thomson	2 holes
1937	Royal St George's	Robert Sweeny	3 & 2
1938	Troon	Charlie Yates	3 & 2
1939	Royal Liverpool	Alex Kyle	2 & 1
1946	Birkdale	James Bruen	4 & 3
1947	Carnoustie	William Turnesa	8 & 6
1948	Royal St George's	Frank Stranahan	5 & 4
1949	Portmarnock	Max McCready	2 & 1

Year	Venue	Winner	Margin
1950	St Andrews	Frank Stranahan	8 & 6
1951	Royal Porthcawl	Richard Chapman	5 & 4
1952	Prestwick	Harvie Ward	6 & 5
1953	Royal Liverpool	Joe Carr	2 holes
1954	Muirfield	Douglas Bachli	2 & 1
1955	Royal Lytham & St Annes	Joseph Conrad	3 & 2
1956	Troon	John Beharrell	5 & 4
1957	Formby	Reid Jack	2 & 1
1958	St Andrews	Joe Carr	3 & 2
1959	Royal St George's	Deane Beman	3 & 2
1960	Royal Portrush	Joe Carr	8 & 7
1961	Turnberry	Michael Bonallack	6 & 4
1962	Royal Liverpool	Richard Davies	1 hole
1963	St Andrews	Michael Lunt	2 & 1
1964	Ganton	Gordon Clark	at 39th
1965	Royal Porthcawl	Michael Bonallack	2 & 1
1966	Carnoustie	Bobby Cole	3 & 2
1967	Formby	Bob Dickson	2 & 1
1968	Troon	Michael Bonallack	7 & 6
1969	Royal Liverpool	Michael Bonallack	3 & 2
1970	Royal County Down	Michael Bonallack	8 & 7
1971	Carnoustie	Steve Melnyk	3 & 2
1972	Royal St George's	Trevor Homer	4 & 3
1973	Royal Porthcawl	Dick Siderowf	5 & 3
1974	Muirfield	Trevor Homer	2 holes
1975	Royal Liverpool	Vinny Giles	8 & 7
1976	St Andrews	Dick Siderowf	at 37th
1977	Ganton	Peter McEvoy	5 & 4
1978	Troon	Peter McEvoy	4 & 3
1979	Hillside	Jay Sigel	3 & 2
1980	Royal Porthcawl	Duncan Evans	4 & 3
1981	St Andrews	Philippe Ploujoux	4 & 2
1982	Royal Cinque Ports	Martin Thompson	4 & 3
1983	Turnberry	Philip Parkin	5 & 4
1984	Formby	Jose Maria Olazabal	5 & 4
1985	Royal Dornoch	Garth McGimpsey	8 & 7
1986	Royal Lytham & St Annes	David Curry	11 & 9
1987	Prestwick	Paul Mayo	3 & 1
1988	Royal Porthcawl	Christian Hardin	1 hole
1989	Royal Birkdale	Stephen Dodd	5 & 3
1990	Muirfield	Rolf Muntz	7 & 6
1991	Ganton	Gary Wolstenholme	8 & 6
1992	Carnoustie	Stephen Dundas	7 & 6
1993	Royal Portrush	Iain Pyman	at 37th

THE US AMATEUR
CHAMPIONSHIP

Year	Venue	Winner	Margin
1895	Newport	Charles Macdonald	12 & 11
1896	Shinnecock Hills	H.J. Whigham	8 & 7
1897	Chicago	H.J. Whigham	8 & 6
1898	Morris County	Findlay Douglas	5 & 3
1899	Owentsia	Herbert Harriman	3 & 2
1900	Garden City	Walter Travis	2 holes
1901	Atlantic City	Walter Travis	5 & 4
1902	Glen View	Louis James	4 & 2
1903	Nassau	Walter Travis	5 & 4
1904	Baltusrol	Chandler Egan	8 & 6
1905	Chicago	Chandler Egan	6 & 5
1906	Englewood	Eben Byers	2 holes
1907	Euclid	Jerome Travers	6 & 5
1908	Garden City	Jerome Travers	8 & 7
1909	Chicago	Robert A. Gardner	4 & 3
1910	Brookline	William Fownes	4 & 3
1911	Apawamis	Harold Hilton	at 37th
1912	Chicago	Jerome Travers	7 & 6
1913	Garden City	Jerome Travers	5 & 4
1914	Ekwanok	Francis Ouimet	6 & 5
1915	Detroit	Robert A. Gardner	5 & 4
1916	Merion	Chick Evans	4 & 3
1919	Oakmont	Davidson Herron	5 & 4
1920	Engineers	Chick Evans	7 & 6
1921	St Louis	Jesse Guilford	7 & 6
1922	Brookline	Jess Sweetser	3 & 2
1923	Flossmoor	Max Marston	at 38th
1924	Merion	Bobby Jones	9 & 8
1925	Oakmont	Bobby Jones	8 & 7
1926	Baltusrol	George von Elm	2 & 1
1927	Minikahda	Bobby Jones	8 & 7
1928	Brae Burn	Bobby Jones	10 & 9
1929	Del Monte	Harrison Johnston	4 & 3
1930	Merion	Bobby Jones	8 & 7
1931	Beverly	Francis Ouimet	6 & 5
1932	Baltimore	Ross Somerville	2 & 1
1933	Kenwood	George Dunlap	6 & 5
1934	Brookline	Lawson Little	8 & 7
1935	Cleveland	Lawson Little	4 & 2
1936	Garden City	Johnny Fischer	at 37th
1937	Alderwood	Johnny Goodman	2 holes
1938	Oakmont	William Turnesa	8 & 7
1939	North Shore	Marvin Ward	7 & 5

Year	Venue	Winner	Margin
1940	Winged Foot	Richard Chapman	11 & 9
1941	Omaha Field	Marvin Ward	4 & 3
1946	Baltusrol	Stanley Bishop	at 37th
1947	Pebble Beach	Robert Riegel	2 & 1
1948	Memphis	William Turnesa	2 & 1
1949	Oak Hill	Charles Coe	11 & 10
1950	Minneapolis	Sam Urzetta	at 39th
1951	Saucon Valley	Billy Maxwell	4 & 3
1952	Seattle	Jack Westland	3 & 2
1953	Oklahoma City	Gene Littler	1 hole
1954	Detroit	Arnold Palmer	1 hole
1955	Virginia	Harvie Ward	9 & 8
1956	Knollwood	Harvie Ward	5 & 4
1957	Brookline	Hillman Robbins	5 & 4
1958	Olympic	Charles Coe	5 & 4
1959	Broadmoor	Jack Nicklaus	1 hole
1960	St Louis	Deane Beman	6 & 4
1961	Pebble Beach	Jack Nicklaus	8 & 6
1962	Pinehurst	Labron Harris	1 hole
1963	Wakonda	Deane Beman	2 & 1
1964	Canterbury	William C. Campbell	1 hole

Competition changed to strokeplay			**Score**
1965	Southern Hills	Bob Murphy	291
1966	Merion	Gary Cowan	285*
1967	Broadmoor	Bob Dickson	285
1968	Scioto	Bruce Fleisher	284
1969	Oakmont	Steve Melnyk	286
1970	Waverley	Lanny Wadkins	279
1971	Wilmington	Gary Cowan	280
1972	Charlotte	Vinny Giles	285

Reverted to matchplay			**Margin**
1973	Inverness	Craig Stadler	6 & 5
1974	Ridgewood	Jerry Pate	2 & 1
1975	Richmond	Fred Ridley	2 holes
1976	Bel-Air	Bill Sander	8 & 6
1977	Aronimink	John Fought	9 & 8
1978	Plainfield	John Cook	5 & 4
1979	Canterbury	Mark O'Meara	8 & 7
1980	Pinehurst	Hal Sutton	9 & 8
1981	Olympic	Nathaniel Crosby	at 37th
1982	Brookline	Jay Sigel	8 & 7
1983	North Shore	Jay Sigel	8 & 7
1984	Oak Tree	Scott Verplank	4 & 3
1985	Montclair	Sam Randolph	1 hole
1986	Shoal Creek	Buddy Alexander	5 & 3

Year	Venue	Winner	Margin
1987	Jupiter Hills	Billy Mayfair	4 & 3
1988	Hot Springs	Eddie Meeks	7 & 6
1989	Merion	Chris Patton	3 & 1
1990	Englewood	Phil Mickelson	5 & 4
1991	Honours Course	Mitch Vosges	7 & 6
1992	Muirfield Village	Justin Leonard	8 & 7
1993	Champions	John Harris	5 & 3

* playoff

THE WALKER CUP

Year	Venue	Winners	Margin
1922	National Golf Links	USA	8-4
1923	St Andrews	USA	6½-5½
1924	Garden City	USA	9-3
1926	St Andrews	USA	6½-5½
1928	Chicago	USA	11-1
1930	Royal St George's	USA	10-2
1932	Brookline	USA	9½-2½
1934	St Andrews	USA	9½-2½
1936	Pine Valley	USA	10½-1½
1938	St Andrews	GB & I	7½-4½
1947	St Andrews	USA	8-4
1949	Winged Foot	USA	10-2
1951	Royal Birkdale	USA	7½-4½
1953	Kittansett	USA	9-3
1955	St Andrews	USA	10-2
1957	Minikahda	USA	8½-3½
1959	Muirfield	USA	9-3
1961	Seattle	USA	11-1
1963	Turnberry	USA	14-10
1965	Baltimore	tie	12-12
1967	Royal St George's	USA	15-9
1969	Milwaukee	USA	13-11
1971	St Andrews	GB & I	13-11
1973	Brookline	USA	14-10
1975	St Andrews	USA	15½-8½
1977	Shinnecock Hills	USA	16-8
1979	Muirfield	USA	15½-8½
1981	Cypress Point	USA	15-9
1983	Royal Liverpool	USA	13½-10½
1985	Pine Valley	USA	13-11
1987	Sunningdale	USA	16½-7½
1989	Peachtree	GB & I	12½-11½
1991	Portmarnock	USA	14-10
1993	Interlachen	USA	19-5

THE LADIES' BRITISH AMATEUR CHAMPIONSHIP

Year	Venue	Winner	Margin
1893	Royal Lytham & St Annes	Lady Margaret Scott	7 & 5
1894	Littlestone	Lady Margaret Scott	3 & 2
1895	Royal Portrush	Lady Margaret Scott	3 & 2
1896	Royal Liverpool	Amy Pascoe	3 & 2
1897	Gullane	Edith Orr	4 & 2
1898	Yarmouth	Lena Thomson	7 & 5
1899	County Down	May Hezlet	2 & 1
1900	Royal North Devon	Rhona Adair	6 & 5
1901	Aberdovey	Miss Graham	3 & 1
1902	Cinque Ports	May Hezlet	at 19th
1903	Royal Portrush	Rhona Adair	4 & 3
1904	Troon	Lottie Dod	1 hole
1905	Cromer	Bertha Thompson	3 & 2
1906	Burnham	Mrs Kennion	4 & 3
1907	County Down	May Hezlet	2 & 1
1908	St Andrews	Maud Titterton	at 19th
1909	Birkdale	Dorothy Campbell	4 & 3
1910	Royal North Devon	Grant Suttie	6 & 4
1911	Royal Portrush	Dorothy Campbell	3 & 2
1912	Turnberry	Gladys Ravenscroft	3 & 2
1913	Royal Lytham & St Annes	Muriel Dodd	8 & 6
1914	Hunstanton	Cecil Leitch	2 & 1
1920	Royal County Down	Cecil Leitch	7 & 6
1921	Turnberry	Cecil Leitch	4 & 3
1922	Prince's	Joyce Wethered	9 & 7
1923	Burnham	Doris Chambers	2 holes
1924	Royal Portrush	Joyce Wethered	7 & 6
1925	Troon	Joyce Wethered	at 37th
1926	Royal St David's	Cecil Leitch	8 & 7
1927	Royal County Down	Simone Thion de la Chaume	5 & 4
1928	Hunstanton	Nanette le Blan	3 & 2
1929	St Andrews	Joyce Wethered	3 & 1
1930	Formby	Diana Fishwick	4 & 3
1931	Portmarnock	Enid Wilson	7 & 6
1932	Saunton	Enid Wilson	7 & 6
1933	Gleneagles	Enid Wilson	5 & 4
1934	Royal Porthcawl	Helen Holm	6 & 5
1935	Royal County Down	Wanda Morgan	3 & 2
1936	Southport & Ainsdale	Pam Barton	5 & 3

Year	Venue	Winner	Margin
1937	Turnberry	Jessie Anderson	6 & 4
1938	Burnham	Helen Holm	4 & 3
1939	Royal Portrush	Pam Barton	2 & 1
1946	Hunstanton	Jean Hetherington	1 hole
1947	Gullane	Babe Zaharias	5 & 4
1948	Royal Lytham & St Annes	Louise Suggs	1 hole
1949	Royal St David's	Frances Stephens	5 & 4
1950	Royal County Down	Vicomtesse de Saint Sauveur	3 & 2
1951	Broadstone	Kitty MacCann	4 & 3
1952	Troon	Moira Paterson	at 39th
1953	Royal Porthcawl	Marlene Stewart	7 & 6
1954	Ganton	Frances Stephens	4 & 3
1955	Royal Portrush	Jessie Valentine	7 & 6
1956	Sunningdale	Margaret Smith	8 & 7
1957	Gleneagles	Philomena Garvey	4 & 3
1958	Hunstanton	Jessie Valentine	1 hole
1959	Ascot	Elizabeth Price	at 37th
1960	Royal St David's	Barbara McIntire	4 & 2
1961	Carnoustie	Marley Spearman	7 & 6
1962	Royal Birkdale	Marley Spearman	1 hole
1963	Royal County Down	Brigitte Varangot	3 & 1
1964	Prince's	Carol Sorenson	at 37th
1965	St Andrews	Brigitte Varangot	4 & 3
1966	Ganton	Elizabeth Chadwick	3 & 2
1967	Royal St David's	Elizabeth Chadwick	1 hole
1968	Walton Heath	Brigitte Varangot	at 20th
1969	Royal Portrush	Catherine Lacoste	1 hole
1970	Gullane	Dinah Oxley	1 hole
1971	Alwoodley	Mickey Walker	3 & 1
1972	Hunstanton	Mickey Walker	2 holes
1973	Carnoustie	Ann Irvin	3 & 2
1974	Royal Porthcawl	Carol Semple	2 & 1
1975	St Andrews	Nancy Syms	3 & 2
1976	Silloth	Cathy Panton	1 hole
1977	Hillside	Angela Uzielli	6 & 5
1978	Notts	Edwina Kennedy	1 hole
1979	Nairn	Maureen Madill	2 & 1
1980	Woodhall Spa	Anne Sander	3 & 1
1981	Caernarvonshire	Belle Robertson	at 20th
1982	Walton Heath	Kitrina Douglas	4 & 2
1983	Silloth	Jill Thornhill	4 & 2
1984	Royal Troon	Jody Rosenthal	4 & 3
1985	Ganton	Lilian Behan	1 hole
1986	West Sussex	Marnie McGuire	2 & 1
1987	Royal St David's	Janet Collingham	at 19th
1988	Royal Cinque Ports	Joanne Furby	4 & 3
1989	Royal Liverpool	Helen Dobson	6 & 5

YEAR	VENUE	WINNER	MARGIN
1990	Dunbar	Julie Hall	3 & 2
1991	Pannal	Valerie Michaud	3 & 2
1992	Saunton	Pernille Pederson	1 hole
1993	Royal Lytham & St Annes	Catriona Lambert	3 & 2

THE US WOMEN'S AMATEUR CHAMPIONSHIP

YEAR	VENUE	WINNER	SCORE
1895	Meadowbrook	Mrs Charles Brown	132

Competition changed to matchplay — MARGIN

YEAR	VENUE	WINNER	MARGIN
1896	Morris County	Beatrix Hoyt	2 & 1
1897	Essex	Beatrix Hoyt	5 & 4
1898	Ardsley	Beatrix Hoyt	5 & 3
1899	Philadelphia	Ruth Underhill	2 & 1
1900	Shinnecock Hills	Frances Griscom	6 & 5
1901	Baltusrol	Genevieve Hecker	5 & 3
1902	Brookline	Genevieve Hecker	4 & 3
1903	Chicago	Bessie Anthony	7 & 6
1904	Merion	Georgianna Bishop	5 & 3
1905	Morris County	Pauline Mackay	1 hole
1906	Brae Burn	Harriot Curtis	2 & 1
1907	Midlothian	Margaret Curtis	7 & 6
1908	Chevy Chase	Katherine Harley	6 & 5
1909	Merion	Dorothy Campbell	3 & 2
1910	Homewood	Dorothy Campbell	2 & 1
1911	Baltusrol	Margaret Curtis	5 & 3
1912	Essex	Margaret Curtis	3 & 2
1913	Wilmington	Gladys Ravenscroft	2 holes
1914	Glen Cove	Mrs Amold Jackson	1 hole
1915	Onwentsia	Mrs C.H. Vanderbeck	3 & 2
1916	Belmont Springs	Alexa Stirling	2 & 1
1919	Shawnee	Alexa Stirling	6 & 5
1920	Mayfield	Alexa Stirling	5 & 4
1921	Hollywood	Marion Hollins	5 & 4
1922	Greenbrier	Glenna Collet	5 & 4
1923	Westchester	Edith Cummings	3 & 2
1924	Rhode Island	Dorothy Campbell Hurd	7 & 6
1925	St Louis	Glenna Collett	9 & 8
1926	Menon	Helen Stetson	3 & 1
1927	Cherry Valley	Miriam Bums Horn	5 & 4
1928	Hot Springs	Glenna Collett	13 & 12
1929	Oakland Hills	Glenna Collett	4 & 3
1930	Los Angeles	Glenna Collett	6 & 5
1931	Buffalo	Helen Hicks	2 & 1
1932	Salem	Virginia Van Wie	10 & 8
1933	Exmore	Virginia Van Wie	4 & 3
1934	Whitemarsh Valley	Virginia Van Wie	2 & 1
1935	Interlachen	Glenna Collett Vare	3 & 2
1936	Canoe Brook	Pam Barton	4 & 3
1937	Memphis	Mrs Julius Page	7 & 6
1938	Westmoreland	Patty Berg	6 & 5
1939	Wee Burn	Betty Jameson	3 & 2
1940	Del Monte	Betty Jameson	6 & 5
1941	Brookline	Betty Hicks Newell	5 & 3
1946	Southern Hills	Babe Zaharias	11 & 9
1947	Franklin Hills	Louise Suggs	2 holes
1948	Del Monte	Grace Lenczyk	4 & 3
1949	Menon	Dorothy Porter	3 & 2
1950	Atlanta	Beverly Hanson	6 & 4
1951	St Paul	Dorothy Kirby	2 & 1
1952	Waverley	Jacqueline Pung	2 & 1
1953	Rhode Island	Mary Lena Faulk	3 & 2
1954	Allegheny	Barbara Romack	4 & 2
1955	Myers Park	Patricia Lesser	7 & 6
1956	Meridian Hills	Marlene Stewart	2 & 1
1957	Del Paso	JoAnne Gunderson	8 & 6
1958	Wee Burn	Anne Quast	3 & 2
1959	Congressional	Barbara McIntire	4 & 3
1960	Tulsa	Joanne Gunderson	6 & 5
1961	Tacoma	Anne Decker	14 & 13
1962	Rochester	Joanne Gunderson	9 & 8
1963	Taconic	Anne Welts	2 & 1
1964	Prairie Dunes	Barbara McIntire	3 & 2
1965	Lakewood	Jean Ashley	5 & 4
1966	Sewickley Heights	Joanne Gunderson Carner	at 41st
1967	Annandale	Mary Lou Dill	5 & 4
1968	Birmingham	JoAnne Gunderson Carner	5 & 4
1969	Las Colinas	Catherine Lacoste	3 & 2
1970	Wee Burn	Martha Wilkinson	3 & 2
1971	Atlanta	Laura Baugh	1 hole
1972	St Louis	Mary Anne Budke	5 & 4
1973	Rochester	Carol Semple	1 hole
1974	Seattle	Cynthia Hill	5 & 4
1975	Brae Burn	Beth Daniel	3 & 2
1976	Del Paso	Donna Horton	2 & 1
1977	Cincinnati	Beth Daniel	3 & 1
1978	Sunnybrook	Cathy Sherk	4 & 3
1979	Memphis	Carolyn Hill	7 & 6
1980	Prairie Dunes	Juli Inkster	2 holes
1981	Waverley	Juli Inkster	1 hole
1982	Broadmoor	Juli Inkster	4 & 3
1983	Canoe Brook	Joanne Pacillo	2 & 1
1984	Seattle	Deb Richard	1 hole
1985	Fox Chapel	Michiko Hattori	5 & 4
1986	Pasatiempo	Kay Cockerill	9 & 7
1987	Barrington	Kay Cockerill	3 & 2
1988	Minikahda	Pearl Sinn	6 & 5
1989	Pinehurst	Vicki Goetze	4 & 3
1990	Canoe Brook	Pat Hurst	at 37th
1991	Prairie Dunes	Amy Fruhwirth	5 & 4
1992	Kemper Lakes	Vicki Goetze	1 hole
1993	San Diego	Jill McGill	1 hole

THE CURTIS CUP

YEAR	VENUE	WINNER	SCORE
1932	Wentworth	USA	5½-3½
1934	Chevy Chase	USA	6½-2½
1936	Gleneagles	tie	4½-4½
1938	Essex	USA	5½-3½
1948	Birkdale	USA	6½-2½
1950	Buffalo	USA	7½-1½
1952	Muirfield	GB & I	5-4
1954	Merion	USA	6-3
1956	Prince's	GB & I	5-4
1958	Brae Burn	tie	4½-4½
1960	Lindrick	USA	6½-2½
1962	Broadmoor	USA	8-1
1964	Royal Porthcawl	USA	10½-7½
1966	Hot Springs	USA	13-5
1968	Royal County Down	USA	10½-7½
1970	Bae Burn	USA	11½-6½
1972	Western Gailes	USA	10-8
1974	San Francisco	USA	13-5
1976	Royal Lytham & St Annes	USA	11½-6½
1978	Apawamis	USA	12-6
1980	St Pierre	USA	13-5
1982	Denver	USA	14½-3½
1984	Muirfield	USA	9½-8½
1986	Prairie Dunes	GB & I	13-5
1988	Royal St George's	GB & I	11-7
1990	Somerset Hills	USA	14-4
1992	Royal Liverpool	GB & I	10-8

INDEX

[Page nos. in **bold** refer to illustrations/photographs]

Index compiled by:
Indexing Specialists,
202 Church Road, Hove,
East Sussex BN3 2DJ

BIBLIOGRAPHY

The following is a list of the books which have provided the chief sources of reference in the preparation and research of this book. Some have proved invaluable; others have been of occasional assistance. In addition, the author has also been greatly helped by several newspaper and magazine articles.

Alliss, Peter (with Michael Hobbs) **The Open** *Collins, London, 1984*

Cornish, Geoffrey S. and Whitten, Ronald E. **The Golf Course** *Windward, Leicester, 1981*

Davis, William H. and the Editors of Golf Digest **Great Golf Courses of the World** *Golf Digest, New York, 1974;*
100 Greatest Golf Courses And Then Some *Golf Digest, New York, 1982*

Davis, William (Editor) **The Punch Book of Golf** *Hutchinson, London, 1973*

Darwin, Bernard **The Golf Courses of the British Isles** *Duckworth, London, 1910*

Dobereiner, Peter **The Glorious World of Golf** *Hamlyn, London, 1973*
The Lord's Taverners Fifty Greatest Golfers *Kingswood/Quixote, London, 1985* (with Peter Alliss, Mark McCormack and Arnold Palmer)
Arnold Palmer's Complete Book of Putting *Stanley Paul, London, 1986* (with Arnold Palmer)
Down The Nineteenth Fairway Andre Deutsch, London, 1982 (Editor)
The Golfers *Collins, London, 1982* (Editor)
Golf Courses of the PGA European Tour *Aurum Press, London, 1992* (with Gordon Richardson and Brian Morgan)

Henderson, Ian T. and Stirk, David **Golf In The Making** *Henderson and Stirk, Winchester, 1979;*
Royal Blackheath *Henderson and Stirk, Winchester, 1981*

Janke, Ken **Golf Is A Funny Game**, *Momentum Books, Ann Arbor, Michigan, 1992*

Keeler, O.B. **The Bobby Jones Story** (edited by Grantland Rice) *Tupper and Love, Atlanta, 1959*

Longhurst, Henry **The Best Of Henry Longhurst** (edited by Mark Wilson and Ken Bowden) *Collins, London, 1979*

Mackenzie, Alister **Dr Mackenzie's Golf Architecture** *Grant Books, Droitwich, 1982 (originally published by Simpkin, Marshall, Hamilton and Kent, London 1920)*

McCormack, Mark H. **The World of Professional Golf** *(Annuals 1967-1994) various publishers*

McDonnell, Michael **The Complete Book of Golf** *Kingswood Press, Tadworth, 1985*

Menzies, Gordon (Editor) **The World of Golf** *BBC, London, 1982*

Parsons, Iain (Editor) **The World Atlas of Golf** *Mitchell Beazley, London, 1976*

Plimpton, George **The Bogey Man** *Harper & Row, New York, 1968*

Price, Charles **The World of Golf** *Random House, New York, 1962;*
Bobby Jones And The Masters *Stanley Paul, London, 1986*

Shelly, Warner **Pine Valley Golf Club, A Chronicle** *Pine Valley Golf Club, Pine Valley, 1982*

Steel, Donald **Golf Records, Facts And Champions** *Guinness Superlatives, Enfield, 1987;*
Classic Golf Links of Great Britain and Ireland *Chapmans, London, 1992,* (with Brian Morgan)

Van Hengel, Steven J.H. **Early Golf** *Frank P. Van Eck, Vaduz, 1985*

Ward-Thomas, Pat **Not Only Golf** *Hodder and Stoughton, London, 1981*

Wilson, Mark (Editor) **Golfer's Handbook 1993** *Macmillan, London, 1993*

Warren Wind, Herbert **The Story of American Golf** *Farrar, Straus, New York, 1948;*
The Lure of Golf *Heinemann, London, 1971;*
Following Through *Ticknor & Fields, New York, 1985;*
The Complete Golfer *Heinemann, London, 1954* (Editor)